CQR Pocke[...]
Spanish II

Learning the following rules and charts will greatly improve your basic Spanish abilities. Pull out this section and keep it with you to study when you have a minute or two.

Direct and indirect object pronouns in Spanish

	DO		IO	
	Singular	Plural	Singular	Plural
First person	*me*	*nos*	*me*	*nos*
Second person	*te*	*vos*	*te*	*vos*
Third person (masculine)	*lo*	*los*	*le*	*les*
Third person (feminine)	*la*	*las*	*le*	*les*

Present tense endings for regular *-ar* verbs

yo	**-o**	nosotros/nosotras	**-amos**
tú	**-as**	vosotros/vosotras	**-áis**
él	**-a**	ellos	**-an**
ella	**-a**	ellas	**-an**
usted	**-a**	ustedes	**-an**

Present tense endings for regular *-er* verbs

yo	**-o**	nosotros/nosotras	**-emos**
tú	**-es**	vosotros/vosotras	**-éis**
él	**-e**	ellos	**-en**
ella	**-e**	ellas	**-en**
usted	**-e**	ustedes	**-en**

Present tense endings for regular *-ir* verbs

yo	**-o**	nosotros/nosotras	**-imos**
tú	**-es**	vosotros/vosotras	**-ís**
él	**-e**	ellos	**-en**
ella	**-e**	ellas	**-en**
usted	**-e**	ustedes	**-en**

Preterit tense endings for regular *-ar* verbs

yo	**-é**	nosotros/ nosotras	**-amos**
tú	**-aste**	vosotros/vosotras	**-asteis**
él	**-ó**	ellos	**-aron**
ella	**-ó**	ellas	**-aron**
usted	**-ó**	ustedes	**-aron**

CQR Pocket Guide
Spanish II

Preterit tense endings for regular *-er* and *-ir* verbs

yo	*-í*	nosotros/nosotras	*-imos*
tú	*-istes*	vosotros/vosotras	*-isteis*
él	*-ió*	ellos	*-ieron*
ella	*-ió*	ellas	*-ieron*
usted	*-ió*	ustedes	*-ieron*

Possessive adjectives

my = *mi* or *mis*

your = *tu* or *tus* (if "you" = *tú*)

your = *su* or *sus* (if "you" = *usted)*

your = *vuestro, vuestra, vuestros,* or *vuestras* (if "you" = *vosotros* or *vosotras)*

his = *su* or *sus*

her = *su* or *sus*

our = *nuestro, nuestra, nuestros,* or *nuestras* (whether "we" is *nosotros* or *nosotras)*

Demonstrative adjectives

Singular	Masculine	Feminine	Plural	Masculine	Feminine
this	este	esta	these	estos	estas
that	ese	esa	those	esos	esas
that (way over there)	aquel	aquella	those (way over there)	aquellos	aquellas

Reflexive pronouns with subject pronouns

yo me	nosotros/nosotras nos
tú te	vosotros/vosotras os
él se	ellos se
ella se	ellas se
usted se	ustedes se

CliffsQuickReview
Spanish II

By Jill Rodriguez

WILEY

Wiley Publishing, Inc.

About the Author

Jill Rodriguez has been teaching Spanish, including Advanced Placement Spanish, for fifteen years and has been named Teacher of the Year, Teacher with the Greatest Impact, and Outstanding Educator during that time. Jill has received college board training for AP Spanish and has helped design the AP curricula. She is the author of Cliffs QuickReview Spanish I and has organized numerous educational tours of Spain and Mexico for many of her students.

Publisher's Acknowledgments

Editorial

Project Editor: Suzanne Snyder

Acquisitions Editor: Roxane Cerda

Copy Editor: Suzanna R. Thompson

Technical Editor: Elsa Pittman

Editorial Assistant: Blair Pottenger

Production

Indexer: Johnna VanHoose

Proofreader: Amy Adrian

Wiley Publishing, Inc. Composition Services

CliffsQuickReview™ Spanish II

Published by
Wiley Publishing, Inc.
909 Third Avenue
New York, NY 10022
www.wiley.com

Copyright © 2003 Wiley Publishing, Inc. New York, New York

Published by Wiley Publishing, Inc., New York, NY
Published simultaneously in Canada

Library of Congress Cataloging-in-Publication Data available from publisher

ISBN: 0-7645-8758-7

Printed in the United States of America

10 9 8 7 6 5 4 3

1O/QT/QT/QT/IN

Table of Contents

INTRODUCTION

CliffsQuickReview *Spanish II* is meant to provide you with the foundations of basic Spanish pronunciation, spelling, and sentence construction. Throughout this book, Spanish grammar is systematically explained in its most simplistic way to an advanced level; topics that were explained in detail in CliffsQuickReview *Spanish I* are reviewed briefly before the introduction of any advanced concept based on previous understanding. If you have already read CliffsQuickReview *Spanish I* or if you have a good foundation in Spanish (two years in high school or one year in college), this book is an appropriate resource to hone your skills to the equivalent of two years of college-level Spanish.

Why You Need This Book

Can you answer "yes" to any of the following questions?

■ Do you need to review the fundamentals of Spanish fast?

■ Do you need a course supplement to the first or second year of a college-level Spanish class?

■ Do you need a concise, comprehensive reference for advanced Spanish grammar concepts?

If so, CliffsQuickReview *Spanish II* is for you!

How to Use This Book

You can use this book in any way that fits your personal style for study and review—you decide what works best with your needs. You can either read the book from cover to cover or just look for the information you want and put the book back on the shelf for later. Here are just a few ways you can search for topics:

■ Use the Pocket Guide to find essential information, such as conjugation charts for regular verbs, pronouns in various different cases, and other basic grammar essentials.

■ Look for areas of interest in the Table of Contents or use the index to find specific topics.

■ Get a glimpse of what you'll gain from a chapter by reading through the Chapter Check-In at the beginning of each chapter.

■ Use the Chapter Checkout at the end of each chapter to gauge your grasp of the important information you need to know.

■ Test your knowledge more completely in the CQR Review and look for additional sources of information in the CQR Resource Center.

■ Use the glossary to find key terms fast. This book defines new terms and concepts where they first appear in the chapter. If a word is bold-faced, you can find a more complete definition in the book's glossary.

■ For helpful lists of antonyms and synonyms, turn to the Appendix located at the back of the book.

■ Flip through the book looking for subject areas at the top of each page until you find what you're looking for. This book is organized to gradually build on key concepts.

Visit Our Web Site

You can access three great learning tools related to CliffsQuickReview *Spanish II* by visiting the www.cliffsnotes.com/extras Web site. Here you will find information on false cognates and idiomatic expressions, as well as access a helpful verb chart of the most common Spanish verbs in the forms and tenses presented in CliffsQuickReview *Spanish II.*

A great resource, www.cliffsnotes.com, features review materials, valuable Internet links, quizzes, and more to enhance your learning. The site also features timely articles and tips, plus downloadable versions of many CliffsNotes books.

When you stop by our site, don't hesitate to share your thoughts about this book or any Wiley product. Just click on the "Contact Us" button. We welcome your feedback!

Chapter 1

SPELLING AND PRONUNCIATION

Chapter Check-In

❏ Spelling words

❏ Pronouncing words

❏ Understanding cognates

❏ Stressing the correct syllable

❏ Knowing when a written accent is necessary

Spanish is very consistent in its spelling and pronunciation rules. Since these rules are simple and easy to learn, anyone can master correctly spelling and pronouncing Spanish words.

The rules presented in this chapter will prepare you to properly pronounce a written word and spell a spoken word. The first step is to forget the limited and chaotic rules of English spelling and, throughout this chapter, focus your attention on the simplicity of Spanish and the consistency of its rules.

A lot of Spanish words look similar to English words, and some are even spelled exactly the same. These words, called **cognates,** are usually easier to spell in Spanish than in English once you learn the pronunciation rules for both consonants and vowels.

Consonants

Consonants in Spanish are generally pronounced like English consonants. Here are some useful rules to follow to eliminate any spelling difficulties.

Double consonants

In English, instances of a double *bb, nn, ss, ff,* and so forth, are common. Spanish, on the other hand, does not have many words with double consonants of the same consonant letter. You can find exceptions to this rule, however, with words containing *ll, rr, cc,* and *nn;* for example, *diccionario, carro, connotación,* and *llave.* Only the single letter *f* is used to make the *f* sound in Spanish. The Spanish never use *ph* to produce the *f* sound, and the letter *p* is always pronounced like the *p* in "papa." If the English word has *ph* or a double *f,* the Spanish cognate will always use one *f;* for example, *fotografía, físico,* and *terrífico.*

There are some important exceptions to the "no double letter" rule. The *ll* that occurs in Spanish is technically not a double *l* but rather a single letter that is pronounced like the consonant *y* in "yellow." In some South American Spanish-speaking countries, the sound of *ll* sounds like a combination of the sound of *sh* and the letter *j* in English. A single *l* sounds like the letter *l* you hear in English words.

Note: On April 27, 1994, the Spanish Language Academies voted and eliminated *ch* and *ll* as separate letters of the Spanish alphabet. Many pre-1994 dictionaries, however, are still in use, and apparently the real Spanish-speaking world continues the thousand-or-so-year habits of the language because *ch* and *ll* are still frequently listed as separate letters and, for example, still occupy one box in a crossword puzzle.

Another letter in Spanish that looks like a double letter is the *rr.* This letter is intended to elicit the rolling sound that is difficult for many who are learning Spanish as a second language. You should roll your tongue when you see the letter *rr* within a word, or when a single *r* is the first letter of a word.

A spelling change is sometimes necessary when two words become one. For example, the *r* in *Costa Rica* is rolled because it is the first letter of a word. The adjective for a native of Costa Rica, however, is only one word, so the *rr* is used in *costarricense* to produce the rolling *r* and maintain the pronunciation.

The only true double consonant in Spanish occurs when two *c*'s are used to produce the *x* sound. In words like *diccionario* and *acceso* the first *c* is hard because it is followed by a consonant and the second *c* is soft because it is followed by *i* or *e.*

Dictionary placement

When looking for a word that starts with *ll* in the dictionary, don't forget that the Spanish side of some dictionaries will list words beginning with *ll* after the words beginning with a single *l*. This will also occur with the letter *ch,* which is also considered a single letter in Spanish and, in most dictionaries, may be found in its own section after the *c* section. *Ch* is easily pronounced (like the sound in "charm" or "Charles"), but, unlike English, *ch* is always pronounced the same way in Spanish.

Dictionary listings may also confuse you when a word includes the Spanish letter *ñ.* The little squiggle over the *n* is called a *tilde,* and its use creates an entirely new letter that follows the *n* section in the dictionary. The *ñ* is pronounced like the *ny* combination in "canyon," or the *ni* combination in "union."

The letter *c*

The letters *k* and *w* do not occur in Spanish words unless the word has been borrowed from another language such as English or even Japanese. For example, *el karate* is considered a "Spanish" noun, even though the *k* is not a Spanish letter.

In Spanish, there are two ways to produce the sound of the English letter *k.* When the letter *c* is followed by an *o, a,* or *u,* it is pronounced like a *k.* The *qu* combination must be used to produce the *k* sound in front of an *e* or *i.* A word that the English borrowed from the Spanish, "mosquito," has already prepared you to pronounce *qu* in Spanish without any *w* sound. Not like "quill," but rather like "tequila."

This rule results from the fact that the letter *c* has "issues." When followed by *o, a, u,* or any consonant, it is pronounced like the *c* in "cat," "coat," or "cut." When *c* is followed by *e* or *i,* it is pronounced like the *c* in "certain" or "cinder."

The letter *g*

The letter *g* in Spanish behaves very much like the letter *c* in that the letter that follows the *g* determines how it is pronounced. The reason the *g* in "go" is pronounced differently than the *g* in "germ" is because there is a "hard *g*" and a "soft *g*" sound. In English and in Spanish, a *g* that is followed by *e* or *i* is generally soft, and any *g* that is followed by *o, a,* or *u* is hard.

The pronunciation of the hard *g* is the same in both languages. The *g* in *gato, gorila,* or *gusto* sounds exactly like the *g* in "goal," "gallant" or "gum." As in English, if a Spanish *g* is followed by an *e* or *i,* it is pronounced soft. However, the soft *g* in Spanish sounds like the English letter *h.* The *g* in *gemelo* or *gitano* sounds like the English *h* in "home" or "head."

The letter *u* is placed between the *g* and *e* or between the *g* and *i* to produce a hard *g* sound in front of an *e* or *i. Guerra* is pronounced "**gay**-ra," and *guido* is pronounced like "**gree**-do" without the *r.* The *u* itself is not pronounced because the intent of the *u* is to produce the hard *g* sound. This is an exception to the rule that all vowels are always pronounced. You are probably already familiar with the words *guerrilla* and *guitarra;* these words can serve as examples in your head to help you avoid the urge to say *gway* or *gwee* when you see the *gue* and *gui* combinations.

If the *gway* or *gwee* sound is desired, the German symbol called an umlaut (a double dot over the *u: ü*) is used to indicate that the *u* should be pronounced like a *w* even if it is in between a *g* and an *i* or a *g* and an *e.* Pronounce the word "bilingual" and then say *bilingüe* with the same *gw* sound.

The letter *j*

The letter *j* is always pronounced like the *h* in "hi" or "hollow." It is difficult to predict whether to use a *g* or *j* when you need to produce a word with the sound of the English *h* followed by an *e* or *i.* For example, *jirafa* and *jefe* are spelled with a *j* and *giro* and *general* are spelled with a *g.* Focus on whether to use a *j* or a *g* when you first learn to spell the word. Words with the *h* sound in front of *o, a,* or *u* (*jota, Japón,* and *julio*) are always spelled with a *j* because a *g* would not produce the *h* sound at all when followed by these letters.

The letter *h*

The Spanish letter *h* is always silent and is generally at the beginning of the word if used at all. There really is no way to predict when a word will begin with a silent *h,* so be sure to focus on the spelling of words that you learn beginning with an *h.*

The letter *d*

The letter *d* basically sounds like an English *d* but is a bit softer in Spanish. At the end of a word, it is not stressed as it is in English. Say the word "paid" out loud and hear the strength of the *d* at the end. It almost creates its own syllable. In Spanish, any *d* at the end of the word is barely pronounced. Say *ciudad* without the *d* at the end and you'll sound like a native.

Remember, the lack of double consonants makes spelling easy. The *d* sound is always a single *d* in any Spanish word.

The letter *t*

Another letter that is softer in Spanish than English is the *t*. It is especially soft when followed by an *r:* The sound of the *tr* in *triple* would sound more like *tl*. Try to say *tratar* without moving your tongue away from the back of your teeth. If you say the *t* as you would in English, you will have a slight accent but will be easily understood. Don't forget that the *t* will never be doubled when spelling Spanish words.

The letters *b* and *v*

Many uneducated Spanish speakers have difficulty determining whether to use a *b* or *v* when spelling a word. Both sound like a combination of *bv*. To make the sound, start out making the *b* sound and slur it into the *v* sound. English speakers usually forget to pronounce the two letters the same, so their instinct is to spell *vivir* or *beber* correctly because, in their minds, the first word still sounds like it begins with a *v* and the second word still sounds like it begins with a *b*. This pronunciation error is helpful with spelling, but until your *b*'s and *v*'s sound like some mixture of both, you'll have an English accent. One helpful point about the similarity of *b* and *v* in Spanish: Sometimes, it can be easy to recognize a word that is similar to English if you imagine the word with a *v* instead of a *b*, or vice versa. For example, the verb *gobernar* means to govern.

Vowels and Dipthongs

Each vowel has only one pronunciation and it will be pronounced that way in every Spanish word. Except for the *gu* and *qu* combination, there are no silent vowels in Spanish. Some vowels will slur together to create a single sound. These vowel combinations are called **dipthongs** and will be explained later in this chapter.

Correct pronunciation of vowels is especially important when you pronounce a word that looks like an English word. Remember, a lot of Spanish words look similar to English words, and some are even spelled exactly the same. However, these cognates are never pronounced exactly like their English equivalents. Also, a Spanish word that is pronounced like an English word will probably be spelled differently in Spanish. When you recognize a cognate, take your time and pronounce the vowels carefully.

Models for vowel pronunciation

A few common Spanish words can serve as models for your pronunciation. Everyone knows how to pronounce the word *taco*. The letters *a* and *o* are always pronounced as they are in *taco*. A heavy Spanish accent will result in English words like "hat" or "can" sounding more like the English words "hot" or "con." That is because the native Spanish speaker is saying the letter *a* the only way it can be said in Spanish. As for the letter *o* in *taco*, it is shorter in Spanish and doesn't end in a *wa* sound.

Another word you have probably learned courtesy of the popularity of Mexican food is *burrito*. The Spanish vowels *u* and *i* are always pronounced as they are in this word.

The final Spanish vowel left to master is the *e*. It is always pronounced like the *e* in *café*. (To see how well you're learning, make sure you are pronouncing the *a* in *café* correctly. It should sound like the *a* in *taco*.) Also, an *e* at the end of a word is not silent as it is in the English word "rake." Remember that there are no silent vowels in Spanish (except for the *qu* and *gu* issue), so you must say *ay* at the end of cognates that end in *e*.

Vowel combinations

The strong vowels are *a, o,* and *e*. When two strong vowels appear next to each other in a word, the result is two separate syllables with both vowels strongly pronounced. If one of the strong vowels is used beside a weak vowel (*i* or *u*), the resulting single syllable, called a **dipthong,** is a slur of the two vowels with the stronger vowel the only one that is clearly heard.

If the weak vowels *i* and *u* are combined, the result is one syllable, with the first weak vowel slurred over and the second one fully pronounced. (Remember that, in the battle of the weak vowels, the last one gets stressed.) When a weak vowel precedes a strong vowel, the weak vowel acts as a consonant. The *u* creates the sound of an English *w;* the *i* sounds like the consonant *y*.

Consonants as vowels

The letter *y* acts as a vowel only when it stands alone or when it is at the end of the word. In such instances, it is pronounced like the *i* in *burrito*. As a consonant, the Spanish *y* sounds just like it does in the English word "you."

Stress and Accentuation

There are easy-to-understand rules explaining why accent marks are used. To start: There is only one kind of accent, only one accent (if any) per word, and it can only be placed on a vowel, never a consonant.

Because the main reason for using an accent mark is to stress a syllable that would not naturally be stressed, you must be prepared to determine which syllable would be stressed naturally. The natural stress of a word follows two simple rules:

■ If a word ends in any consonant other than *n* or *s,* the natural stress will be on the last syllable.

■ If a word ends in a vowel or the letter *n* or *s,* the natural stress is on the next-to-last syllable.

If the word is supposed to be pronounced with the stress somewhere other than the rules require, a written accent mark indicates which syllable to stress.

The main purpose of writing an accent mark is to indicate that this particular word is supposed to be stressed somewhere other than the syllable where it would be stressed naturally if it followed the rules. This leads to some predictable rules within the rules. For example, there are hundreds of words that are cognates of English words that end in *-tion* like "nation," "liberation," or "condition." These words end in *-ción* in Spanish: *nación, liberación,* and *condición.* The rule states that a word that ends in an *n* has the natural stress on the next to the last syllable, but these words are supposed to be stressed on the last syllable as opposed to the stress on the first syllable in English, so an accent mark is written on the last vowel, which is the *o.*

If a syllable is added to the end of a word, the natural stress of the word is changed. This happens when you make a word plural by adding *-es.* The accent mark on a word like *nación* served the purpose of placing the stress on the *o,* but the plural word ends in *s,* so the natural stress would already be on the next-to-last syllable, which is now the *o.* Thus, you must remove the accent mark on the plural form of a word ending in *-ción* because the stress is naturally on the *o* in *-ciones.*

The previous lesson on dipthongs and the strong and weak vowels becomes important when you are trying to decide whether a word needs a written accent mark. Remember that one strong and one weak vowel together create one syllable. For example, the word *iglesia* ends in the vowel *a* so the stress naturally falls on the next to the last syllable, the *e*, according to the general rule. Thus, it does not carry a written accent. It is common, however, to see an accent on the -*ía* ending. That is because an accent mark can be used to indicate that the softer vowel is to be pronounced as well as the stronger. This creates two separate syllables and the stress will be on the accented syllable.

Understanding these rules helps you not only to know whether to write an accent when spelling a word that you hear, but also to pronounce a word that you are reading with the stress on the correct syllable.

Another reason for writing an accent mark has nothing to do with pronunciation. It is used to differentiate between two words that are otherwise spelled the same but have different meanings. For example, the word *sí* means "yes" and the word *si* means "if." Although the accent makes the spelling different, only the context of a spoken sentence will provide a clue as to which of the two words is appropriate.

Chapter Checkout

For the following words, use the rules you have learned and underline where the stress would naturally fall.

1. *diaria*

2. *examen*

3. *iniciar*

The words below have Spanish cognates that are very similar. Can you predict how they would be spelled?

4. professor

5. organization

6. photo

Answers: 1. *diaria* **2.** *examen* **3.** *iniciar* **4.** *profesor* **5.** *organización* **6.** *foto*

Chapter 2

REVIEW OF SENTENCE AND QUESTION STRUCTURE

Chapter Check-In

❑ Writing complete sentences

❑ Using interrogative pronouns

❑ Creating and answering questions

Basic Sentence Structure

The only requirements for a complete sentence are a subject and a verb. The subject is the person or thing that is responsible for the action of the verb. The verb, of course, is the action word, and is conjugated in the correct form to agree with the subject. In Spanish, the subject (when stated) comes before the verb just like in an English sentence. There is a tendency in Spanish to eliminate the subject pronoun because the form of the verb indicates what person the subject is. If the verb form has more than one potential subject (like *él, ella,* and *Ud.*), simply look for context clues in the sentence or in the preceding sentences to determine the subject. There are many other parts of speech that can make a sentence more complex, but you will not master them until later in this book. For now, simply think of a sentence as <u>subject</u> + **verb** + rest of sentence. The examples below demonstrate the relationship between the subject and verb of a sentence. In each sentence below, the verb is in boldface and the subject is underlined. This will be continued later in the chapter, so use these examples of simple sentences to get used to seeing the subject underlined and the verb in boldface.

*Julieta **compra** una coca cola.*

Julieta **buys** a Coke.

*Tú **miras** la televisión.*

You **watch** TV.

*Gonzalo **visita** a sus abuelos. **Viven** en Ecuador.*

Gonzalo **visits** his grandparents. (They) **live** in Ecuador.

*Soledad **termina** su examen.*

Soledad **finishes** her test.

Remember that a pronoun not only replaces a noun, but it also replaces all of the descriptive words that go with the noun. Thus, a pronoun eliminates the noun and all the words that modify (describe) it. In the sentences below, the pronoun "she" replaces the noun "woman," but also eliminates all of the modifiers that accompany "woman."

An extremely beautiful woman wearing a gold gown arrived at the party. She was the center of attention.

It would sound ridiculous to say, "An extremely beautiful she wearing the gown was the center of attention." Just remember that when a noun has any modifiers, such as adjectives or articles, those modifiers disappear when that noun becomes a pronoun.

Subject Pronouns

Every sentence must have a subject. Any pronoun used to replace a noun that serves as the subject of the sentence comes from the subject case and is called a "subject pronoun." Subject pronouns have been used throughout this text in conjugation charts; the order in which subject pronouns appear in conjugation charts is important because the other cases of pronouns are written in the same order.

The order and grouping of the pronouns in Table 2-1 is consistently followed in the other cases presented in this chapter. Notice that *nosotros/nosotras* is across from *yo; vosotros/vosotras* is across from *tú; él* is across from *ellos; ella* is across from *ellas;* and *usted* is across from *ustedes.* It is important to maintain this form when you write the pronouns in a conjugation chart.

Table 2-1   Subject Pronoun Chart

yo	nosotros/nosotras
tú	vosotros/vosotras
él	ellos
ella	ellas
usted	ustedes

The pronouns listed above are arranged in a chart form that is used for grammatical explanations. Grammatical terms such as "first person singular" or "third person plural" are often used to identify pronouns listed in a specific order. Each different pronoun case is listed in the same order as the subject pronouns listed above. Any new pronoun case presented in this book will be in the same order as the subject case.

The pronouns in the top row (*yo* and *nosotros*) are called first person pronouns. On the left is the first person singular (*yo*) and on the right is the first person plural (*nosotros*). In English, when I have a group with me, the plural of "I" is "we." The same is true in Spanish, the plural of *yo* is *nosotros* (or *nosotras* if we are all females).

Pronouns in the second row are second person pronouns (*tú* and *vosotros/vosotras*). On the left, *tú* refers to one person; on the right, *vosotros* or *vosotras* refers to more than one person, as in the English "you guys" or "y'all."

The pronouns in the third, fourth, and fifth rows are called third person pronouns. There is a third person singular pronoun for each gender: *él* and *ella*. The third person plural also specifies gender (*ellos* or *ellas*); you use it when talking about any group of people or things that does not include yourself.

In English, because things or inanimate objects do not have gender, the pronoun "it" is used to represent a thing or inanimate object that is the subject of the sentence. There is no Spanish equivalent to the subject pronoun "it" because, in Spanish, all nouns are either masculine or feminine. If you want to say something such as, "It's important," or, "It's raining," you simply use the *él* form of the verb with no subject pronoun.

In the subject pronoun chart, *usted* and *ustedes* are tricky. Even though they both mean "you" and "you" is a second person pronoun in English, these two "respectful" pronouns are treated as third person pronouns in Spanish (and, thus, are listed with the third person pronouns).

The second person pronoun in English is "you." This is an extremely vague pronoun because it can refer to one person or to more than one person (as in "you guys" or "y'all"). Spanish, however, has singular and plural versions of "you." The singular pronoun *usted* is often abbreviated *Ud,* and the plural version (*ustedes*) is abbreviated as *Uds.*

Usted, however, is not always the appropriate pronoun to use for "you": The pronoun *tú* is the informal way to say "you." *Tú* is used when you are speaking to someone younger than you or to someone who is a close friend or family member. You must consider whether you should use the "friendly" or "informal" *tú,* or the "respectful" or "formal" *usted,* depending on the age and position of the person you are calling "you."

It is always safer to use the *usted* way of saying "you" unless you are absolutely certain that you won't be insulting someone by using the informal *tú* pronoun. (Although, in our current culture, some people don't want to be referred to as *usted* because they say it makes them feel old.) The plural form of *tú* is *vosotros* or *vosotras,* which is rarely used outside of Spain. Latin Americans generally use *ustedes* for the plural of both *tú* and *usted.* Some people don't bother to learn the *vosotros/vosotras* pronoun because *ustedes* can be used as the plural form of "you" for any situation. Because Spanish is new to you, it's easier to use *ustedes* any time you want to address a group as "you guys" or "y'all."

There is not always an easy match between English and Spanish pronouns. The list below is not presented in standard chart form, but, rather, is meant to help you understand what each of the subject pronouns means.

> *yo* = I
> *tú* = you (informal)
> *usted (Ud.)* = you (formal)
> *ustedes (Uds.)* = you (plural)
> *él* = he
> *ella* = she
> *nosotros* = we
> *nosotras* = we (feminine)
> *ellos* = they
> *ellas* = they (feminine)

Subject pronouns in Spanish are generally not capitalized unless they are the first word in a sentence. Notice, however, that the abbreviated forms *Ud.* and *Uds.* are always capitalized, although the longer versions (*usted* and *ustedes*) are not capitalized except when they're the first word in a sentence. You don't think about the fact that the English pronoun "I" is always capitalized, but you must remember that the Spanish equivalent (*yo*) is not capitalized unless it is the first word of the sentence.

Remember that if you want to understand the explanations about pronouns throughout this chapter, it is important to know that the top row is called first person (*yo* and *nosotros/nosotras*). The second row is called the second person (*tú* and *vosotros/vosotras*), and anything lower on the chart is called the third person (*él, ella, usted, ellos, ellas,* and *ustedes*).

The pronouns in the left-hand column of the chart are all singular (*yo, tú, él, ella,* and *usted*) and those on the right-hand side are their plural equivalents. The plural of *yo* is *nosotros/nosotras,* the plural of *tú* is *vosotros/vosotras,* the plural of *él* is *ellos,* the plural of *ella* is *ellas,* and the plural of *usted* is *ustedes.*

Interrogative Pronouns (Question Words)

People sometimes find grammatical terms such as **interrogative pronouns** scary. If you count yourself among those who do, think of interrogative pronouns as "question words." A question word is actually a pronoun because it is used in place of whatever noun would answer the question.

Notice that *all* question words have accent marks. When you learn a word with an accent mark, it is helpful to say it out loud and clap your hands on the syllable with the accent mark. This will not only remind you to stress that syllable, but it will also help you remember that the word has an accent mark.

¿Quién?	who
¿Quiénes?	who plural (used when you assume the answer is more than one person)
¿Qué?	what
¿Cuál?	which, what
¿Cuáles?	which ones, what (in front of a plural noun)
¿Cómo?	how
¿Dónde?	where
¿Cuándo?	when
¿Cuánto?	how much (used in front of a singular, masculine noun)
¿Cuánta?	how much (used in front of a singular, feminine noun)

> *¿Cuántos?*   how many (used in front of a plural, masculine noun)
>
> *¿Cuántas?*   how many (used in front of a plural, feminine noun)
>
> *¿Por qué?*   why (because of what)
>
> *¿Para qué?*   why (for what purpose)

Most of the question words have exact equivalents in Spanish and English. But there are a few issues you must understand to use the correct question word in context. There are three Spanish pronouns that can be translated by the English word "what." Unfortunately, they are not interchangeable; there are, however, some simple rules to govern their usage.

"What" rule 1

Always use *qué* to mean "what" directly in front of any noun.

> *¿Qué coche* **condujiste** *tú?*
>
> What car did you drive?
>
> *¿Qué programas* **prefieren** *ellos?*
>
> What programs do they prefer?

"What" rule 2

Qué is used in front of any form of the verb *ser* ("to be") when asking for a definition or an explanation. That is, use *qué* when you are really asking, "What does it mean?" or "What is it?"

Cuál is used to mean "what" in front of any form of the verb *ser* when you are asking for a specific answer.

To understand the difference between "*qué es . . .*" and "*cuál es . . .*," consider the difference between these two answers to the question "What is your address?"

A. My address is the house number, street name, city, state, and ZIP code where I live.

B. My address is 322 4th St., Carrollton, OH 44615.

Answer A is obviously the response to a question asking for a definition or explanation of the word "address." This is the type of answer that is elicited from the question:

> *¿Qué es dirección?*
>
> What is address? (or, "Give me an explanation or definition of the word 'address.'")

Answer B is the type of response you would most likely give if you heard the question, "What is your address?" However, notice that the question word *cuál* must be used in front of the verb "to be" in Spanish if you hope to get a specific answer rather than a generalized definition.

> *¿Cuál es tu dirección?*
> What is your address? (or, "Give me a specific place.")

To better illustrate the difference, the following questions have completely different answers because of the different question words used.

Question 1. *¿Qué es la fecha?*
What is the date?

Answer 1. *La fecha es el día, mes y año.*
The date is the day, month, and year.

Question 2. *¿Cuál es la fecha?*
What is the date?

Answer 2. *La fecha es el 5 de junio del 2002.*
The date is June 5, 2002.

Question 1 uses the word *qué* in front of *es*. It is asking for an explanation or definition of the word *fecha*. Answer 1 explains what *fecha* means.

Question 2 uses the word *cuál* in front of *es*. It is asking for a specific answer, so Answer 2 provides a specific date.

"What" rule 3

Cómo is often used as a response when one fails to hear a comment and would like it repeated. In English, when someone says something you don't hear, you say, "What?" If this happens in Spanish, the one-word response, *¿Cómo?* is appropriate. That does not, however, mean that *cómo* can be used to mean "What?" in any other situation.

Creating and Answering Questions

The simplest questions to create are "yes or no" questions. They are actually much easier in Spanish than they are in English. For example, how do you make a "yes or no" question out of the sentence, "Erin dates Mario"? You put the word "does" in front and change the form of the verb "to date." **Does** <u>Erin</u> **date** Mario?

The helping verb "to do" is rarely used in simple English sentences, although it is necessary for questions. An English "yes or no" question is formed using a helping verb. This verb has different forms including "do," "does," and in the past tense the form "did." The sentences below use the helping verb forms "do" or "does":

I **do need** this job. She **does read** a lot. Normally, it sounds funny to use a helping verb in a sentence, but when you want to make a "yes or no" question out of a sentence, the helping verb forms "do" or "does" are necessary. To form a question in English, the helping verb switches places with the subject of the sentence.

> **Do** I **need** this job?
> **Does** she **read** a lot?

Even though you already know how to make a sentence into a "yes or no" question in English, it's helpful to realize that part of what you do is to switch the subject with the helping verb ("do" or "does"). The words "do" or "does," however, do not translate in a Spanish question because Spanish does not use helping verbs to create questions; it simply switches the subject and the main verb. Don't, therefore, be tempted to find the Spanish equivalent of "do" or "does" when you see a question starting with "do" or "does" in English. Instead, you need to apply a simple, three-step process to create the Spanish question.

1. Remove the "do" or "does" from the English question.
2. Translate the remaining sentence into Spanish, conjugating the verb to go with the subject.
3. Switch the subject with the verb and add the question marks.

Here's an example: **Do** I **need** this job?

Use the three-step process to translate this into Spanish.

1. Remove the "do" or "does" from the English question (I **need** this job).
2. Translate the remaining sentence into Spanish, carefully conjugating the verb to agree with the subject (Yo **necesito** *este trabajo*).
3. Switch the subject and the verb and add the question marks (**¿Necesito** yo *este trabajo?*).

Writing questions with question words

To write a Spanish question that begins with a question word (such as "how," "where," "when"), start by pretending the question word is not there. Without the question word, you will be able to create a simple "yes or no" question by switching the subject and verb.

Most questions that begin with a question word are created exactly like a "yes or no" question, with the question word in front. Take the question "Does she speak Russian?" (*¿Habla ella ruso?*). Several question words could simply be placed in front of the question to elicit more information than a "yes or no" answer.

How does she speak Russian?

¿Cómo **habla** *ella ruso?*

Where does she speak Russian?

¿Dónde **habla** *ella ruso?*

When does she speak Russian?

¿Cuándo **habla** *ella ruso?*

Why does she speak Russian?

¿Por qué **habla** *ella ruso?*

How much does she speak Russian?

¿Cuánto **habla** *ella ruso?*

All of the above questions can be created simply by first switching the subject and the verb to create a "yes or no" question, then placing the specific question word at the beginning of the sentence.

Some question words are used a little differently. These question words actually serve as the subject of the question. The question "Who speaks Russian?" uses the pronoun "who" as the subject. The pronoun *quién* is the subject of the Spanish question: *¿Quién* **habla** *ruso?*

These questions are actually created in exactly the same way in Spanish and English, but since Spanish has both singular and plural versions of "who," you have to think about one extra thing in Spanish: You must conjugate the verb to agree with the subject.

The singular pronoun *quién* is meant to represent one person, so use the *él* form of the verb, which is the form you would use if one person were the subject of the sentence. The plural version of who, *quiénes,* is meant to represent several people. It requires you to use the *ellos* form of the verb with it. (Note: When the question words *quién* and *quiénes* are preceded by a preposition such as *a* [*a quién*] or *de* [*de quién*], they will not be the subject of the sentence.)

¿Quiénes **juegan** *al vólibol?*

Who is playing volleyball? (assuming that more than one person is playing volleyball)

¿Quién **baila** *con Shakita?*

Who is dancing with Shakita? (assuming that only one person is dancing with Shakita)

Notice that when the question word serves as the subject, there is no need to switch the subject and verb. There are a few other question words that can act as the subject of the sentence.

¿Cuántos **asisten** *a la universidad?* (*cuántos* is the subject, *asisten* is the verb)

How many attend the university? ("how many" is the subject, "attend" is the verb)

¿Cuáles **tienen** *más de diez cuartos?*

Which ones have more than ten rooms?

The question word *cuántos* can be used in another type of question. This is a simple "yes or no" question with the question word placed in front. For example:

¿Come Julieta? (*Julieta* is the subject, *come* is the verb)

Does Julieta eat? ("Julieta" is the subject, "eat" is the verb)

As long as you have established what is being eaten, you can simply put the question word for "how many" in front of this "yes or no" question. In the above question, however, Julieta is the subject. If *cuántos* were the subject, the verb *comer* would be in the *ellos* form and Julieta would be the one being eaten.

¿Cuántos [tacos, burritos, etc.] **come** *Julieta?* How many [. . .] does Julieta eat?

The pronouns below can be used to create both kinds of questions. Questions using these pronouns will not always have the subject and verb switched, because sometimes the pronouns are actually the subject of the sentence. When this is the case, the verb will be conjugated in the *él* form if the question word is singular and in the *ellos* form if the question word is plural.

cuánto	how much (used to replace or modify a masculine noun)
cuánta	how much (used to replace or modify a feminine noun)
cuántos	how many (plural, masculine)
cuántas	how many (plural, feminine)
cuál	which
cuáles	which ones (plural)

How to use the right pronoun to answer a question

In answering a question, you must first listen for or look carefully at the subject used in the question to determine the correct subject to use in your response. You can either memorize the charts below (see tables 2-2 and 2-3) to determine how to answer the question, or you can think about which pronoun you'd use to answer the question in English. In other words, if a question is addressed to you, you'd answer with "I" both in English and Spanish. It is always better to understand than memorize. Once you understand tables 2-2 and 2-3, you can refer to them while you are still learning, but you will quickly find that you no longer need to do so.

Table 2-2   Determining the Subject for the Response to a Question

If the subject of the question is	Answer with
tú or *usted*	*yo*
ustedes	*nosotros/nosotras*
any name(s) *y tú*	*nosotros/nosotras,* or name(s) *y yo*
any name(s) *y usted*	*nosotros/nosotras,* or name(s) *y yo*

For example:

> *¿Hablas tú español? Sí, yo hablo español.*
> Do you speak Spanish? Yes, I speak Spanish.

> *¿Hablan ustedes español? Sí, nosotros hablamos español.*
> Do you guys speak Spanish? Yes, we speak Spanish.

¿Hablan Marco y tú español? Sí, nosotros hablamos español. **Or** *Sí, Marco y yo hablamos español.*

Do you and Marco speak Spanish? Yes, we speak Spanish. **Or** Yes, Marco and I speak Spanish.

The reverse of these is also true. If the subject of the question is y*o,* the subject of the answer is *tú* and if the subject of the question is *tú,* the subject of the answer is *yo.* Since there are some options, you have to determine the specific pronoun depending on the context of the question.

Table 2-3   The Reverse of Table 2-2

If the subject of the question is	*Answer with*
yo	*tú*
nosotros/nosotras	*ustedes*
any name(s) *y yo*	*ustedes,* or name(s) *y usted,* or name(s) *y tú*

When a question is asked about someone else, use either the person's name or the appropriate third person pronoun in your response. To answer these types of questions, you do not have to change the subject or the verb form. Simply answer *sí* or *no,* and put the subject back in front of the verb to change the question into a basic sentence. If there is a question word, fill in any information requested.

¿Baila ella? Sí, ella baila.

Does she dance? Yes, she dances.

¿Trabaja María? Sí, María trabaja.

Does María work? Yes, María works.

¿Cuándo trabaja María? María trabaja mañana.

When does María work? María works tomorrow.

Chapter Checkout

Translate the following questions to Spanish.

1. Do they practice?
2. Why does Elisa run?
3. How do Raúl and I dance?

Answer the following questions using the appropriate subject pronoun and correctly conjugated form of the verb.

4. *¿Quieres comer?*

5. *¿Gastan Uds. todo el dinero?*

6. *¿Canta Rosita bien?*

Decide whether to use *qué* or *cuál* in the following questions.

7. *¿_____libro tienes en tu bolsa?*

8. *¿_____ es una telenovela?*

Answers: 1. *¿Practican ellos?* **2.** *¿Por qué corre Elisa?* **3.** *¿Cómo bailamos Raúl y yo?* **4.** *Sí, yo quiero comer.* **5.** *Sí, nosotros gastamos todo el dinero.* **6.** *Sí, Rosita canta bien.* **7.** *Qué* **8.** *Qué*

Chapter 3

REVIEW OF THE PRESENT TENSE INDICATIVE

Chapter Check-In

❑ Conjugating irregular verbs

❑ Predicting irregular verb patterns

❑ Recognizing verbs with prefixes

This chapter reviews some of the irregularities of verbs in the present tense. You probably remember that some irregular verbs have predictable irregularities. Once you learn the patterns, these verbs will be as easy to conjugate as regular verbs. To build both your vocabulary and your ability to know which verbs have irregular forms, you should learn the list of verbs that follows the explanation of the most common irregularity patterns.

Certain irregular verbs, however, follow no pattern and since you won't be able to predict the ending, you will have to learn each specific form of those verbs.

Yo Irregulars

Verbs in Spanish that are completely regular in the present tense except for the *yo* form are called *yo* **irregulars.** There is an entirely new tense called the present subjunctive, which you will learn in Chapter 7. This tense is based on the *yo* form, so it will be extremely important to know the irregular *yo* form of the useful verbs below and remember that all of the other forms of these verbs are regular. Verbs with a similar irregular *yo* form are grouped together to help you remember them.

It is quite common to make verbs by adding a prefix to a simple verb. The verb with the prefix is conjugated like the simple verb, so look for examples of this at the end of each list of verbs. Also, learn to predict the conjugation patterns when you notice that a new verb has a prefix preceding a simple verb that you already know how to conjugate.

Just in case you forget the regular present tense endings of verbs, tables 3-1, 3-2, and 3-3 can help refresh your memory. The *yo* form is not included in these charts because it will be irregular for the first group of verbs you will learn.

Table 3-1   Regular -*ar* Verb Endings

Subject	Ending	Subject	Ending
yo	-??	nosotros/nosotras	-amos
tú	-as	vosotros/vosotras	-áis
él	-a	ellos	-an
ella	-a	ellas	-an
usted	-a	ustedes	-an

Table 3-2   Regular -*er* Verb Endings

Subject	Ending	Subject	Ending
yo	-??	nosotros/nosotras	-emos
tú	-es	vosotros/vosotras	-éis
él	-e	ellos	-en
ella	-e	ellas	-en
usted	-e	ustedes	-en

Table 3-3   Regular -*ir* Verb Endings

Subject	Ending	Subject	Ending
yo	-??	nosotros/nosotras	-imos
tú	-es	vosotros/vosotras	-ís
él	-e	ellos	-en
ella	-e	ellas	-en
usted	-e	ustedes	-en

-*oy* verbs

There are two extremely important verbs that are irregular only because the *yo* form of the verb ends in -*oy*. These two verbs are *dar* (to give) and *estar* (to be). The rest of the forms of the verbs have regular endings, but notice in Table 3-4 that the verb *estar* has accent marks on all forms *except* the first-person pronouns (*yo* and *nosotros/nosotras*). The verb *dar* is completely regular in all forms except *yo* and does not have any accents.

Table 3-4   Conjugation Chart for the Verb *Estar* (to Be)

Subject	Verb	Subject	Verb
yo	estoy	nosotros/nosotras	estamos
tú	estás	vosotros/vosotras	estáis
él	está	ellos	están
ella	está	ellas	están
usted	está	ustedes	están

-*go* verbs

Another specific type of "*yo* irregular" includes verbs whose *yo* form ends in -*go* even though there is not a single *g* in the infinitive. The simplest and most common -*go* verbs are regular in all forms except *yo*, so only the irregular *yo* form is listed below.

hacer (to make, to do)	*yo* form: *hago*
poner (to put)	*yo* form: *pongo*
valer (to be worth)	*yo* form: *valgo*
salir (to leave)	*yo* form: *salgo*
caer (to fall)	*yo* form: *caigo*
raer (to scrape, rub off)	*yo* form: *raigo*
traer (to bring)	*yo* form: *traigo*

Atraer (to attract), *contraer* (to contract), *retraer* (to bring back), and *sustraer* (to subtract) are good examples of verbs composed of a basic verb that you know (in this case, *traer*) and different prefixes (*a-*, *con-*, *re-*, and *sus-*). You should be able to predict the *yo* form of these verbs (*atraigo*, *contraigo*, *retraigo*, and *sustraigo*).

Three common *-go* verbs are also stem-changing verbs. The conjugation patterns of stem-changing verbs is explained later in this chapter, but the irregular *-go* ending of the *yo* form is included below to keep the list of *-go* verbs complete.

tener (to have [possession])	*yo* form: *tengo*
venir (to come)	*yo* form: *vengo*
decir (to say, to tell)	*yo* form: *digo*

-zco verbs

Normally, you cannot predict whether a verb will be irregular in its *yo* form unless you already know how to conjugate the verb. There is one rule, however, that is generally consistent: If the infinitive of the verb ends in a vowel followed by *-cer* or *-cir,* the *yo* form of the verb will end in *-zco.* Remember, there are three common verbs that do not follow the *-zco* rule. They are *hacer* (to do, to make), *decir* (to say, to tell), and *satisfacer* (to satisfy). Instead, they follow the *-go* rule. *Hacer* and *satisfacer* are regular in all other forms. *Decir* is irregular in all forms.

The following verbs all have a *yo* form that ends in *-zco.* They are regular in all other forms.

aborrecer (to hate)	*yo* form: *aborrezco*
agradecer (to thank)	*yo* form: *agradezco*
aparecer (to appear)	*yo* form: *aparezco*
complacer (to please, to gratify)	*yo* form: *complazco*
conocer (to know, to be acquainted with)	*yo* form: *conozco*
crecer (to grow)	*yo* form: *crezco*
establecer (to establish)	*yo* form: *establezco*
merecer (to deserve)	*yo* form: *merezco*
nacer (to be born)	*yo* form: *nazco*
obedecer (to obey)	*yo* form: *obedezco*
ofrecer (to offer)	*yo* form: *ofrezco*
permanecer (to remain)	*yo* form: *permanezco*
pertenecer (to belong)	*yo* form: *pertenezco*
yacer (to lie down)	*yo* form: *yazco*

Desaparecer (to disappear) is a good example of a basic verb that you know (*aparecer*) and a prefix (*des-*). *Desconocer* (to be ignorant) and *reconocer* (to recognize) are also good examples of a basic verb that you know (*conocer*) and different prefixes (*des-* and *re-*).

Many verbs end in *-ucir;* these are regular in all forms but the *yo* form, which ends in *-zco.*

conducir (to drive)	*yo* form: *conduzco*
deducir (to deduce)	*yo* form: *deduzco*
introducir (to introduce)	*yo* form: *introduzco*
lucir (to wear, to light up, to display)	*yo* form: *luzco*
producir (to produce)	*yo* form: *produzco*
reducir (to reduce)	*yo* form: *reduzco*
traducir (to translate)	*yo* form: *traduzco*

Deslucir (to tarnish) is a good example of a basic verb that you know (*lucir*) and a prefix (*des-*).

The above verbs are grouped together because they all end in a **vowel** followed by *-cer* or *-cir* and, therefore, have a *yo* form ending in *-zco.* Another predictable irregular *yo* form occurs when a verb ends in a **consonant** followed by *-cer* or *-cir.* In this case, the *yo* form will end in *-zo* rather than *-zco.*

ejercer (to practice, to exercise)	*yo* form: *ejerzo*
esparcir (to scatter)	*yo* form: *esparzo*
vencer (to conquer)	*yo* form: *venzo*
zurcir (to mend)	*yo* form: *zurzo*

Convencer (to convince, to persuade) is a good example of a basic verb you know (*vencer*) and a prefix (*con-*).

Verbs ending in *-ger* or *-gir*

Whenever the letter *g* is followed by an *e* or an *i,* it will have a soft *g* sound, like the letter *h* in English. When *g* is followed by *o, u,* or *a,* it will have a hard *g* sound, as in the English word "good." Conjugated forms of a verb should maintain the same sound as the infinitive form. Because the *yo* form in the present tense usually ends in *-o,* the *-go* ending sounds like the English word "go." A verb that ends in *-ger* or *-gir* must maintain a soft *g* sound, so the *yo* form will change the spelling from *g* to *j.* Some of the verbs in this list are "stem-changers." The stem change is included in parentheses after the infinitive, and the *yo* form will reflect this change. Stem-changers are explained later in this chapter. If there is nothing in parentheses after the verb, you can assume that it is regular in all present tense forms (except that the *g* changes to *j* in the *yo* form).

afligir (to afflict, to grieve)	*yo* form: *aflijo*
coger (to catch, to seize, to grab)	*yo* form: *cojo*
colegir (*e>i*) (to deduce)	*yo* form: *colijo*
corregir (*e>i*) (to correct)	*yo* form: *corrijo*
dirigir (to direct)	*yo* form: *dirijo*
elegir (*e>i*) (to elect)	*yo* form: *elijo*
exigir (to demand, to require)	*yo* form: *exijo*
fingir (to pretend)	*yo* form: *finjo*
proteger (to protect)	*yo* form: *protejo*
sumergir (to immerse, to submerge)	*yo* form: *sumerjo*
surgir (to surge)	*yo* form: *surjo*

Escoger (to choose) and *recoger* (to gather, to pick up) are good examples of a basic verb that you know (*coger*) and different prefixes (*es-* and *re-*). You should be able to predict the *yo* form of these verbs.

When a verb ends in -*guir,* the letter *u* is there only to maintain the hard *g* sound. You do not pronounce the *u* in the infinitive, and you should not pronounce it in any of the conjugated forms. However, when the letter *u* is placed between a *g* and an *o* or between a *g* and an *a,* pronunciation rules require that you say the *u*. Because the *yo* form of these verbs ends in -*o,* the *u* is dropped in the *yo* form to maintain the same sound as the infinitive. Verbs that behave like this include those listed below.

distinguir (to distinguish)	*yo* form: *distingo*
extinguir (to extinguish)	*yo* form: *extingo*
seguir (*e>i*) (to follow, to continue)	*yo* form: *sigo*

Conseguir (to get), *perseguir* (to persecute, to pursue), and *proseguir* (to continue, to proceed) are good examples of a basic verb that you know (*seguir*) and different prefixes (*con-, per-,* and *pro-*). You should be able to predict the *yo* form of these verbs if you remember the stem change.

Ver and saber

Two other verbs have unique *yo* forms: Both *ver* and *saber* are regular -*er* verbs in all forms but the *yo* form, but their *yo* forms are completely different.

ver (to see)	*yo* form: *veo*
saber (to know [a fact])	*yo* form: *sé*

Extra *Y* Verbs

Another predictable verb pattern has spelling changes in forms other than *yo:* Any verb that ends in *-uir* (except for those that end in *-guir*) adds a *y* before the normal ending in all forms but *nosotros/nosotras* and v*osotros/vosotras*. Table 3-5 serves as an example for all the verbs in the list that follows.

Table 3-5   Conjugation Chart for the Verb *Construir* (to Build)

Subject	Verb	Subject	Verb
yo	construyo	nosotros/nosotras	construimos
tú	construyes	vosotros/vosotras	construís
él	construye	ellos	construyen
ella	construye	ellas	construyen
usted	construye	ustedes	construyen

concluir	(to conclude)	*yo* form: *concluyo*
constituir	(to constitute)	*yo* form: *constituyo*
contribuir	(to contribute)	*yo* form: *contribuyo*
destruir	(to destroy)	*yo* form: *destruyo*
fluir	(to flow)	*yo* form: *fluyo*
huir	(to run away, to flee)	*yo* form: *huyo*
incluir	(to include)	*yo* form: *incluyo*

Influir (to influence) is a good example of a basic verb you know (*fluir*) and a prefix (*in-*).

All the above verbs are conjugated exactly like *construir*. The verb *oír* (to hear) is similar, but *oír* is also a *-go* verb in its *yo* form, and has an accent on the infinitive and in the *nosotros/nosotras* and *vosotros/vosotras* forms. See Table 3-6, for example.

Table 3-6   Conjugation Chart for the Verb *Oír* (to Hear)

Subject	Verb	Subject	Verb
yo	oigo	nosotros/nosotras	oímos
tú	oyes	vosotros/vosotras	oís
él	oye	ellos	oyen
ella	oye	ellas	oyen
usted	oye	ustedes	oyen

Stem-Changing Verbs in the Present Tense

For the verbs presented so far, the ending is what is irregular. There is, however, a different kind of predictable verb conjugation in which the stem of the verb changes and the endings are normal—even the *yo* form! The stem of a verb is what is left when you remove the infinitive ending (*-ar, -er,* or *-ir*).

Because the stem of the verb changes, these verbs are called stem-changing verbs, or stem-changers. You must learn each particular verb and remember that it is a stem-changer. It is impossible to identify that a verb is a stem-changer by simply looking at the infinitive unless you recognize a previously learned stem-changer with a prefix.

The hardest part about stem-changers is that you have to memorize the verbs in which stem changes occur. Once you memorize the type of stem change a verb undergoes, the actual patterns of the stem-changing verbs are quite simple; because all the conjugation endings are regular, conjugating these verbs is easy.

For all stem-changers, it is always the stressed syllable that changes. Stem-changing verbs are so common that most dictionaries inform you of the stem change in the entry even before giving the verb's translation.

There are basically three different ways in which the stem of a verb can change in the present tense. The verbs listed below are grouped according to the type of stem change they undergo. When you learn the meanings of the verbs below, memorize what kind of stem change each undergoes as well.

The patterns for stem-changing verbs are very consistent. All forms of the verb will undergo a stem change except for *nosotros/nosotras* and *vosotros/vosotras*. The best way to see the patterns is to consider a few examples.

e>ie stem-changers

The most common stem change is *e>ie*. That means the stressed letter *e* in the stem of the verb will change to *ie* in certain forms of the verb. If a verb has two *e*'s in the stem, it will always be the second *e* that undergoes a stem change. In the lists and charts below, the specific *e* that changes to *ie* is underlined.

The verb *cerrar* is typical of an *-ar* verb with an *e>ie* stem change. In Table 3-7, the *ie* is underlined where the stem change occurs. Notice that *nosotros/nosotras* and *vosotros/vosotras* do not undergo a stem change.

Table 3-7 **Conjugation Chart for the Verb** *Cerrar* **(to Close)**

Subject	Verb	Subject	Verb
yo	c*ie*rro	nosotros/nosotras	cerramos
tú	c*ie*rras	vosotros/vosotras	cerráis
él	c*ie*rra	ellos	c*ie*rran
ella	c*ie*rra	ellas	c*ie*rran
usted	c*ie*rra	ustedes	c*ie*rran

All the *e>ie* stem-changing verbs listed below include the stem change in parentheses after the infinitive. You should remember the verbs with the *e>ie* as a part of the infinitive in Spanish so that you will be able to conjugate these verbs correctly.

Listed below are some commonly used *-ar* verbs that undergo an *e>ie* stem change exactly like that shown in Table 3-7.

acertar (*e>ie*)	to guess, to get correct
apretar (*e>ie*)	to tighten, to squeeze
atravesar (*e>ie*)	to cross
cerrar (*e>ie*)	to close
comenzar (*e>ie*)	to begin (interchangeable with *empezar*)
confesar (*e>ie*)	to confess
despertar (*e>ie*)	to wake up
empezar (*e>ie*)	to begin (interchangeable with *comenzar*)
gobernar (*e>ie*)	to govern
helar (*e>ie*)	to freeze
negar (*e>ie*)	to deny
pensar (*e>ie*)	to think
quebrar (*e>ie*)	to break
recomendar (*e>ie*)	to recommend
remendar (*e>ie*)	to patch
sentarse (*e>ie*)	to sit down
temblar (*e>ie*)	to tremble
tropezar (*e>ie*) (*con*)	to stumble, to bump into

Encerrar (*e>ie*) (to enclose) is a good example of a basic verb that you know (*cerrar*) and a prefix (*en-*).

The verb *perder* is a typical -*er* verb with an *e>ie* stem change. The forms of this verb presented in Table 3-8 serve as an example for all the verbs listed below.

Table 3-8   Conjugation Chart for the Verb *Perder* (to Lose)

Subject	Verb	Subject	Verb
yo	pierdo	nosotros/nosotras	perdemos
tú	pierdes	vosotros/vosotras	perdéis
él	pierde	ellos	pierden
ella	pierde	ellas	pierden
usted	pierde	ustedes	pierden

Notice that, in the verbs below, the -*er* ending is not part of the stem, so *perder* and *querer* only have one *e* in the stem. When verbs like *defender* and *entender* have two *e*'s in the stem, the second one, closer to the end, will undergo a stem change. See Table 3-9 for a sample conjugation chart.

The following list includes common -*er* verbs that undergo the stem change *e>ie*.

ascender (*e>ie*)	to ascend (to go up)
descender (*e>ie*)	to descend (to go down)
defender (*e>ie*)	to defend
encender (*e>ie*)	to light
entender (*e>ie*)	to understand
perder (*e>ie*)	to lose
querer (*e>ie*)	to want

Table 3-9   Conjugation Chart for the Verb *Defender* (to Defend)

Subject	Verb	Subject	Verb
yo	defiendo	nosotros/nosotras	defendemos
tú	defiendes	vosotros/vosotras	defendéis
él	defiende	ellos	defienden

(continued)

Table 3-9 *(continued)*

Subject	Verb	Subject	Verb
ella	defiende	ellas	defienden
usted	defiende	ustedes	defienden

For *-ir* verbs that undergo the stem change *e>ie,* all follow the same patterns as the verb *mentir* in Table 3-10. Use this conjugation chart as an example for the forms of the verbs in the list that follows.

Table 3-10 Conjugation Chart for the Verb *Mentir* (to Tell a Lie)

Subject	Verb	Subject	Verb
yo	miento	nosotros/nosotras	mentimos
tú	mientes	vosotros/vosotras	mentís
él	miente	ellos	mienten
ella	miente	ellas	mienten
usted	miente	ustedes	mienten

Some of the most common *-ir* verbs that undergo an *e>ie* stem change are listed below.

advertir (e>ie)	to advise, to warn
convertir (e>ie)	to convert
hervir (e>ie)	to boil
mentir (e>ie)	to tell a lie
preferir (e>ie)	to prefer
referir (e>ie)	to refer
sentir (e>ie)	to feel, to regret
sugerir (e>ie)	to suggest

Consentir (e>ie) (to consent) is a good example of a basic verb that you know (*sentir*) and a prefix (*con-*).

Notice that the verb *preferir* has two *e*'s in the stem. Whenever there are two *e*'s in the stem of a verb, it is the second one that undergoes a stem change. The conjugated forms of *preferir* are somewhat difficult to picture, so take a good look at Table 3-11 that follows. When pronouncing these verb forms, remember to say every vowel.

Table 3-11   Conjugation Chart for the Verb *Preferir* (to Prefer)

Subject	Verb	Subject	Verb
yo	prefiero	nosotros/nosotras	preferimos
tú	prefieres	vosotros/vosotras	preferís
él	prefiere	ellos	prefieren
ella	prefiere	ellas	prefieren
usted	prefiere	ustedes	prefieren

Tener and *venir* are *e>ie* stem-changers that also have an irregular *yo* form. You may remember that these two verbs were listed with the *-go* verbs under the *yo* irregulars. That is because the *yo* form of each of these verbs ends in *-go;* the rest of the forms, however, follow the *e>ie* stem-changing patterns. These verbs are very common, so be sure to learn the conjugation charts in Table 3-12 and Table 3-13.

Table 3-12   Conjugation Chart for the Verb *Tener* (to Have)

Subject	Verb	Subject	Verb
yo	tengo	nosotros/nosotras	tenemos
tú	tienes	vosotros/vosotras	tenéis
él	tiene	ellos	tienen
ella	tiene	ellas	tienen
usted	tiene	ustedes	tienen

Table 3-13   Conjugation Chart for the Verb *Venir* (to Come)

Subject	Verb	Subject	Verb
yo	vengo	nosotros/nosotras	venimos
tú	vienes	vosotros/vosotras	venís
él	viene	ellos	vienen
ella	viene	ellas	vienen
usted	viene	ustedes	vienen

The forms for both verbs are very similar, but you should be careful to notice that the *nosotros/nosotras* and *vosotros/vosotras* endings are different for *venir* because it is an *-ir* verb and *tener* is an *-er* verb.

o>ue stem-changers

The second-most common type of stem change that occurs in Spanish verbs is *o>ue.* Now that you understand how to conjugate stem-changing verbs in general, learning about the verbs with an *o>ue* stem change will be relatively easy.

Common *-ar* verbs that undergo a stem change *o>ue:*

acordar (o>ue)	to agree upon
acostarse (o>ue)	to go to bed
almorzar (o>ue)	to eat lunch
aprobar (o>ue)	to approve
contar (o>ue)	to count, to tell a story
costar (o>ue)	to cost
encontrar (o>ue)	to find
mostrar (o>ue)	to show (interchangeable with *demostrar*)
probar (o>ue)	to prove
recordar (o>ue)	to remember, to remind
rogar (o>ue)	to pray
sonar (o>ue)	to sound
soñar (o>ue) (con)	to dream
tostar (o>ue)	to toast
volar (o>ue)	to fly

Demostrar (o>ue) is a good example of a basic verb that you know (*mostrar*) and a prefix (*de-*). The verb *demostrar* is interchangeable with *mostrar* because they both mean "to show."

Common *-er* verbs that undergo a stem change *o>ue:*

doler (o>ue)	to ache, to hurt
morder (o>ue)	to bite
mover (o>ue)	to move
poder (o>ue)	to be able
resolver (o>ue)	to resolve
soler (o>ue)	to be accustomed to
volver (o>ue)	to return

Devolver (o>ue) (to return an object, to give something back) and *envolver (o>ue)* (to wrap up) are good examples of a basic verb that you know (*volver*) and different prefixes (*de-* and *en-*).

By now, you understand that a stem-changing verb will have regular verb endings, so Table 3-14 is the only example of an *o>ue* stem-changer.

Table 3-14   Conjugation Chart for the Verb *Mover* (to Move)

Subject	Verb	Subject	Verb
yo	muevo	nosotros/nosotras	movemos
tú	mueves	vosotros/vosotras	movéis
él	mueve	ellos	mueven
ella	mueve	ellas	mueven
usted	mueve	ustedes	mueven

The following verbs also undergo an *o>ue* stem change; because they are -*ir* verbs, however, the *nosotros/nosotras* ending is -*imos*.

Common -*ir* verbs that stem change *o>ue:*

dormir (*o>ue*)   to sleep

morir (*o>ue*)   to die

The verb *jugar* is usually listed with the *o>ue* stem-changing verbs because it follows the same pattern. However, you may notice there is no *o* to change to *ue* in the verb *jugar*. It is the only *u>ue* stem-changer in the Spanish language. Because it means "to play" (a sport or game), it's a popular word in both Spanish- and English-speaking cultures. See Table 3-15 for the unusual verb forms of *jugar*.

Table 3-15   Conjugation Chart for the Verb *Jugar* (to Play)

Subject	Verb	Subject	Verb
yo	juego	nosotros/nosotras	jugamos
tú	juegas	vosotros/vosotras	jugáis
él	juega	ellos	juegan
ella	juega	ellas	juegan
usted	juega	ustedes	juegan

e>i stem-changers

Here's a test of your grasp of formal logic: All *e>i* stem-changing verbs are *-ir* verbs, but not all *-ir* verbs are *e>i* stem-changers. Consider the earlier list of *e>ie* stem-changers; some of them are *-ir* verbs. This means that when you learn an *-ir* verb that undergoes a stem change, you have to be careful to remember whether it undergoes an *e>ie* or *e>i* stem change. Fortunately, the list of *e>i* stem-changing verbs is short, and it is true that only *-ir* verbs can undergo an *e>i* stem change.

Common *e>i* stem-changing verbs:

bendecir (e>i)	to bless
colegir (e>i)	to deduce
competir (e>i)	to compete
corregir (e>i)	to correct
decir (e>i)	to say, to tell
despedirse (e>i)	to say goodbye
elegir (e>i)	to elect
freír (e>i)	to fry
gemir (e>i)	to grumble, to groan
maldecir (e>i)	to curse
medir (e>i)	to measure
pedir (e>i)	to request
reír (e>i)	to laugh
repetir (e>i)	to repeat
seguir (e>i)	to follow, to continue
servir (e>i)	to serve
sonreír (e>i)	to smile
vestir (e>i)	to dress

Despedir (e>i) (to fire), *impedir (e>i)* (to impede, to prevent), and *desvestir (e>i)* (to undress) are good examples of basic verbs that you know (*pedir* and *vestir*) and a prefix (*des-* and *im-*).

Because all the above verbs are *-ir* verbs, you only need one example of the conjugation chart for these verbs. All *e>i* stem-changers will be conjugated like *servir* in Table 3-16.

Table 3-16   Conjugation Chart for the Verb *Servir* (to Serve)

Subject	Verb	Subject	Verb
yo	sirvo	nosotros/nosotras	servimos
tú	sirves	vosotros/vosotras	servís
él	sirve	ellos	sirven
ella	sirve	ellas	sirven
usted	sirve	ustedes	sirven

The Really Irregular Verbs

Some verbs are so irregular that the infinitive of the verb looks nothing like its conjugated forms. One of the most irregular verbs in Spanish—*ir*, which means "to go" (see Table 3-17)—is also the most common, so you see the conjugated forms of this verb often. Notice that the entire verb looks like the *-ir* infinitive ending. However, it is conjugated nothing at all like a normal *-ir* verb. Be aware that each conjugation in the chart below is the entire form of the verb that should be used with each pronoun.

Table 3-17   Present Tense Conjugation Chart for the Verb *Ir* (to Go)

Subject	Verb	Subject	Verb
yo	voy	nosotros/nosotras	vamos
tú	vas	vosotros/vosotras	vais
él	va	ellos	van
ella	va	ellas	van
usted	va	ustedes	van

Once you get used to thinking that *voy, vas, va, vamos, vais,* and *van* all mean "go" or "goes," it is hard to remember that the infinitive is *ir.*

The verb *ser* means "to be." Remember that although Table 3-18 is full of little words, they are not endings; rather, they are the entire conjugated verb form.

Table 3-18   Present Tense Conjugation Chart for the Verb *Ser* (to Be)

Subject	Verb	Subject	Verb
yo	soy	nosotros/nosotras	somos
tú	eres	vosotros/vosotras	sois
él	es	ellos	son
ella	es	ellas	son
usted	es	ustedes	son

Chapter Checkout

Write the correct present tense form of the verb to agree with the subject pronoun in parentheses.

1. *sustraer* (*yo*)
2. *entender* (*tú*)
3. *pedir* (*ellos*)
4. *fingir* (*yo*)
5. *quebrar* (*él*)
6. *perseguir* (*Uds.*)
7. *distribuir* (*ella*)

Answers: 1. *sustraigo* **2.** *entiendes* **3.** *piden* **4.** *finjo* **5.** *quiebra* **6.** *persiguen* **7.** *distribuye*

Chapter 4
REVIEW OF THE PAST TENSES

Chapter Check-In

❑ Conjugating regular verbs in the preterit and imperfect

❑ Predicting irregular preterit patterns

❑ Learning the three imperfect verbs

Spanish has two past tenses, the preterit and the imperfect. The preterit tense is used to indicate completed actions in the past. The imperfect is used to describe and indicate ongoing or incomplete actions in the past. The imperfect tense is ironically named because it has only three irregular verbs. In contrast, there are many irregular preterit forms that undergo several spelling changes. Once you are able to conjugate verbs correctly in both tenses, you must also learn to differentiate between the two Spanish past tenses by learning the situations in which each tense is appropriate— a topic that will be presented later in this book. For now, this chapter focuses on reviewing how to conjugate verbs in the past.

Regular Verbs in the Preterit Tense

Verbs that are regular in the present tense are not necessarily regular in the preterit. Because the preterit irregulars are presented later in this chapter, only regular verbs in the preterit are used as examples in this section. To conjugate a regular verb in the preterit tense, remove the infinitive ending and add the preterit endings presented below. For an *-ar* verb that is regular in the preterit, use the endings in Table 4-1. Because *-er* and *-ir* verbs are conjugated exactly alike in the preterit tense, both use the endings in Table 4-3.

Table 4-1   Preterit Endings for Regular *-ar* Verbs

Subject	Ending	Subject	Ending
yo	-é	nosotros/nosotras	-amos
tú	-aste	vosotros/vosotras	-asteis
él	-ó	ellos	-aron
ella	-ó	ellas	-aron
usted	-ó	ustedes	-aron

In the present tense, the *yo* form ends in *-o*, but in the preterit tense, the *él, ella,* and *usted* forms end in *-ó*. Be sure to notice the accent mark on the preterit forms because that is the only difference between the *yo* form of the present tense and the *él* form of the preterit tense. There is also an accent mark on the *yo* form of all regular preterit verbs. Pronounce these words with the stress on the last syllable.

Notice that regular *-ar* verbs have the same *nosotros/nosotras* form in the preterit as they do in the present tense. The only way to know whether it is in the preterit or present tense is by considering the context of the sentence.

Cantar (to sing) is a regular verb in the preterit, so it serves as a good example. Table 4-2 is a conjugation chart for the verb *cantar* in the preterit tense. Because the preterit is a past tense, these forms translate to the English past tense form: "sang."

Table 4-2   Preterit Forms of the Regular *-ar* Verb *Cantar*

Subject	Verb	Subject	Verb
yo	canté	nosotros/nosotras	cantamos
tú	cantaste	vosotros/vosotras	cantasteis
él	cantó	ellos	cantaron
ella	cantó	ellas	cantaron
usted	cantó	ustedes	cantaron

As you can see in Table 4-3, the endings for *-er* and *-ir* verbs are the same for regular verbs in the preterit tense.

Table 4-3   Preterit Endings for Regular -er Verbs and Regular -ir Verbs

Subject	Ending	Subject	Ending
yo	-í	nosotros/nosotras	-imos
tú	-iste	vosotros/vosotras	-isteis
él	-ió	ellos	-ieron
ella	-ió	ellas	-ieron
usted	-ió	ustedes	-ieron

The *nosotros/nosotras* form of an *-ir* verb is exactly the same in the present and preterit tenses.

Beber (to drink) is a regular *-er* verb in the preterit. The preterit forms in Table 4-4 translate to the English past tense form: "drank."

Table 4-4   Preterit Forms of the Regular -er Verb Beber

Subject	Verb	Subject	Verb
yo	bebí	nosotros/nosotras	bebimos
tú	bebiste	vosotros/vosotras	bebisteis
él	bebió	ellos	bebieron
ella	bebió	ellas	bebieron
usted	bebió	ustedes	bebieron

The verb *vivir* (to live) is a good example of a regular *-ir* verb in the preterit. Table 4-5 serves as a sample conjugation for all *-ir* verbs in the preterit.

Table 4-5   Preterit Forms of the Regular -ir Verb Vivir

Subject	Verb	Subject	Verb
yo	viví	nosotros/nosotras	vivimos
tú	viviste	vosotros/vosotras	vivisteis
él	vivió	ellos	vivieron
ella	vivió	ellas	vivieron
usted	vivió	ustedes	vivieron

Verbs with Spelling Changes in the Preterit Tense

The spelling and pronunciation rules of Spanish are extremely consistent, and a conjugated form of the verb may have to change its spelling in order to maintain the pronunciation of the infinitive. In the *yo* form of some verbs, adding *-í* or *-é* to the base of the verb changes the pronunciation of the word, so the spelling is changed to elicit the same basic sound as the infinitive.

Verbs that end in *-car*

The vowel that follows the letter *c* determines whether it is pronounced hard (like a *k*) or soft (like an *s*). The *c* is pronounced soft when followed by an *i* or an *e*; it is pronounced hard when followed by an *o, a,* or *u*. Thus, a verb ending in *-car* has the hard *c* sound in its infinitive form. All the conjugated forms must maintain this sound, but the preterit *yo* ending causes problems. The *c* becomes a soft sound when you add *-é* to the stem, which is unacceptable for a *-car* verb. For this reason, the letter *c* changes to *qu* in the *yo* form. Pronounce the ending (*-qué*) like the English name "Kay." The letter *u* is never pronounced when it follows a *q*. The combination of letters *qu* is always pronounced like a *k*, not like the sound in the English word "queen." Table 4-6 is the preterit conjugation chart for the verb *practicar* (to practice), whose conjugation is typical of all regular verbs that end in *-car*, including those in the list that follows Table 4-6. To simplify the rule: If a verb ends in *-car*, change the *c* to *qu* in the *yo* form of the preterit.

Table 4-6   Preterit Forms of the Verb *Practicar* (to Practice)

Subject	Verb	Subject	Verb
yo	practiqué	nosotros/nosotras	practicamos
tú	practicaste	vosotros/vosotras	practicasteis
él	practicó	ellos	practicaron
ella	practicó	ellas	practicaron
usted	practicó	ustedes	practicaron

Some common verbs ending in -*car:*

aparcar	to park	preterit *yo* form: *aparqué*
aplicar	to apply	preterit *yo* form: *apliqué*
buscar	to seek, to look for	preterit *yo* form: *busqué*
clarificar	to clarify	preterit *yo* form: *clarifiqué*
clasificar	to classify	preterit *yo* form: *clasifiqué*
colocar	to place, to put	preterit *yo* form: *coloqué*
comunicar	to communicate	preterit *yo* form: *comuniqué*
dedicar	to dedicate	preterit *yo* form: *dediqué*
destacar	to stand out	preterit *yo* form: *destaqué*
educar	to educate	preterit *yo* form: *eduqué*
empacar	to pack	preterit *yo* form: *empaqué*
explicar	to explain	preterit *yo* form: *expliqué*
fabricar	to make	preterit *yo* form: *fabriqué*
indicar	to indicate	preterit *yo* form: *indiqué*
justificar	to justify	preterit *yo* form: *justifiqué*
marcar	to mark	preterit *yo* form: *marqué*
masticar	to chew	preterit *yo* form: *mastiqué*
pescar	to fish	preterit *yo* form: *pesqué*
publicar	to publish	preterit *yo* form: *publiqué*
sacar	to take out	preterit *yo* form: *saqué*
significar	to mean	preterit *yo* form: *signifiqué*
tocar	to touch, to play a musical instrument	preterit *yo* form: *toqué*

Verbs that end in -*gar*

The Spanish letter *g* behaves a lot like the letter *c.* The vowel that follows the letter *g* determines whether it is pronounced hard (like the *g* in "girl") or soft (like the *g* in "gem"). Infinitives that end in -*gar* are pronounced with a hard *g* sound. To prevent this hard *g* from becoming a soft *g* with the addition of the preterit *yo* ending (-*é*), the letter *u* is added between the *g* and *e* to maintain the sound of the infinitive. This *yo* ending (-*gué*) sounds like the English word "gay."

Table 4-7 is the preterit conjugation chart for the verb *cargar* (to load), which serves as a good example for these types of verbs.

Table 4-7   Preterit Forms of the Verb *Cargar* (to Load)

Subject	Verb	Subject	Verb
yo	cargué	nosotros/nosotras	cargamos
tú	cargaste	vosotros/vosotras	cargasteis
él	cargó	ellos	cargaron
ella	cargó	ellas	cargaron
usted	cargó	ustedes	cargaron

The following -*gar* verbs are conjugated like *cargar* in the preterit tense. They are regular in all forms except that you must change the *g* to *gu* before the regular *yo* ending.

Some common verbs ending in -*gar:*

agregar	to add	preterit *yo* form: *agregué*
apagar	to extinguish, to turn off	preterit *yo* form: *apagué*
cargar	to load	preterit *yo* form: *cargué*
encargar	to put in charge, to entrust	preterit *yo* form: *encargué*
entregar	to hand in, to hand over	preterit *yo* form: *entregué*
jugar	to play a sport	preterit *yo* form: *jugué*
llegar	to arrive	preterit *yo* form: *llegué*
obligar	to compel, to oblige	preterit *yo* form: *obligué*
pegar	to hit, to stick, to glue	preterit *yo* form: *pegué*
regar	to water (a plant)	preterit *yo* form: *regué*
segar	to mow (the lawn)	preterit *yo* form: *segué*
tragar	to swallow	preterit *yo* form: *tragué*
vagar	to wander	preterit *yo* form: *vagué*

Verbs that end in -*zar*

You may have already learned a simple rule about the letter *z* in Spanish: "Whenever *z* is followed by *e*, it changes to *c*." This rule is important in the preterit tense of verbs ending in -*zar* because the *z* must change to *c* before adding the -*é* ending in the *yo* form. The preterit conjugation of the verb *rezar* (to pray) in Table 4-8 is an example of how to conjugate the -*zar* verbs in the list that follows.

Table 4-8   Preterit Forms of the Verb *Rezar* (to Pray)

Subject	Verb	Subject	Verb
yo	recé	nosotros/nosotras	rezamos
tú	rezaste	vosotros/vosotras	rezasteis
él	rezó	ellos	rezaron
ella	rezó	ellas	rezaron
usted	rezó	ustedes	rezaron

Common verbs that end in *-zar:*

autorizar	to authorize	preterit *yo* form: *autoricé*
abrazar	to embrace, to hug	preterit *yo* form: *abracé*
alcanzar	to reach	preterit *yo* form: *alcancé*
almorzar	to eat lunch	preterit *yo* form: *almorcé*
amenazar	to threaten	preterit *yo* form: *amenacé*
avanzar	to advance	preterit *yo* form: *avancé*
comenzar	to begin	preterit *yo* form: *comencé*
empezar	to begin	preterit *yo* form: *empecé*
gozar	to enjoy	preterit *yo* form: *gocé*
lanzar	to throw	preterit *yo* form: *lancé*
organizar	to organize	preterit *yo* form: *organicé*
realizar	to fulfill, to realize (one's dream)	preterit *yo* form: *realicé*
rezar	to pray	preterit *yo* form: *recé*
simbolizar	to symbolize	preterit *yo* form: *simbolicé*
trazar	to trace	preterit *yo* form: *tracé*
tropezar	to stumble, to trip	preterit *yo* form: *tropecé*

i to *y*

A spelling change is necessary in certain forms in the preterit when the stem of the verb ends in a vowel. If the letter *i* is surrounded by two other vowels, you must change the *i* to *y.* The *-er* and *-ir* preterit endings cause the *i* to change to *y* in the third person forms (*él, ella, usted, ellos, ellas,* and *ustedes*). An accent will be added to any other *i* in the conjugation chart. Look carefully at the accent marks in Table 4-9. This conjugation chart of the verb *creer* (to believe) serves as an example for the verbs in the list that follows.

Table 4-9   Preterit Forms of the Verb *Creer* (to Believe)

Subject	Verb	Subject	Verb
yo	creí	nosotros/nosotras	creímos
tú	creíste	vosotros/vosotras	creísteis
él	creyó	ellos	creyeron
ella	creyó	ellas	creyeron
usted	creyó	ustedes	creyeron

Other verbs that have a base ending in a vowel are also conjugated like *creer*. Many of these verbs end in *-uir*:

caer	to fall
construir	to construct, to build
contribuir	to contribute
creer	to believe
destruir	to destroy
distribuir	to distribute
fluir	to flow
huir	to flee, to run away
incluir	to include
influir	to influence
leer	to read
oír	to hear
poseer	to possess
proveer	to provide

Verbs ending in *-guir* are exceptions to the above rule because of the special issue posed by the *g*. The verb *seguir* (to follow, to continue) appears to have spelling issues, but actually it does not. As you can see in Table 4-10, although it looks very strange, it is conjugated like an *-ir* stem-changing verb.

Table 4-10   Preterit Forms of the Verb *Seguir* (to Follow, to Continue)

Subject	Verb	Subject	Verb
yo	seguí	nosotros/nosotras	seguimos
tú	seguiste	vosotros/vosotras	seguisteis

Subject	Verb	Subject	Verb
él	siguió	ellos	siguieron
ella	siguió	ellas	siguieron
usted	siguió	ustedes	siguieron

The verb *traer* (to bring) is also an exception; because it is completely irregular, it is presented later in this chapter.

-ar or *-er* Verbs in the Preterit Tense

No *-ar* or *-er* verbs undergo a stem change in the preterit. Remember that *-ar* and *-er* verbs that undergo a stem change in the present tense *do not* undergo a stem change in the preterit. The verb *pensar* (to think) is a good example of this. Look carefully at the forms in Table 4-11 and notice the lack of stem change in the preterit.

Table 4-11   Preterit Forms of the Verb *Pensar* (to Think)

Subject	Verb	Subject	Verb
yo	pensé	nosotros/nosotras	pensamos
tú	pensaste	vosotros/vosotras	pensasteis
él	pensó	ellos	pensaron
ella	pensó	ellas	pensaron
usted	pensó	ustedes	pensaron

Stem-Changers in the Preterit Tense

An *-ir* verb that undergoes a stem change in the present tense will undergo a stem change in the preterit in the third person forms (*él, ella, usted, ellos, ellas,* and *ustedes*). Any *-ir* verb that undergoes an *o>ue* stem change in the present tense undergoes an *o>u* stem change in the preterit. Table 4-12 demonstrates the preterit patterns for *morir* (to die), an *-ir* verb that undergoes an *o>ue* stem change in the present tense. The verb *dormir* (to sleep) is conjugated in exactly the same manner.

Table 4-12   Preterit Forms of *Morir* (to Die)

Subject	Verb	Subject	Verb
yo	morí	nosotros/nosotras	morimos
tú	moriste	vosotros/vosotras	moristeis
él	murió	ellos	murieron
ella	murió	ellas	murieron
usted	murió	ustedes	murieron

There are several *-ir* verbs that undergo an *e>ie* stem change in the present tense. Any *-ir* verb that undergoes an *e>ie* stem change in the present tense undergoes an *e>i* stem change in the preterit in the third person forms (*él, ella, usted, ellos, ellas,* and *ustedes*). Table 4-13 represents the conjugation chart for all the verbs in the list that follows. Notice that, just as in the present tense, it is the second *e* in *preferir* (to prefer) that undergoes a change.

Table 4-13   Preterit Forms of *Preferir* (to Prefer)

Subject	Verb	Subject	Verb
yo	preferí	nosotros/nosotras	preferimos
tú	preferiste	vosotros/vosotras	preferisteis
él	prefirió	ellos	prefirieron
ella	prefirió	ellas	prefirieron
usted	prefirió	ustedes	prefirieron

Common verbs conjugated like *preferir* in the preterit tense:

advertir	to advise, to warn
convertir	to convert
hervir	to boil
mentir	to tell a lie
preferir	to prefer
sentir	to feel, to regret

An *-ir* verb that undergoes an *e>i* stem change in the present tense will also undergo an *e>i* stem change in the preterit, but only in the third person forms (*él, ella, usted, ellos, ellas,* and *ustedes*). The verbs that follow Table 4-14 are all conjugated like *servir* (to serve).

Table 4-14   Preterit Forms of *Servir* (to Serve)

Subject	Verb	Subject	Verb
yo	serví	nosotros/nosotras	servimos
tú	serviste	vosotros/vosotras	servisteis
él	sirvió	ellos	sirvieron
ella	sirvió	ellas	sirvieron
usted	sirvió	ustedes	sirvieron

Common verbs conjugated like *servir* in the preterit tense:

impedir	to impede, to prevent
medir	to measure
pedir	to request
repetir	to repeat
seguir	to follow
vestirse	to dress oneself, to get dressed

Morphing Irregulars in the Preterit Tense

Some verbs are irregular in the preterit tense because the stem of the verb morphs into something very different from the infinitive. These verbs are not stem-changers because they do not follow the patterns that stem-changing verbs follow. The morphing verbs do, however, have consistent preterit irregularities that you can predict if you know they are morphing verbs. These verbs also consistently use the special set of irregular endings found in Table 4-15. All the preterit-morphing verbs listed below use these endings rather than the regular preterit endings. Notice that there are no written accent marks on any form.

Table 4-15   Endings for Preterit-Morphing Verbs

Subject	Ending	Subject	Ending
yo	-e	nosotros/nosotras	-imos
tú	-iste	vosotros/vosotras	-isteis
él	-o	ellos	-ieron
ella	-o	ellas	-ieron
usted	-o	ustedes	-ieron

u-stem verbs

Some verbs have a *u* as part of the stem in the preterit even though they do not have a *u* in the infinitive. The morph listed next to the verbs below is used in place of the stem of the verb for every form of the preterit conjugation. All of the following verbs use the endings from Table 4-15 to form the preterit.

andar (to walk)	changes to *anduv-*
estar (to be)	changes to *estuv-*
poner (to put)	changes to *pus-*
poder (to be able)	changes to *pud-*
saber (to know)	changes to *sup-*
tener (to have)	changes to *tuv-*

Memorize the forms of *tener* in the preterit (Table 4-16) and chant them like a mantra. Not only is the verb *tener* (to have) extremely common, but knowing how to conjugate it in the preterit tense will also help you to remember the patterns for all of the *u*-stem verbs listed above.

Table 4-16 Preterit Forms of *Tener* (to Have)

Subject	Verb	Subject	Verb
yo	tuve	nosotros/nosotras	tuvimos
tú	tuviste	vosotros/vosotras	tuvisteis
él	tuvo	ellos	tuvieron
ella	tuvo	ellas	tuvieron
usted	tuvo	ustedes	tuvieron

i-stem verbs

Another group of preterit-morphing verbs have an irregular stem that includes the letter *i*. These verbs use the irregular endings in Table 4-15. The *i*-stem verbs that follow are conjugated like *venir* (to come) in the preterit tense (see Table 4-17).

hacer (to make, to do)	changes to *hic-*
querer (to want, to love)	changes to *quis-*
venir (to come)	changes to *vin-*

Remember that preterit-morphing verbs do not conjugate like stem-changers in the preterit tense, even though some of them may be stem-changers in the present tense.

Table 4-17   Preterit Forms of *Venir* (to Come)

Subject	Verb	Subject	Verb
yo	vine	nosotros/nosotras	vinimos
tú	viniste	vosotros/vosotras	vinisteis
él	vino	ellos	vinieron
ella	vino	ellas	vinieron
usted	vino	ustedes	vinieron

Even though *hacer* uses the same endings as *venir* in the preterit, there is one spelling change that you have to make on the *él, ella,* and *usted* forms of *hacer* to preserve the soft *c* sound. As you can see in Table 4-18, you must change the *c* to a *z* in front of the *-o* ending.

Table 4-18   Preterit Forms of *Hacer* (to Make, to Do)

Subject	Verb	Subject	Verb
yo	hice	nosotros/nosotras	hicimos
tú	hiciste	vosotros/vosotras	hicisteis
él	hizo	ellos	hicieron
ella	hizo	ellas	hicieron
usted	hizo	ustedes	hicieron

j-stem verbs

The group of preterit-morphing verbs with a stem ending in *j* use the same endings as the other preterit-morphing verbs with one exception: Notice that the third-person plural ending of the verb *traer* in Table 4-19 is *-eron.* When the irregular stem ends in *j*, the *ellos, ellas,* and *ustedes* ending drops the letter *i* and becomes *-jeron.* All the following verbs are conjugated like *traer* in the preterit.

conducir (to drive, to lead)	changes to *conduj-*
decir (to say, to tell)	changes to *dij-*
producir (to produce)	changes to *produj-*
traducir (to translate)	changes to *traduj-*

Table 4-19   Preterit Forms of *Traer* (to Bring)

Subject	Verb	Subject	Verb
yo	traje	nosotros/nosotras	trajimos
tú	trajiste	vosotros/vosotras	trajisteis
él	trajo	ellos	trajeron
ella	trajo	ellas	trajeron
usted	trajo	ustedes	trajeron

The Truly Irregular Verbs in the Preterit

A few verbs in the preterit follow no patterns and must be memorized. The verbs *ir* (to go) and *ser* (to be) are conjugated exactly the same in the preterit. The context of a sentence determines which verb is being used. Also, any form of *ir* is always followed by the preposition *a*. Table 4-20 presents the preterit forms of two of the most common verbs in the Spanish language.

Table 4-20   Preterit Forms of the Verbs *Ir* (to Go) and *Ser* (to Be)

Subject	Verb	Subject	Verb
yo	fui	nosotros/nosotras	fuimos
tú	fuiste	vosotros/vosotras	fuisteis
él	fue	ellos	fueron
ella	fue	ellas	fueron
usted	fue	ustedes	fueron

Dar (to give) and *ver* (to see) are usually learned together in the preterit because their forms are similar. *Ver* uses the regular endings for a normal *-er* verb in the preterit and is only irregular because it does not have accent marks. The verb *dar* is strange because it is conjugated like *ver* even though it is an *-ar* verb. Notice that there are no accents on any of the forms in Table 4-21 and that the forms of *dar* are not the normal forms for an *-ar* verb.

Table 4-21   Preterit Forms of *Dar* (to Give)

Subject	Verb	Subject	Verb
yo	di	nosotros/nosotras	dimos
tú	diste	vosotros/vosotras	disteis
él	dio	ellos	dieron
ella	dio	ellas	dieron
usted	dio	ustedes	dieron

Regular Verbs in the Imperfect

The formation of verbs in the preterit is much more difficult than in the imperfect. If you do not like learning irregularities, you will find the imperfect tense the most "perfect" tense. Only three verbs in the entire language are irregular in the imperfect tense.

The *-ar* endings found in Table 4-22 are used for every *-ar* verb in the imperfect. There is not a single *-ar* verb that is irregular in the imperfect tense. There are no spelling changes and no stem changes in any verb in this tense. Notice that the *yo* form is exactly like the *él, ella,* and *usted* forms. Use a pronoun to specify the subject if it is not clear in a sentence. Also notice that only the *nosotros/nosotras* form carries a written accent mark.

Table 4-22   Imperfect Tense Endings for All *-ar* Verbs

Subject	Ending	Subject	Ending
yo	-aba	nosotros/nosotras	-ábamos
tú	-abas	vosotros/vosotras	-abais
él	-aba	ellos	-aban
ella	-aba	ellas	-aban
usted	-aba	ustedes	-aban

A stem-changing verb like *empezar* (to begin) does not undergo a stem change in the imperfect. Notice in Table 4-23 that the verb *empezar* is completely regular in all forms of the imperfect tense.

Table 4-23   Imperfect Tense Forms of the Verb *Empezar* (to Begin)

Subject	Verb	Subject	Verb
yo	empezaba	nosotros/nosotras	empezábamos
tú	empezabas	vosotros/vosotras	empezabais
él	empezaba	ellos	empezaban
ella	empezaba	ellas	empezaban
usted	empezaba	ustedes	empezaban

The endings in Table 4-24 are used for both *-ir* and *-er* verbs. *Ser, ir,* and *ver* (discussed later in this chapter) are the only three irregular verbs in the imperfect tense; for every other *-er* and *-ir* verb, use the endings in Table 4-24. Notice that all imperfect tense forms of *-er* and *-ir* verbs have a written accent mark on the letter *i.*

Table 4-24   Imperfect Tense Forms of Regular *-er* and *-ir* Verbs

Subject	Ending	Subject	Ending
yo	-ía	nosotros/nosotras	-íamos
tú	-ías	vosotros/vosotras	-íais
él	-ía	ellos	-ían
ella	-ía	ellas	-ían
usted	-ía	ustedes	-ían

A regular verb like *escribir* (to write), conjugated in Table 4-25, serves as a good example of an *-ir* verb in the imperfect tense.

Table 4-25   Imperfect Tense Forms of *Escribir* (to Write)

Subject	Verb	Subject	Verb
yo	escribía	nosotros/nosotras	escribíamos
tú	escribías	vosotros/vosotras	escribíais

Subject	Verb	Subject	Verb
él	escribía	ellos	escribían
ella	escribía	ellas	escribían
usted	escribía	ustedes	escribían

The -er verbs use the exact same endings in the imperfect tense as the -ir verbs. The verb *entender* (to understand) is a good example; notice in Table 4-26 that *entender* does not undergo a stem change in the imperfect tense as it does in the present.

Table 4-26   Imperfect Tense Forms of *Entender* (to Understand)

Subject	Verb	Subject	Verb
yo	entendía	nosotros/nosotras	entendíamos
tú	entendías	vosotros/vosotras	entendíais
él	entendía	ellos	entendían
ella	entendía	ellas	entendían
usted	entendía	ustedes	entendían

The Three Imperfect Irregular Verbs

The verbs *ir* (to go), *ver* (to see), and *ser* (to be) are completely irregular in the imperfect tense. Note that the forms of the verbs *ir* (Table 4-27) and *ser* (Table 4-28) show the complete imperfect conjugation, not just an ending.

Table 4-27   Imperfect Tense Forms of the Verb *Ir* (to Go)

Subject	Verb	Subject	Verb
yo	iba	nosotros/nosotras	íbamos
tú	ibas	vosotros/vosotras	ibais
él	iba	ellos	iban
ella	iba	ellas	iban
usted	iba	ustedes	iban

Table 4-28 Imperfect Tense Forms of the Verb *Ser* (to Be)

Subject	Verb	Subject	Verb
yo	era	nosotros/nosotras	éramos
tú	eras	vosotros/vosotras	erais
él	era	ellos	eran
ella	era	ellas	eran
usted	era	ustedes	eran

The verb *ver* is barely irregular. In Table 4-29, notice that *ver* has the regular endings for an -*er* verb. Rather than removing the -*er* from the infinitive, remove only the *r* and put *ve* in front of the regular endings.

Table 4-29 Imperfect Tense Forms of the Verb *Ver* (to See)

Subject	Verb	Subject	Verb
yo	veía	nosotros/nosotras	veíamos
tú	veías	vosotros/vosotras	veíais
él	veía	ellos	veían
ella	veía	ellas	veía
usted	veía	ustedes	veía

Chapter Checkout

For the following sentences, conjugate the verb in parentheses in the imperfect tense to agree with the subject of the sentence.

1. *Cada día yo _____ a la casa de mi abuela cuando yo era joven.* (*ir*)
2. *Carmen, Raquel y Angelita _____ producciones dramáticas muy buenas en la escuela secundaria.* (*hacer*)
3. *Lorenzo y su hermano _____ deportistas cuando niños.* (*ser*)
4. *Olivia _____ que trabajar.* (*tener*)

Using the verb in parentheses, write the correct form of the verb in the preterit tense for each of the following sentences. Do not forget to consider the subject and use the appropriate verb form.

5. *Ayer yo ____ para España. (salir)*

6. *Anoche mi padre ____ a visitarme. (venir)*

7. *El año pasado Julieta y Consuelo ____ un nuevo disco. (producir)*

8. *Las casas ____ destruidas por el terremoto. (ser)*

9. *Yo ____ al fútbol anoche. (jugar)*

Answers: 1. *iba* **2.** *hacían* **3.** *eran* **4.** *tenía* **5.** *salí* **6.** *vino* **7.** *produjeron* **8.** *fueron* **9.** *jugué*

Chapter 5
NEW VERB TENSES

Chapter Check-In

❑ Recognizing English future/conditional tense constructions

❑ Conjugating verbs in the future/conditional tense

❑ Creating future/conditional tense verb forms

❑ Using the future/conditional tense in sentences

The Future Tense

In Spanish, the future tense is an extremely easy tense to use because it is created by a special verb conjugation. The first step to understanding the Spanish future tense is to realize that its structure is completely different than it is in English. A Spanish verb in the future tense is only one word, whereas in English the future tense requires at least two words: "will" or "shall," which are placed in front of the verb in an affirmative sentence; in a negative sentence, the English future tense requires that "will not" or "shall not" precede the verb. To confuse matters, English speakers also have many colloquial methods of creating the future tense. The expressions "going to" or "gonna" are often used in affirmative sentences, and "won't" or "not gonna" are often used in negative sentences. The future in Spanish is much more clear and simple. It is simply a matter of learning to conjugate the verb in the future tense forms. There are no tricky helping verbs or confusing slang expressions as there are in English.

Using the future tense in sentences

The future tense is used in sentences when the action of the verb will happen in the future. There are many ways to express this in English, and they all require more than one word. Here are several examples of the future tense in English in simple affirmative and negative sentences.

I shall study. He will not study.

I'll study. He won't study.

I am going to study. He is not going to study.

I'm gonna study. He's not gonna study.

Here's an English grammar tidbit for you to note: You may be surprised to find that it is grammatically correct to use "shall" instead of "will" as the helping verb to create the future tense when the subject of the sentence is "I" or "we."

Any of the above sentences can be written in Spanish by using the future tense conjugation of the verb.

Yo estudiaré. Él no estudiará.

Do not get confused by the English words "will," "won't," or "gonna." Just conjugate the verb in the future tense form to go with the subject. No helping verb is necessary, and a negative sentence in Spanish simply places the word *no* in front of the conjugated verb.

There is another way in Spanish to indicate that the action of the verb is in the future without using the future tense. The formula you use is:

present tense of the verb *ir* + *a* + infinitive.

This formula is illustrated in the following sentences, which are followed by their English equivalents.

Yo voy a estudiar. Él no va a estudiar.

I shall study. (I'm going to study.) He will not study. (He's not going to study.)

Because this method requires only the ability to conjugate the verb *ir* in the present tense, students of Spanish use it often until they learn to use the actual future tense. In reality, it does not matter whether you use the actual future tense or the "*ir* + *a* + infinitive" formula.

Regular verbs

So far, all the tenses for which we have learned the conjugated forms have required that we remove the infinitive ending. That means that you must remove the -*ar*, -*er*, or -*ir* ending from the verb before adding the appropriate ending for the form and tense.

The future tense is unusual because the endings for each form are added to the entire infinitive. Because the entire infinitive is used, there is no need for three different conjugation charts for the three different kinds of infinitives

(*-ar, -er,* and *-ir* verbs). The verb endings in Table 5-1 are added to the infinitive of any regular verb to create the future tense. The 12 verbs that are irregular in the future tense are presented in the next section, so for now, just remember to use the entire infinitive plus the endings in Table 5-1.

Table 5-1   Future Tense Verb Endings

Subject	Ending	Subject	Ending
yo	-é	nosotros/nosotras	-emos
tú	-ás	vosotros/vosotras	-éis
él	-á	ellos	-án
ella	-á	ellas	-án
usted	-á	ustedes	-án

Notice that all the future tense endings have an accent except for the *nosotros/nosotras* form.

Now look over Table 5-2, Table 5-3, and Table 5-4. These serve as examples of verb conjugation charts for regular *-ar, -er,* and *-ir* verbs. Notice that the exact same endings are used for all three types of verbs in the future tense.

Table 5-2   A Regular *-ar* Verb in the Future Tense

Subject	Verb	Subject	Verb
yo	hablaré	nosotros/nosotras	hablaremos
tú	hablarás	vosotros/vosotras	hablaréis
él	hablará	ellos	hablarán
ella	hablará	ellas	hablarán
usted	hablará	ustedes	hablarán

Table 5-3   A Regular *-er* Verb in the Future Tense

Subject	Verb	Subject	Verb
yo	comeré	nosotros/nosotras	comeremos
tú	comerás	vosotros/vosotras	comeréis
él	comerá	ellos	comerán
ella	comerá	ellas	comerán
usted	comerá	ustedes	comerán

Table 5-4   A Regular -*ir* Verb in the Future Tense

Subject	Verb	Subject	Verb
yo	escribiré	nosotros/nosotras	escribiremos
tú	escribirás	vosotros/vosotras	escribiréis
él	escribirá	ellos	escribirán
ella	escribirá	ellas	escribirán
usted	escribirá	ustedes	escribirán

Irregular verbs

The good news is that the same endings used to create the future tense of regular verbs are used to create the future tense of irregular verbs. What makes a verb irregular in the future tense is that the infinitive must be changed before you add the future tense ending. There are only 12 basic verbs that are irregular in the future tense. The irregularities for the "dirty dozen" follow certain patterns that make them easier to memorize.

Five irregular verbs simply drop the *e* of the infinitive (see Table 5-5).

Table 5-5   The Irregular Verbs That Drop the *e* of the Infinitive

Infinitive	Changes to . . .	Future Tense Ending
saber (to know)	sabr-	yo sabré (I shall know)
querer (to want)	querr-	tú querrás (you will want)
poder (to be able)	podr-	él podrá (he will be able)
haber (helping verb)	habr-	ellas habrán (they will have)
caber (to fit)	cabr-	Uds. cabrán (you all will fit)

Table 5-6   The Future Tense of an Irregular Verb That Drops the Last *e* of the Infinitive

Subject	Verb	Subject	Verb
yo	sabré	nosotros/nosotras	sabremos
tú	sabrás	vosotros/vosotras	sabréis
él	sabrá	ellos	sabrán
ella	sabrá	ellas	sabrán
usted	sabrá	ustedes	sabrán

Most often, *haber* is conjugated to go with the subject and is used with a past participle to create the perfect tenses. Since you have just learned to conjugate *haber* in the future tense, you will be able to create the future perfect tense. The past participle form of the verb as well as the construction of the perfect tenses will be introduced in Chapter 6.

Five other irregulars change the last vowel of the infinitive to the letter *d*. These are called "*e* to *d, i* to *d* oddities" and are shown in Tables 5-7 and 5-8.

Table 5-7   The Irregular Verbs That Change the Vowel of the Infinitive to *d*

Infinitive	Changes to . . .	Future Tense Ending
venir (to come)	*vendr-*	*yo vendré* (I shall come)
valer (to be worth)	*valdr-*	*él valdrá* (he will be worth)
tener (to have)	*tendr-*	*Eva tendrá* (Eva will have)
salir (to leave)	*saldr-*	*tú saldrás* (you will leave)
poner (to put)	*pondr-*	*ellos pondrán* (they will put)

Table 5-8   The Future Tense of an Irregular Verb That Changes the Vowel of the Infinitive to *d*

Subject	Verb	Subject	Verb
yo	*tendré*	*nosotros/nosotras*	*tendremos*
tú	*tendrás*	*vosotros/vosotras*	*tendréis*
él	*tendrá*	*ellos*	*tendrán*
ella	*tendrá*	*ellas*	*tendrán*
usted	*tendrá*	*ustedes*	*tendrán*

The final two verbs are irregular in the future tense because they drop the letters *e* and *c* from the infinitive. Notice in tables 5-9 and 5-10 that the *e* and *c* are not in the same order for both verbs:

Table 5-9   The Irregular Verbs That Drop *e* and *c* from the Infinitive

Infinitive	Changes to . . .	Future Tense Ending
decir (to say, to tell)	*dir-*	*tú dirás* (you will tell)
hacer (to make, to do)	*har-*	*yo haré* (I will make)

Table 5-10   The Future Tense of an Irregular Verb That Drops the *e* and *c* of the Infinitive

Subject	Verb	Subject	Verb
yo	diré	nosotros/nosotras	diremos
tú	dirás	vosotros/vosotras	diréis
él	dirá	ellos	dirán
ella	dirá	ellas	dirán
usted	dirá	ustedes	dirán

Don't forget that there are several verbs that add a prefix to a basic verb (see Table 5-11). For example, the verb *imponer* is the verb *poner* with a prefix. These verbs are conjugated exactly like the basic verb without the prefix (but have a totally new meaning). The following verbs are irregular in the future tense because they are based on one of the "dirty dozen."

Table 5-11   Verbs That Add a Prefix to a Basic Irregular Verb

Infinitive	Changes to . . .	Future Tense Ending
suponer (to suppose)	supondr-	yo supondré (I'll suppose)
imponer (to impose)	impondr-	tú impondrás (you'll impose)
componer (to compose)	compondr-	Carlos compondrá (Carlos will compose)
disponer (to dispose)	dispondr-	Cristina y yo dispondremos (Cristina and I will dispose)

Did you notice that most of the "*poner* verbs" are easy to recognize if you change the *n* to *s*? For example, *imponer* means "to impose" and *componer* means "to compose." Look at the conjugation chart in Table 5-12 and you will notice that every form is exactly like the chart for *poner* except that the prefix *com-* has been added to the beginning of each form.

Table 5-12   The Future Tense of a Verb Like *Poner*

Subject	Verb	Subject	Verb
yo	compondré	nosotros/nosotras	compondremos
tú	compondrás	vosotros/vosotras	compondréis

(continued)

Table 5-12 *(continued)*

Subject	Verb	Subject	Verb
él	compondrá	ellos	compondrán
ella	compondrá	ellas	compondrán
usted	compondrá	ustedes	compondrán

Note that not all the verbs that end like *decir* (see Table 5-13) have the same conjugation endings of the "root verb" in the future tense. For example, *bendecir, predecir,* and *maldecir* are regular verbs in the future tense: *bendeciré, predeciré,* and *maldeciré* (see Table 5-14).

Table 5-13   The Future Tense of a Verb Like *Decir*

Subject	Verb	Subject	Verb
yo	contradiré	nosotros/nosotras	contradiremos
tú	contradirás	vosotros/vosotras	contradiréis
él	contradirá	ellos	contradirán
ella	contradirá	ellas	contradirán
usted	contradirá	ustedes	contradirán

Table 5-14   Verbs Like *Decir* That Are Regular in the Future

Infinitive	Future Tense Ending
predecir (to predict)	Isabel y Rafael predecirán (Isabel and Rafael will predict)
bendecir (to bless)	tu bendecirás (you will bless)

Verbs like *tener* will change the last vowel of the infinitive to the letter *d*. See Tables 5-15 and 5-16.

Table 5-15   Verbs Like *Tener*

Infinitive	Changes to . . .	Future Tense Ending
detener (to detain)	detendr-	nosotras detendremos (we will detain)
obtener (to obtain)	obtendr-	Ud. obtendrá (you will obtain)
mantener (to maintain)	mantendr-	yo mantendré (I shall maintain)

Table 5-16   The Future Tense of a Verb Like *Tener*

Subject	Verb	Subject	Verb
yo	detendré	nosotros/nosotras	detendremos
tú	detendrás	vosotros/vosotras	detendréis
él	detendrá	ellos	detendrán
ella	detendrá	ellas	detendrán
usted	detendrá	ustedes	detendrán

The verb *satisfacer* is always conjugated like *hacer*, so it will also be irregular in the future tense, as you can see in Tables 5-17 and 5-18.

Table 5-17   Verbs Like *Hacer*

Infinitive	Changes to ...	Future Tense Ending
satisfacer (to satisfy)	satisfar-	nosotras satisfaremos (we will satisfy)
rehacer (to redo, to do over)	rehar-	él rehará (he will redo)
deshacer (to undo, to destroy)	deshar-	yo desharé (I will undo)

Table 5-18   The Future Tense of *Satisfacer*

Subject	Verb	Subject	Verb
yo	satisfaré	nosotros/nosotras	satisfaremos
tú	satisfarás	vosotros/vosotras	satisfaréis
él	satisfará	ellos	satisfarán
ella	satisfará	ellas	satisfarán
usted	satisfará	ustedes	satisfarán

Although you might not be able to predict that *satisfacer* is conjugated like *hacer*, many other verbs are easy to predict. Any time you remove the first few letters and you find a verb that looks exactly like a verb you've learned, it will probably be conjugated like the verb you already know in all tenses and forms. For example, you can probably see that the verb *proponer* is conjugated like *poner*. If you've paid close attention, you can also predict that *proponer* means "to propose." What would the *yo* form of the future tense of *sobresalir* be? Because the *yo* form of *salir* is *saldré,* the answer is *sobresaldré.* You can follow this same process for many other irregular verbs.

The Conditional Tense

The conditional tense is usually introduced with the future tense because the two tenses have much in common. For example, the same verbs that are irregular in the future tense are also irregular in the conditional tense in exactly the same way. The conditional tense also requires you to use the entire infinitive, only with different endings. Because the future and conditional tenses are created in a similar fashion, it is very easy to learn to conjugate verbs in the conditional tense once you have learned the future tense; the meanings of the two tenses, however, are not similar at all.

Using the conditional tense in sentences

The conditional is used when the action of the verb would happen only if a certain condition were met. In an English sentence in the conditional tense, the helping verb "would" is placed in front of the main verb, which is usually followed by the words "if" or "but." In the sentences, "I would study if I had my book" or "He would study but he doesn't have his book," the condition that needs to be met in order for studying to happen is "having a book." In the following example, you must infer the condition that must be met before Benjamin can visit his grandma.

> *Benjamín visitaría a su abuela pero ella vive en Europa.*
> Benjamin would visit his grandmother but she lives in Europe.

The above sentence implies that the condition that must be met before Benjamin visits his grandma is that she would have to move closer to him.

In Spanish, when the conditional tense is followed by *si* ("if"), the next verb is in a tense called the imperfect (past) subjunctive, which will be introduced in Chapter 14. In the following examples, *tuviera* is the past subjunctive form of the verb *tener.*

> *Yo hablaría español si yo tuviera mi diccionario.*
> I would speak Spanish if I had my dictionary.

> *Britanía viajaría a África si tuviera el dinero.*
> Britanía would travel to Africa if she had the money.

The English language has a bad habit of using the same word to mean completely different things. Unfortunately, when an English sentence places the helping verb "would" in front of the verb, it does not always mean that you will use the conditional tense in a Spanish translation. Sometimes, the English language uses the helping verb "would" to indicate a repetitive action in the past. For example, the sentence "I would study every night when I was in high school" would not be translated using the conditional tense because it is not actually saying "I would study if . . ." or "I would study but . . ." This sentence does not imply that a condition must be met in order for the action of the verb to happen. Technically, in the above sentence, "would study" means "used to study." Thus, in Spanish, the verb would be conjugated in the imperfect tense to indicate an ongoing or repetitive action in the past.

Although the above explanation may sound confusing, there is an easy way to determine whether you need to use the conditional or the imperfect tense. If an English sentence has the word "would" in front of the verb, try changing "would" to "used to." If it still sounds right, use the imperfect. If not, use the conditional tense.

Read the following sentences and consider in which sentence you can change the underlined "would" to "used to."

> *Cuando niña, Tatiana hablaba con su tía todas las noches.*
> As a child, Tatiana <u>would</u> speak with her aunt every night.

> *Tatiana hablaría con su tía si ella tuviera teléfono.*
> Tatiana <u>would</u> speak to her aunt if she had a phone.

It doesn't sound quite right to say "Tatiana used to speak to her aunt if she had a phone." Therefore, the second sentence should be translated in the conditional tense. It sounds perfectly correct to say, however, "As a child, Tatiana used to speak with her aunt every night"; thus, you know that the imperfect is the appropriate tense to use in the Spanish translation.

Regular verbs

To create the conditional tense of regular verbs, the conditional ending for each form is added to the entire infinitive. Because the entire infinitive is used, there is no need for three different conjugation charts for the three different kinds of infinitives (-*ar*, -*er*, and -*ir* verbs). The endings in Table 5-19 are added to the entire infinitive of any regular verb to create the conditional tense. The 12 verbs that are irregular in the future tense are also irregular in the conditional tense.

Table 5-19   Conditional Tense Verb Endings

Subject	Ending	Subject	Ending
yo	-ía	nosotros/nosotras	-íamos
tú	-ías	vosotros/vosotras	-íais
él	-ía	ellos	-ían
ella	-ía	ellas	-ían
usted	-ía	ustedes	-ían

Notice in the examples of regular verbs conjugated in the conditional tense (see tables 5-20, 5-21, and 5-22) that the entire infinitive is simply placed in front of the conditional tense endings from Table 5-19.

Table 5-20   A Regular -ar Verb in the Conditional Tense

Subject	Verb	Subject	Verb
yo	trabajaría	nosotros/nosotras	trabajaríamos
tú	trabajarías	vosotros/vosotras	trabajaríais
él	trabajaría	ellos	trabajarían
ella	trabajaría	ellas	trabajarían
usted	trabajaría	ustedes	trabajarían

Table 5-21   A Regular -er Verb in the Conditional Tense

Subject	Verb	Subject	Verb
yo	sería	nosotros/nosotras	seríamos
tú	serías	vosotros/vosotras	seríais
él	sería	ellos	serían
ella	sería	ellas	serían
usted	sería	ustedes	serían

Table 5-22   A Regular -*ir* Verb in the Conditional Tense

Subject	Verb	Subject	Verb
yo	iría	nosotros/nosotras	iríamos
tú	irías	vosotros/vosotras	iríais
él	iría	ellos	irían
ella	iría	ellas	irían
usted	iría	ustedes	irían

Irregular verbs

As you now know, the good news about the conditional tense is that, like the future tense, it has only 12 verbs that are irregular—and these are the same verbs that are irregular in the future tense. The irregulars listed below follow exactly the same patterns as well.

Five irregular verbs simply drop the *e* of the infinitive (see tables 5-23 and 5-24):

Table 5-23   The Irregular Verbs That Drop the *e* of the Infinitive

Infinitive	Changes to . . .	Conditional Tense Ending
saber (to know)	sabr-	yo sabría (I would know)
querer (to want)	querr-	tú querrías (you would want)
poder (to be able)	podr-	él podría (he would be able)
haber (helping verb)	habr-	ellas habrían (they would have)
caber (to fit)	cabr-	Uds. cabrían (you all would fit)

Table 5-24   The Conditional Tense of an Irregular Verb That Drops the Last *e* of the Infinitive

Subject	Verb	Subject	Verb
yo	querría	nosotros/nosotras	querríamos
tú	querrías	vosotros/vosotras	querríais
él	querría	ellos	querrían
ella	querría	ellas	querrían
usted	querría	ustedes	querrían

Five other irregulars change the last vowel of the infinitive to the letter *d* (see Tables 5-25 and 5-26):

Table 5-25   The Irregular Verbs That Change the Vowel of the Infinitive to *d*

Infinitive	Changes to ...	Conditional Tense Ending
venir (to come)	*vendr-*	*yo vendría* (I would come)
valer (to be worth)	*valdr-*	*él valdría* (he would be worth)
tener (to have)	*tendr-*	*Eva tendría* (Eva would have)
salir (to leave)	*saldr-*	*tú saldrías* (you would leave)
poner (to put)	*pondr-*	*ellos pondrían* (they would put)

The conjugation chart of the verb *venir* in Table 5-26 is an example of this type of verb in the conditional tense.

Table 5-26   The Conditional Tense of an Irregular Verb That Changes the Vowel of the Infinitive to *d*

Subject	Verb	Subject	Verb
yo	*vendría*	*nosotros/nosotras*	*vendríamos*
tú	*vendrías*	*vosotros/vosotras*	*vendríais*
él	*vendría*	*ellos*	*vendrían*
ella	*vendría*	*ellas*	*vendrían*
usted	*vendría*	*ustedes*	*vendrían*

The final two verbs, *hacer* and *decir* are irregular in the conditional tense because they drop the letters *e* and *c* from the infinitive. Notice that the *e* and *c* are not in the same order for both verbs (see Table 5-27).

Table 5-27   The Irregular Verbs That Drop *e* and *c* from the Infinitive

Infinitive	Changes to ...	Conditional Tense Ending
decir (to say, to tell)	*dir-*	*tú dirías* (you would tell)
hacer (to make, to do)	*har-*	*yo haría* (I would make)

Table 5-28   The Conditional Tense of an Irregular Verb That Drops the _e_ and _c_ of the Infinitive

Subject	Verb	Subject	Verb
yo	haría	nosotros/nosotras	haríamos
tú	harías	vosotros/vosotras	haríais
él	haría	ellos	harían
ella	haría	ellas	harían
usted	haría	ustedes	harían

Chapter Checkout

Translate the following sentences using the future tense.

1. The students will learn a lot.

2. Ana will tell the truth.

3. Linda and I will have a house.

4. I shall go to the store.

Translate the following phrases using the conditional tense.

5. Gabriela would want . . .

6. Anita would come . . .

7. Gloria would arrive . . .

8. I would put . . .

Answers: 1. _Los estudiantes aprenderán mucho._ **2.** _Ana dirá la verdad._ **3.** _Linda y yo tendremos una casa._ **4.** _Yo iré a la tienda._ **5.** _Gabriela querría . . ._ **6.** _Anita vendría . . ._ **7.** _Gloria llegaría . . ._ **8.** _Yo pondría . . ._

Chapter 6

THE PERFECT TENSES

Chapter Check-In

❑ Creating and recognizing the past participle form

❑ Using the helping verb *haber*

❑ Understanding compound tenses

In grammar terms, the word "perfect" indicates completion. The perfect tenses focus not on the moment something is done, but rather a moment by which it has been done. A perfect tense is created by using a helping verb with a past participle. The helping verb in English is "have." Used with a past participle it creates a perfect tense; for example, "I have studied." The tense of the helping verb determines which perfect tense is created. For example, the past tense of "have" is "had," and when it is followed by a past participle, "he had written," the past perfect is created. Spanish uses the helping verb *haber* followed by a past participle to create the perfect tenses; therefore, knowing how to conjugate *haber* in different tenses allows you to create different perfect tenses. For example, the future tense of *haber* is used to create a future perfect tense. There is a perfect tense to go with every possible tense you can conjugate.

The Past Participle

The **past participle** is a specific form of the verb that usually ends in *-ado* or *-ido*. This is not a conjugated form because it does not change to agree with the subject. The past participle verb form has two uses.

■ It may be used after a conjugated form of the helping verb, *haber,* as part of a compound verb (a verb tense that requires more than one word to create). When used as a verb, it always ends in *-o* because it does not need to agree with the subject in number or gender. This type of past participle will be called the "pure past participle" in this chapter to indicate that you should not mess with its ending.

■ It is the base form used to create an adjective from a verb. When used as an adjective, the past participle verb form must be adapted to match the gender and number of the noun it modifies. Just about every verb can be made into an adjective by using its past participle form.

Learning to recognize and use past participles will increase your Spanish language powers tremendously. The creation and use of the past participle form of the verb as well as the use of the past participle as an adjective are explained in the following sections.

Regular past participles

No verb undergoes a stem change in its past participle form, and all *-ar* verbs have regular past participle forms. To create the past participle form of an *-ar* verb, replace the *-ar* infinitive ending with *-ado*. In the examples in Table 6-1, you may notice that the English past participle sometimes looks and sounds just like the English past tense but that the Spanish past participle form is entirely different from the past tense.

Table 6-1   Past Participle Form of -ar Verbs

Infinitive	Past Participle
cantar (to sing)	*cantado* (sung)
tomar (to take)	*tomado* (taken)
cerrar (to close)	*cerrado* (closed)
jugar (to play)	*jugado* (played)
pensar (to think)	*pensado* (thought)

Because an English past participle is so similar to the English past tense, recognizing a past participle written in English is much more difficult than it is in Spanish. To thoroughly understand this concept, let's quickly review this point of English grammar. Most English speakers were forced to learn the past participle as one of three forms of a verb. You may remember chanting: "swim, swam, swum," "drink, drank, drunk," "write, wrote, written," and "bring, brought, brought." Can you fill in the blanks below?

do, did, _____

take, took, _____

think, thought, _____

Whether or not you remember the correct answers (done, taken, and thought) for these particular blanks, any memory of these verb threesomes indicates that some elementary school teacher was trying to teach you that the past tense and the past participle form of a verb may be but are not always the same. Most people chanted away without realizing that they were chanting the present tense, past tense, and past participle form of each verb. Now we confuse English past participles with the past tense because, for some verbs, the past participle form looks and sounds exactly like the past tense.

When an English verb ends in *-ed* it may be in its past participle form or in a past tense conjugation. There is only one way to know for sure that it is a past participle rather than the past tense: A past participle is always preceded by some form of the helping verb "to have" (namely, have, has, or had). For example:

Yesterday, I <u>wrote </u>(past tense).

I **have** <u>written</u> (past participle).

Last week, I <u>called</u> (past tense).

I **have** <u>called</u> (past participle) many times.

Yesterday, he <u>did</u> (past tense) his homework.

He **has** <u>done</u> (past participle) it every day.

Past participle forms never look like past tense forms in Spanish, and there are not many verbs with a past participle ending other than *-ido* or *-ado*. The regular past participles of *-er* and *-ir* verbs are exactly alike (see Table 6-2). The few irregularly formed past participles are listed in Table 6-3. Any *-ir* or *-er* verb that does not appear on the irregular list has a past participle formed by removing the *-er* or *-ir* infinitive ending and replacing it with *-ido*. Remember that a Spanish past participle form never undergoes a stem change.

Table 6-2 Past Participle Forms of Regular -er and -ir Verbs

Infinitive	*Past Participle*
beber (to drink)	*bebido* (drunk)
prometer (to promise)	*prometido* (promised)
preferir (to prefer)	*preferido* (preferred)
vestir (to dress)	*vestido* (dressed)

Irregular past participles

Table 6-3 lists the 12 verbs with irregular past participle forms. Notice that most irregulars end in -*to* or -*cho*.

Table 6-3   Verbs with Irregular Past Participle Forms

Infinitive	Past Participle
abrir (to open)	*abierto* (opened)
cubrir (to cover)	*cubierto* (covered)
decir (to say)	*dicho* (said)
freír (to fry)	*frito* (fried)
hacer (to make)	*hecho* (made)
imprimir (to print)	*impreso* (printed)
morir (to die)	*muerto* (dead)
poner (to put)	*puesto* (put)
resolver (to resolve)	*resuelto* (resolved)
romper (to break)	*roto* (broken)
ver (to see)	*visto* (seen)
volver (to return)	*vuelto* (returned)

Many of the above verbs are also used with prefixes. The following verbs have the same past participle form (after the prefix) as the simple verbs above:

> *bendecir* (to bless)
> *componer* (to compose)
> *descubrir* (to discover)
> *deshacer* (to undo)
> *devolver* (to return something)
> *disponer* (to put)
> *exponer* (to expose)
> *imponer* (to impose)
> *rehacer* (to redo, to remake)
> *revolver* (to turn around, to turn over)

Note: Because *satisfacer* (to satisfy) is always formed like *hacer,* its past participle is *satisfecho.*

To preserve the stress on the correct syllable, any verb that ends in -*aer*, -*eer*, or -*oír* will have an accent on the *i* of its past participle ending (see Table 6-4).

Table 6-4   Past Participles with Accents

Infinitive	*Past Participle*
caer (to fall)	*caído* (fallen)
creer (to believe)	*creído* (believed)
leer (to read)	*leído* (read)
oír (to hear)	*oído* (heard)
reír (to laugh)	*reído* (laughed)
traer (to bring)	*traído* (brought)

The following verbs with prefixes also have an accent on the -*ído* of the past participle form:

> *atraer* (to attract)
> *distraer* (to distract)
> *sonreír* (to smile)
> *sustraer* (to subtract)

The Helping Verb *Haber*

The compound tenses in English are created by using the past participle form after a conjugated form of the helping verb "to have" ("has," "have," or "had"). Unfortunately, the English language also has a verb of possession that looks and sounds exactly the same. Which of the following sentences includes the helping verb?

> I **have** studied.
> I **have** a book.

The only way to know that the first "have" is a helping verb is to notice that it is followed by a verb in its past participle form. When you are writing a Spanish sentence, you need to determine whether you are stating that someone has (possesses) something, which requires the verb *tener* ("to have"), or that someone has done something, which requires you to create a compound tense by using the Spanish helping verb *haber* ("to have done . . .").

The only other use for *haber* that doesn't create a compound tense is when *haber* is used idiomatically to indicate existence. It is irregular in the present tense when used this way: The word *hay* is followed by singular or plural objects to express "there is" or "there are."

> *Hay un concierto de Orishas este fin de semana.*
> There's an Orishas concert this weekend.

> *Hay muchos admiradores de este grupo aquí.*
> There are many of this group's fans here.

In other tenses, the third person singular (*él*) form of the verb is used regardless of the number of what follows.

> *Había un partido de vólibol ayer.*
> There was a volleyball game yesterday. (imperfect)

> *Había muchos espectadores en el gimnasio.*
> There were many spectators in the gym. (imperfect)

> *Habrá otra competencia mañana.*
> There will be another competition tomorrow. (future)

> *Habrá cinco equipos en el torneo.*
> There will be five teams in the tournament. (future)

> *Habría más pero uno se canceló.*
> There would be more but one was cancelled. (conditional)

Compound Tenses

The verb *haber* is placed in front of a "pure past participle" to create a compound tense. The past participle never changes, but the helping verb must be conjugated to agree with the subject. The tense in which the helping verb is conjugated will determine which of the compound tenses is being constructed.

Present perfect

Table 6-5 presents the verb *haber* alone, but in reality, any form of the helping verb *haber* is almost always followed by a past participle.

Table 6-5   Present Tense Conjugation Chart for the Helping Verb *Haber*

Subject	Verb	Subject	Verb
yo	he	nosotros/nosotras	hemos
tú	has	vosotros/vosotras	habéis
él	ha	ellos	han
ella	ha	ellas	han
usted	ha	ustedes	han

See Table 6-6 for an example of *haber* being used to create the present perfect tense. Notice that only the conjugated forms of *haber* change; the past participle form does not change.

Table 6-6   Present Perfect Tense Conjugation Chart for *Llamar* (to Call)

Subject	Verb	Subject	Verb
yo	he llamado	nosotros/nosotras	hemos llamado
tú	has llamado	vosotros/vosotras	habéis llamado
él	ha llamado	ellos	han llamado
ella	ha llamado	ellas	han llamado
usted	ha llamado	ustedes	han llamado

The present perfect tense illustrated above is translated as: "I have called," "you have called," "we have called," "they have called," and so on.

Use the present perfect to indicate that the action of the verb has been completed prior to the present. The present tense conjugation of *haber* places the point of view in the present but the perfect tense indicates completion. For this reason, the present perfect can actually be used like the preterit to indicate "completedness." For example, *Yo he estudiado* (I have studied) in the present perfect expresses the same meaning as *Yo estudié* (I studied) in the preterit but focuses a little more on the fact that the action is presently completed.

Past perfect (pluperfect)

The **past perfect (pluperfect) tense** is formed like the present perfect except that the helping verb is conjugated in a past tense. But, because there are two simple past tenses in Spanish, you must know that the imperfect tense rather than the preterit is used to create what is called the pluperfect tense. The imperfect tense conjugation of the verb *haber* is used with the past participle of the main verb. Notice in Table 6-7 that the imperfect tense forms of the helping verb are all regular.

Table 6-7   Past Perfect (Pluperfect) Tense Conjugation Chart for *Escribir* (to Write)

Subject	Verb	Subject	Verb
yo	había escrito	nosotros/nosotras	habíamos escrito
tú	habías escrito	vosotros/vosotras	habíais escrito
él	había escrito	ellos	habían escrito
ella	había escrito	ellas	habían escrito
usted	había escrito	ustedes	habían escrito

The past perfect tense illustrated above is translated as: "I had written," "you had written," "he had written," "we had written," "they had written," and so on.

The past perfect (pluperfect) tense is used when you are speaking about a time in the past and you want to indicate that something had already been completed before that time. For example,

> *Yo había llamado dos veces antes de visitarles* **ayer**
> I had called twice before visiting them **yesterday**

establishes that you are referring to a past time.

Preterit perfect (past anterior)

The pluperfect explained above is also called the past perfect because it is what a Spanish speaker will naturally use to express the fact that an action was already completed at some point in the past. When the past participle is used with a helping verb conjugated in the preterit rather than the imperfect, the tense is called the **preterit perfect** or **past anterior.** The preterit perfect expresses the same idea as the past perfect but is rarely used in spoken Spanish. You are most likely to encounter the preterit perfect in literature, where it is easy to understand. You will probably be safe to use the past perfect tense consistently in spoken Spanish and need only be aware that the preterit perfect illustrated in Table 6-8 has the same meaning.

Table 6-8   Preterit Perfect (Past Anterior) Tense Conjugation Chart for *Cenar* (to Dine)

Subject	Verb	Subject	Verb
yo	hube cenado	nosotros/nosotras	hubimos cenado
tú	hubiste cenado	vosotros/vosotras	hubisteis cenado
él	hubo cenado	ellos	hubieron cenado
ella	hubo cenado	ellas	hubieron cenado
usted	hubo cenado	ustedes	hubieron cenado

Because there is only one past tense in English, the preterit perfect tense is translated the same as the imperfect: "I had dined," "you had dined," "he had dined," "we had dined," "they had dined," and so on.

Future perfect (future anterior)

The **future perfect tense** is predictably created by using the future tense of the helping verb with the past participle. Notice in Table 6-9 that *haber* is one of the few verbs that is irregular in the future tense.

Table 6-9   Future Perfect Tense Conjugation Chart for *Ganar* (to Win, to Earn)

Subject	Verb	Subject	Verb
yo	habré ganado	nosotros/nosotras	habremos ganado
tú	habrás ganado	vosotros/vosotras	habréis ganado
él	habrá ganado	ellos	habrán ganado
ella	habrá ganado	ellas	habrán ganado
usted	habrá ganado	ustedes	habrán ganado

The future perfect tense illustrated above is equivalent to the following English expressions: "I will have earned," "you will have earned," "she will have earned," "they will have earned," and so on.

The future perfect is used to express an action in the future that will be completed before another action that is yet to occur. For example,

*Para el fin de semana, yo **habré leído** su libro*

means

By the end of the week, I **will have read** his book.

The adverb *ya* ("already") is often used with the future perfect. On standardized tests, *ya* in front of the blank may be a clue to use the future perfect tense, although other tenses may also be appropriate. For example,

*Ellos **ya** **habrán terminado** su clase cuando reparen el **acondicionador de aire***

means

They <u>already</u> **will have finished** their class when they repair the air conditioner.

The future tense is sometimes used to express conjecture or the probability of an action occurring in the present. The future perfect tense can be used in a similar fashion to express the probability that an action has currently been completed:

Ellos habrán llegado al aeropuerto.

They have arrived at the airport. (probably)

Ella habrá llamado para hacer reservaciones.

She has called to make reservations. (supposition)

Conditional perfect

The conditional conjugation of *haber* is completely regular. When used with a past participle, the result is a statement contrary to reality; the action of the verb would have been completed if some condition had been met: "I would have done something if . . ." This is called the **conditional perfect.**

Table 6-10   Conditional Perfect Tense Conjugation Chart for *Ir* (to Go)

Subject	Verb	Subject	Verb
yo	habría ido	nosotros/nosotras	habríamos ido
tú	habrías ido	vosotros/vosotras	habríais ido

(continued)

Table 6-10 *(continued)*

Subject	Verb	Subject	Verb
él	habría ido	ellos	habrían ido
ella	habría ido	ellas	habrían ido
usted	habría ido	ustedes	habrían ido

The conditional perfect tense illustrated above is translated as: "I would have gone," "you would have gone," "she would have gone," "we would have gone," "they would have gone," and so on.

The conditional perfect can also be used to express probability or conjecture about the completion of an action prior to some point in the past:

> *El habría ganado una beca antes de asistir a esa universidad.*
>
> He would have won a scholarship before attending that university. (I bet)
>
> *La jefe le habría prometido el puesto cuando empezó a trabajar aquí.*
>
> The boss must have promised him the position when he started to work here. (pure conjecture)

Chapter Checkout

In the following sentences, fill in the blanks using the perfect tense indicated. Conjugate *haber* in the first blank and use the past participle of the verb indicated in parentheses in the second blank.

1. *Ahora las gitanas* _____ _____ *su baile flamenco.* (*terminar*, present perfect)

2. *Simón* _____ _____ *a su abogado para mañana.* (*escribir*, future perfect)

3. *Lidia nunca* _____ _____ *pasteles hasta el año pasado en Puerto Rico.* (*comer*, past perfect)

4. *Benito* _____ _____ *su tarea pero su amigo le llamó.* (*hacer*, conditional perfect)

Answers: 1. *han terminado* **2.** *habrá escrito* **3.** *había comido* **4.** *habría hecho*

Chapter 7
SUBJUNCTIVE MOOD I

Chapter Check-In

❑ Creating the present tense subjunctive conjugations

❑ Mastering the irregular verbs in the subjunctive

❑ Understanding when the subjunctive is necessary

The subjunctive is a mood rather than a tense, and within the subjunctive mood there are several tenses. English does not use a subjunctive mood, so the Spanish present subjunctive tense, when translated to English, sounds just like the present tense. In Spanish, the subjunctive present tense is used about as often as the regular present tense that you have already learned. The "regular" present tense is called the indicative present tense. Like the subjunctive, the indicative has several tenses. Every verb tense you have learned so far is one of the indicative tenses. The subjunctive tenses are used in specific situations, which are explained at the end of the chapter.

The Present Subjunctive

The first step to using the subjunctive present tense is learning to create the conjugated forms of a verb in the present subjunctive. Because it is a present tense, the present subjunctive is based on the forms of the present tense that you already know. If you know all the irregularities of the indicative present tense, you will find the present subjunctive an easy tense to conjugate. Because there are a lot of issues in the present tense, you may want to review Chapter 3 before continuing.

Creating present subjunctive verb forms

There are three steps you can chant when creating a present subjunctive verb form:

1. form of *yo*
2. drop the -*o*
3. add the opposite endings

Of course, chanting the above does no good if you do not understand what it means in application. First of all, you must think of the *yo* form of the indicative present tense that you already know. For 99.9% of Spanish verbs, you simply drop the -*o* ending of the *yo* form and add a present tense subjunctive ending to what is left. (Only a few verbs in the Spanish language have a *yo* form that doesn't end in -*o,* and all these are irregular in the present subjunctive. You'll learn those later.) Because the *yo* form no longer ends in -*o,* the present subjunctive *yo* form looks exactly like the *él/ella/Ud.* form. Use the appropriate subject pronoun to specify the subject. The reason the "chant" says to add the opposite endings is because -*er* and -*ir* verbs use -*ar* verb endings, and you must use the normal -*er* endings with -*ar* verbs.

Present subjunctive of -*ar* verbs

Table 7-1, below, will help you understand that the verb endings used for -*ar* verbs in the present tense subjunctive are like those used for the regular present tense of -*er* verbs.

Table 7-1   Present Subjunctive Endings for -*ar* Verbs

Subject	Ending	Subject	Ending
yo	-e	nosotros/nosotras	-emos
tú	-es	vosotros/vosotras	-éis
él	-e	ellos	-en
ella	-e	ellas	-en
usted	-e	ustedes	-en

Look over the present subjunctive conjugations of the regular -*ar* verb *escuchar* in Table 7-2.

Table 7-2   Present Subjunctive Conjugation Chart for *Escuchar* (to Listen)

Subject	Verb	Subject	Verb
yo	escuche	nosotros/nosotras	escuchemos
tú	escuches	vosotros/vosotras	escuchéis
él	escuche	ellos	escuchen
ella	escuche	ellas	escuchen
usted	escuche	ustedes	escuchen

Verbs that end in *-car, -gar,* and *-zar*

Any verb that ends in *-car, gar,* or *-zar* will use the endings and rules explained above for creating the present subjunctive, but to preserve the correct pronunciation of that letter, it will undergo a spelling change in the letter that precedes the subjunctive ending. You learned about a similar spelling change in the preterit tense that happens for the same reason, but in the preterit, this spelling change affects only the *yo* form. In the present subjunctive, the spelling change occurs in all forms.

To maintain the hard *c* sound (like a *k*), use *qu* rather than *c* in all forms of the present subjunctive for any verb whose infinitive form ends in *-car*.

Table 7-3   Present Subjunctive Conjugation Chart for *Buscar* (to Search)

Subject	Verb	Subject	Verb
yo	busque	nosotros/nosotras	busquemos
tú	busques	vosotros/vosotras	busquéis
él	busque	ellos	busquen
ella	busque	ellas	busquen
usted	busque	ustedes	busquen

Table 7-4 provides the subjunctive forms of common *-car* verbs. Because the *él* form is the same as the *yo* form, it is not listed.

Table 7-4 Common Verbs That End in -*car* and Their Subjunctive Forms

Infinitive	*Subjunctive Endings*
aparcar (to park)	*aparque, aparques, aparquemos, aparquéis, aparquen*
aplicar (to apply)	*aplique, apliques, apliquemos, apliquéis, apliquen*
buscar (to seek)	*busque, busques, busquemos, busquéis, busquen*
clarificar (to clarify)	*clarifique, clarifiques, clarifiquemos, clarifiquéis, clarifiquen*
clasificar (to classify)	*clasifique, clasifiques, clasifiquemos, clasifiquéis, clasifiquen*
colocar (to place, to put)	*coloque, coloques, coloquemos, coloquéis, coloquen*
comunicar (to communicate)	*comunique, comuniques, comuniquemos, comuniquéis, comuniquen*
dedicar (to dedicate)	*dedique, dediques, dediquemos, dediquéis, dediquen*
destacar (to stand out)	*destaque, destaques, destaquemos, destaquéis, destaquen*
educar (to educate)	*eduque, eduques, eduquemos, eduquéis, eduquen*
empacar (to pack)	*empaque, empaques, empaquemos, empaquéis, empaquen*
explicar (to explain)	*explique, expliques, expliquemos, expliquéis, expliquen*
fabricar (to make)	*fabrique, fabriques, fabriquemos, fabriquéis, fabriquen*
indicar (to indicate)	*indique, indiques, indiquemos, indiquéis, indiquen*
justificar (to justify)	*justifique, justifiques, justifiquemos, justifiquéis, justifiquen*
marcar (to mark)	*marque, marques, marquemos, marquéis, marquen*

Infinitive	Subjunctive Endings
masticar (to chew)	*mastique, mastiques, mastiquemos, mastiquéis, mastiquen*
pescar (to fish)	*pesque, pesques, pesquemos, pesquéis, pesquen*
publicar (to publish)	*publique, publiques, publiquemos, publiquéis, publiquen*
sacar (to take out)	*saque, saques, saquemos, saquéis, saquen*
significar (to mean)	*signifique, signifiques, signifiquemos, signifiquéis, signifiquen*
tocar (to touch)	*toque, toques, toquemos, toquéis, toquen*

To maintain the hard *g* sound (like the *g* in "go"), use *gu* rather than *g* in all forms of the present subjunctive for any verb whose infinitive form ends in -*gar*.

Table 7-5   Present Subjunctive Conjugation Chart for *Pagar* (to Pay)

Subject	Verb	Subject	Verb
yo	pague	nosotros/nosotras	paguemos
tú	pagues	vosotros/vosotras	paguéis
él	pague	ellos	paguen
ella	pague	ellas	paguen
usted	pague	ustedes	paguen

The verbs in Table 7-6 undergo the *g* to *gu* spelling change in all forms of the subjunctive. If the verb is a stem-changer, the change will be apparent in all forms but *nosotros/nosotras* and *vosotros/vosotras*. A more thorough explanation of stem-changers in the subjunctive can be found later in this chapter. Because the *él* form is the same as the *yo* form, it is not listed.

Table 7-6   **Common Verbs That End in -*gar* and Their Subjunctive Forms**

Infinitive	Subjunctive Endings
agregar (to add)	*agregue, agregues, agreguemos, agreguéis, agreguen*
ahogar (to drown)	*ahogue, ahogues, ahoguemos, ahoguéis, ahoguen*
apagar (to extinguish, to turn off)	*apague, apagues, apaguemos, apaguéis, apaguen*
cargar (to load)	*cargue, cargues, carguemos, carguéis, carguen*
castigar (to punish)	*castigue, castigues, castiguemos, castiguéis, castiguen*
colgar (to hang)	*cuelgue, cuelgues, colguemos, colguéis, cuelguen*
encargar (to put in charge)	*encargue, encargues, encarguemos, encarguéis, encarguen*
entregar (to hand over)	*entregue, entregues, entreguemos, entreguéis, entreguen*
jugar (to play)	*juegue, juegues, juguemos, juguéis, jueguen*
llegar (to arrive)	*llegue, llegues, lleguemos, lleguéis, lleguen*
madrugar (to rise early)	*madrugue, madrugues, madruguemos, madruguéis madruguen*
negar (to deny)	*niegue, niegues, neguemos, neguéis, nieguen*
obligar (to obligate)	*obligue, obligues, obliguemos, obliguéis, obliguen*
pegar (to hit)	*pegue, pegues, peguemos, peguéis, peguen*
regar (to water a plant)	*riegue, riegues, reguemos, reguéis, rieguen*
rogar (to beg)	*ruegue, ruegues, roguemos, roguéis, rueguen*
segar (to mow the lawn)	*siegue, siegues, seguemos, seguéis, sieguen*
tragar (to swallow)	*trague, tragues, traguemos, traguéis, traguen*
vagar (to wander)	*vague, vagues, vaguemos, vaguéis, vaguen*

There is a consistent rule in Spanish that dictates that the letter *z* change to a *c* when followed by an *e*. This spelling change occurs in every subjunctive conjugated form of any verb that ends in -*zar*.

Look at the conjugation chart in Table 7-7 and use it as an example for the -*zar* verbs in Table 7-8.

Table 7-7   Present Subjunctive Conjugation Chart for *Abrazar* (to Hug)

Subject	Verb	Subject	Verb
yo	abrace	nosotros/nosotras	abracemos
tú	abraces	vosotros/vosotras	abracéis
él	abrace	ellos	abracen
ella	abrace	ellas	abracen
usted	abrace	ustedes	abracen

Table 7-8 provides the subjunctive forms of common -*zar* verbs. Because the *él* form is the same as the *yo* form, it is not listed.

Table 7-8   Common Verbs That End in -*zar* and Their Subjunctive Forms

Infinitive	Subjunctive Endings
abrazar (to hug)	abrace, abraces, abracemos, abracéis, abracen
autorizar (to authorize)	autorice, autorices, autoricemos, autoricéis, autoricen
alcanzar (to reach)	alcance, alcances, alcancemos, alcancéis, alcancen
almorzar (to eat lunch)	almuerce, almuerces, almorcemos, almorcéis, almuercen
amenazar (to threaten)	amenace, amenaces, amenacemos, amenacéis, amenacen
avanzar (to advance)	avance, avances, avancemos, avancéis, avancen
comenzar (to begin)	comience, comiences, comencemos, comencéis, comiencen
empezar (to begin)	empiece, empieces, empecemos, empecéis, empiecen
gozar (to enjoy)	goce, goces, gocemos, gocéis, gocen

(continued)

Table 7-8 *(continued)*

Infinitive	Subjunctive Endings
lanzar (to throw)	*lance, lances, lancemos, lancéis, lancen*
organizar (to organize)	*organice, organices, organicemos, organicéis, organicen*
realizar (to fulfill)	*realice, realices, realicemos, realicéis, realicen*
rezar (to pray)	*rece, reces, recemos, recéis, recen*
simbolizar (to symbolize)	*simbolice, simbolices, simbolicemos, simbolicéis, simbolicen*
trazar (to trace)	*trace, traces, tracemos, tracéis, tracen*
tropezar (to stumble)	*tropiece, tropieces, tropecemos, tropecéis, tropiecen*

Notice that *-ar* verbs do not undergo a stem change in the *nosotros/nosotras* or *vosotros/vosotras* forms but do undergo a stem change in all other forms.

Present subjunctive of *-er* and *-ir* verbs

The earlier chant still applies when you conjugate *-er* and *-ir* verbs in the subjunctive present tense:

1. form of *yo*
2. drop the *-o*
3. add the opposite endings

As you can see in Table 7-9, the endings for *-er* and *-ir* verbs in the present subjunctive look like the *-ar* endings in the regular (indicative) present tense, except that the *yo* form is exactly like the *él* form.

Table 7-9 **Present Subjunctive Conjugation Chart for *-er* and *-ir* Verbs**

Subject	Ending	Subject	Ending
yo	*-a*	*nosotros/nosotras*	*-amos*
tú	*-as*	*vosotros/vosotras*	*-áis*
él	*-a*	*ellos*	*-an*
ella	*-a*	*ellas*	*-an*
usted	*-a*	*ustedes*	*-an*

The verb *escribir* is a regular *-ir* verb so, in the present subjunctive, it takes regular *-ar* endings (see Table 7-10).

Table 7-10   Present Subjunctive Conjugation Chart for *Escribir* (to Write)

Subject	Verb	Subject	Verb
yo	escriba	nosotros/nosotras	escribamos
tú	escribas	vosotros/vosotras	escribáis
él	escriba	ellos	escriban
ella	escriba	ellas	escriban
usted	escriba	ustedes	escriban

Yo Irregulars

Because the first step to creating a subjunctive conjugation is to determine the *yo* form of the regular present tense, any verb that is irregular in the *yo* form of the present tense will carry that irregularity in all forms of the subjunctive present tense. It is very important to go back to Chapter 3 and review the different types of irregularities you will need to know in order to conjugate a verb correctly in the subjunctive.

-go verbs

Table 7-11 presents the present subjunctive conjugation of *tener*, a *-go* verb. More verbs that behave like *tener* are listed in Table 7-12. Only the *yo/él* form is listed because, by now, you should be able to ascertain the other forms.

Table 7-11   Present Subjunctive Conjugation Chart for *Tener* (to Have)

Subject	Verb	Subject	Verb
yo	tenga	nosotros/nosotras	tengamos
tú	tengas	vosotros/vosotras	tengáis
él	tenga	ellos	tengan
ella	tenga	ellas	tengan
usted	tenga	ustedes	tengan

Table 7-12   The *Yo/Él* Form of -*go* Verbs in the Present Subjunctive

Infinitive	Present Subjunctive Yo/Él Form
atraer (to attract)	*atraiga*
caer (to fall)	*caiga*
contraer (to contract)	*contraiga*
decir (to say, to tell)	*diga*
hacer (to make, to do)	*haga*
oír (to hear)	*oiga*
poner (to put)	*ponga*
raer (to scrape)	*raiga*
retraer (to bring back)	*retraiga*
salir (to leave)	*salga*
sustraer (to subtract)	*sustraiga*
traer (to bring)	*traiga*
valer (to be worth)	*valga*
venir (to come)	*venga*

-*zco* verbs

In general, any verb that ends in a vowel followed by -*cer* or -*cir* will have a *yo* form that ends in -*zco*. Therefore, all forms of the present subjunctive for these verbs will reflect the *yo* form, as demonstrated in Table 7-13.

Table 7-13   Present Subjunctive Conjugation Chart for *Conocer* (to Know, to Be Acquainted With)

Subject	Verb	Subject	Verb
yo	*conozca*	*nosotros/nosotras*	*conozcamos*
tú	*conozcas*	*vosotros/vosotras*	*conozcáis*
él	*conozca*	*ellos*	*conozcan*
ella	*conozca*	*ellas*	*conozcan*
usted	*conozca*	*ustedes*	*conozcan*

All the following verbs are conjugated like *conocer* with the *-zca, -zcas, -zca, -zcamos, -zcáis,* and *-zcan* endings. The present subjunctive *yo/él* form of each verb follows its translation in Table 7-14, below. The rest of the subjunctive endings follow the regular subjunctive ending patterns discussed earlier in this chapter.

Table 7-14   The *Yo/Él* Form of *-zco* Verbs in the Present Subjunctive

Infinitive	Present Subjunctive Yo/Él Form
aborrecer (to hate)	aborrezca
agradecer (to thank)	agradezca
aparecer (to appear)	aparezca
crecer (to grow)	crezca
desaparecer (to disappear)	desaparezca
desconocer (to be ignorant)	desconozca
establecer (to establish)	establezca
merecer (to deserve)	merezca
nacer (to be born)	nazca
obedecer (to obey)	obedezca
ofrecer (to offer)	ofrezca
permanecer (to remain)	permanezca
pertenecer (to belong)	pertenezca
complacer (to please, to gratify)	complazca
reconocer (to recognize)	reconozca
yacer (to lie down)	yazca

Table 7-15 lists several verbs that end in *-ucir.* They also have *-zca, -zcas, -zca, -zcamos, -zcáis,* and *-zcan* endings. The present subjunctive *yo/él* form of each verb follows its translation.

Table 7-15 The *Yo/Él* Form of *-ucir* Verbs in the Present Subjunctive

Infinitive	Present Subjunctive Yo/Él Form
conducir (to drive)	*conduzca*
deducir (to deduce)	*deduzca*
deslucir (to tarnish)	*desluzca*
introducir (to introduce)	*introduzca*
lucir (to light up, to display)	*luzca*
producir (to produce)	*produzca*
reducir (to reduce)	*reduzca*
traducir (to translate)	*traduzca*

-zo verbs

A verb that ends in a consonant followed by *-cer* has a *yo* form ending in *-zo*. Therefore, all forms of the present subjunctive for these verbs will reflect the *yo* form, as demonstrated in Table 7-16.

Table 7-16 Present Subjunctive Conjugation Chart for *Ejercer* (to Exercise, to Practice a Profession)

Subject	Verb	Subject	Verb
yo	ejerza	nosotros/nosotras	ejerzamos
tú	ejerzas	vosotros/vosotras	ejerzáis
él	ejerza	ellos	ejerzan
ella	ejerza	ellas	ejerzan
usted	ejerza	ustedes	ejerzan

The verbs in Table 7-17 are conjugated like *ejercer* with the *-za, -zas, -za, -zamos, -záis,* and *-zan* endings. The present subjunctive *yo/él* form of each verb follows its translation.

Table 7-17   The *Yo/Él* Form of *-zo* Verbs in the Present Subjunctive

Infinitive	Present Subjunctive Yo/Él Form
convencer (to convince, to persuade)	*convenza*
esparcir (to scatter)	*esparza*
vencer (to conquer)	*venza*
zurcir (to mend)	*zurza*

-gir verbs

A verb that ends in *-gir* in its infinitive form must change the *g* to *j* to maintain the soft *g* sound in all forms of the present subjunctive. Table 7-18 presents the present subjunctive forms for the verb *dirigir*. All the other verbs ending in *-gir* are listed in Table 7-19.

Table 7-18   Present Subjunctive Conjugation Chart for *Dirigir* (to Direct)

Subject	Verb	Subject	Verb
yo	dirija	nosotros/nosotras	dirijamos
tú	dirijas	vosotros/vosotras	dirijáis
él	dirija	ellos	dirijan
ella	dirija	ellas	dirijan
usted	dirija	ustedes	dirijan

The verbs in the list below undergo a spelling change in every form of the subjunctive present tense. The verbs followed by an asterisk also undergo an *e>i* stem change in all forms.

Table 7-19   The *Yo/Él* Form of *-gir* Verbs in the Present Subjunctive

Infinitive	Present Subjunctive Yo/Él Form
afligir (to afflict, to grieve)	*aflija*
coger (to catch, to seize, to grab)	*coja*
*colegir** (to deduce)	*colija*

(continued)

Table 7-19 *(continued)*

Infinitive	Present Subjunctive Yo/Él Form
*corregir** (to correct)	*corrija*
escoger (to choose)	*escoja*
dirigir (to direct)	*dirija*
*elegir** (to elect)	*elija*
exigir (to demand, to require)	*exija*
fingir (to pretend)	*finja*
proteger (to protect)	*proteja*
recoger (to gather, to pick up)	*recoja*
sumergir (to immerse)	*sumerja*
surgir (to surge)	*surja*

-guir verbs

A verb that ends in *-guir* includes a *u* in its infinitive form only to attain a hard *g* sound. In all forms of the subjunctive, you must drop that *u;* because the *g* is now followed by an *a,* it is already pronounced hard. Table 7-20 presents the present subjunctive forms for the verb *seguir.* All the other verbs ending in *-guir* are listed in Table 7-21. There is, however, one extra issue: *Seguir* is a stem-changer, and the *e* changes to *i* in all forms of the present subjunctive.

Table 7-20 **Present Subjunctive Conjugation Chart for *Seguir***
(to Continue, to Follow)

Subject	Verb	Subject	Verb
yo	siga	nosotros/nosotras	sigamos
tú	sigas	vosotros/vosotras	sigáis
él	siga	ellos	sigan
ella	siga	ellas	sigan
usted	siga	ustedes	sigan

The verbs in Table 7-21 drop the *u* in every form of the subjunctive present tense. The verbs followed by an asterisk also undergo an *e>i* stem change in all forms.

Table 7-21   The *Yo/Él* Form of -*guir* Verbs in the Present Subjunctive

Infinitive	Present Subjunctive Yo/Él Form
conseguir* (to get)	consiga
distinguir (to distinguish)	distinga
extinguir (to extinguish)	extinga
perseguir* (to persecute, to pursue)	persiga
proseguir* (to continue, to proceed)	prosiga

-*uir* verbs that add a *y*

Any verb that ends in -*uir* (except -*guir* verbs) will have a *y* in front of the subjunctive ending for all forms.

Table 7-22   Conjugation Chart for the Verb *Contribuir* (to Contribute)

Subject	Verb	Subject	Verb
yo	contribuya	nosotros/nosotras	contribuyamos
tú	contribuyas	vosotros/vosotras	contribuyáis
él	contribuya	ellos	contribuyan
ella	contribuya	ellas	contribuyan
usted	contribuya	ustedes	contribuyan

All of the following verbs in Table 7-23 are conjugated like *contribuir* with a *y* in front of the ending for every form.

Table 7-23   The *Yo/Él* Form of -*uir* Verbs That Change *i* to *y* in the Present Subjunctive

Infinitive	Present Subjunctive Yo/Él Form
concluir (to conclude)	concluya
constituir (to constitute)	constituya
construir (to build, to construct)	construya
contribuir (to contribute)	contribuya

(continued)

Table 7-23 *(continued)*

Infinitive	Present Subjunctive Yo/Él Form
destruir (to destroy)	*destruya*
fluir (to flow)	*fluya*
huir (to run away, to flee)	*huya*
incluir (to include)	*incluya*
influir (to influence)	*influya*

Stem-Changers in the Present Subjunctive

Any verb that undergoes a stem change in the present tense undergoes the same stem change in the present subjunctive in all forms except *nosotros/nosotras* and *vosotros/vosotras*. Only -*ir* verbs undergo a stem change in the *nosotros/nosotras* and *vosotros/vosotras* forms and, only in these forms, they undergo *o>u* or *e>i* stem changes. Notice that *mostrar* (Table 7-24) and *entender* (Table 7-25) do not undergo a stem change in the *nosotros/nosotras* and *vosotros/vosotras* forms, but *dormir* (Table 7-26) does because it is an -*ir* verb.

Table 7-24   Subjunctive Present Tense for *Mostrar* (to Show)

Subject	Verb	Subject	Verb
yo	muestre	nosotros/nosotras	mostremos
tú	muestres	vosotros/vosotras	mostréis
él	muestre	ellos	muestren
ella	muestre	ellas	muestren
usted	muestre	ustedes	muestren

Table 7-25   Subjunctive Present Tense for *Entender* (to Understand)

Subject	Verb	Subject	Verb
yo	entienda	nosotros/nosotras	entendamos
tú	entiendas	vosotros/vosotras	entendáis
él	entienda	ellos	entiendan

Subject	Verb	Subject	Verb
ella	entienda	ellas	entiendan
usted	entienda	ustedes	entiendan

Table 7-26   Subjunctive Present Tense for *Dormir* (to Sleep)

Subject	Verb	Subject	Verb
yo	duerma	nosotros/nosotras	durmamos
tú	duermas	vosotros/vosotras	durmáis
él	duerma	ellos	duerman
ella	duerma	ellas	duerman
usted	duerma	ustedes	duerman

The verb *jugar* (to play) is exceptionally tricky because it is a stem-changer and also undergoes a spelling change. Because *jugar* is a very common verb, it is worth learning the forms in Table 7-27.

Table 7-27   Subjunctive Present Tense for *Jugar* (to Play)

Subject	Verb	Subject	Verb
yo	juegue	nosotros/nosotras	juguemos
tú	juegues	vosotros/vosotras	juguéis
él	juegue	ellos	jueguen
ella	juegue	ellas	jueguen
usted	juegue	ustedes	jueguen

Truly Irregular Verbs in the Present Subjunctive

Any verb that does not end in *-o* in the regular (indicative) present tense will be irregular in the present subjunctive because, in these cases, you cannot just take the *yo* form and drop the *o*. The five verbs in this category are conjugated in tables 7-28, 7-29, 7-30, 7-31, and 7-32.

The verb *dar* (see Table 7-28) has an accent on the forms that look like the preposition *de* to differentiate the verb forms from the preposition. In addition, the *vosotros/vosotras* form does not have an accent because it is only one syllable. The verb *estar* (see Table 7-29) has accents on all forms except the *nosotros/nosotras* form because of the general rule of accentuation.

Table 7-28   Subjunctive Present Tense for *Dar* (to Give)

Subject	Verb	Subject	Verb
yo	dé	nosotros/nosotras	demos
tú	des	vosotros/vosotras	deis
él	dé	ellos	den
ella	dé	ellas	den
usted	dé	ustedes	den

Table 7-29   Subjunctive Present Tense for *Estar* (to Be)

Subject	Verb	Subject	Verb
yo	esté	nosotros/nosotras	estemos
tú	estés	vosotros/vosotras	estéis
él	esté	ellos	estén
ella	esté	ellas	estén
usted	esté	ustedes	estén

Table 7-30   Subjunctive Present Tense for *Ir* (to Go)

Subject	Verb	Subject	Verb
yo	vaya	nosotros/nosotras	vayamos
tú	vayas	vosotros/vosotras	vayáis
él	vaya	ellos	vayan
ella	vaya	ellas	vayan
usted	vaya	ustedes	vayan

Table 7-31   Subjunctive Present Tense for *Saber* (to Know)

Subject	Verb	Subject	Verb
yo	sepa	nosotros/nosotras	sepamos
tú	sepas	vosotros/vosotras	sepáis
él	sepa	ellos	sepan
ella	sepa	ellas	sepan
usted	sepa	ustedes	sepan

Table 7-32   Subjunctive Present Tense for *Ser* (to Be)

Subject	Verb	Subject	Verb
yo	sea	nosotros/nosotras	seamos
tú	seas	vosotros/vosotras	seáis
él	sea	ellos	sean
ella	sea	ellas	sean
usted	sea	ustedes	sean

Chapter Checkout

Write the correct present tense subjunctive form of the verb to agree with the subject pronoun in parentheses.

1. *traer* (*yo*)
2. *perder* (*tú*)
3. *pedir* (*ellos*)
4. *afligir* (*yo*)
5. *dar* (*él*)
6. *perseguir* (*Uds.*)
7. *contribuir* (*ella*)

Answers: 1. *traiga* **2.** *pierdas* **3.** *pidan* **4.** *aflija* **5.** *dé* **6.** *persigan* **7.** *contribuya*

Chapter 8
SUBJUNCTIVE MOOD II

Chapter Check-In

❑ Understanding when to use the subjunctive mood
❑ Mastering the irregular verbs in the subjunctive
❑ Understanding when the subjunctive is necessary

When to Use the Subjunctive Mood

Most of us are baffled by the subjunctive mood because it is so subjective! After all, how do you know in what mood the speaker is? By using a simple thought process, however, you can determine which mood (subjunctive or indicative) is appropriate for any context.

The best way to learn when to use the subjunctive mood is to understand the different reasons or psychological states that cause a Spanish speaker to use the subjunctive. The problem with this approach, however, is that an English speaker does not think like a Spanish speaker, so it is difficult for an English speaker to understand the reasons for using the subjunctive. Therefore, until you understand the subtleties of the subjunctive mood, you can memorize vocabulary lists that represent the reasons to use the subjunctive.

To determine the correct mood of the verb, you will have to analyze the entire sentence structure. Most sentences have an independent clause and at least one dependent clause, joined by a conjunction. Most often, the conjunction is the word *que* (or includes the word *que*). For example:

Ellas dudan que yo recuerde sus cumpleaños.
They doubt that I will remember their birthdays.

Nosotras queremos que ellos bailen con nosotras.
We want them to dance with us.

Que, the conjunction that generally joins two clauses in Spanish, is the key word. The thought expressed in the clause in front of *que* often determines the mood of the verb after *que.* The term **subjunctive indicators** is used for the collection of verbs that express the types of thoughts that cause the subjunctive to be used after *que.*

Subjunctive Indicators

The subjunctive indicators are easier to learn if you understand the basic reasons to use the subjunctive that each list represents. The mnemonic device **WEIRD** may help you remember the five basic reasons for using the subjunctive:

Wish

Emotion

Impersonal Expressions

Requests

Doubt (of existence or of occurrence)

With practice, you will better understand what types of verbs, conjunctions, or situations are followed by the subjunctive. The following explanations that introduce each group of subjunctive indicators will help you understand why these lead to the use of the subjunctive. Again, it is preferable to understand the concept of the subjunctive, but you can memorize the list of verbs generally followed by the subjunctive until you attain that understanding. You should at least memorize the five categories for subjunctive indicators and try to recognize any verb that could be listed as an example for any one of these categories; most likely, it will indicate that you will use the subjunctive after *que* if one of these verbs is in front of *que.*

Wishes

If the point of a sentence is to express a hope, desire, or need, the subjunctive is used for the verb that is wished. When the first clause indicates that what follows is not necessarily a reality, but rather something the subject of the first clause desires or needs, the verb after *que* must be in the subjunctive. It does not matter whether these are basic sentences or questions, nor does it matter whether they are affirmative or negative. You must use the subjunctive after *que* if one of these verbs of desire is somewhere before *que.*

In the sample sentences below, the subjunctive indicator is boldface and the verb that is conjugated in the subjunctive mood is underlined. Pay attention to what the subjunctive conjugation looks like and what verb was used in the beginning of the sentence that required the present subjunctive conjugation after *que*.

desear = to desire, to want

*Él no **desea** que yo lo <u>llame</u>.*

He doesn't want me to call him.

esperar = to hope

*Mi perro **espera** que <u>demos</u> un paseo.*

My dog hopes that we take a walk.

necesitar = to need

***Necesitamos** que tú nos <u>presentes</u> a tus padres.*

We need you to introduce us to your parents.

querer (e>ie) = to want

*Carlos no **quiere** que su hija <u>toque</u> el tambor.*

Carlos does not want his daughter to play the drums.

Long before you ever heard of the subjunctive, you learned to use verbs with an infinitive. In "two-verb" sentences where there is no change of subject (and no *que*), the first verb is conjugated and the second is in the infinitive form. These verbs are often used without *que*, but only if the subject is the same for both verbs.

Yo quiero bailar.

I want to dance.

Who wants? I do. Who dances? I do.

Él desea comprar una computadora nueva.

He wants to buy a new computer.

Who wants? He does. Who buys? He does.

Esperamos ganar muchos partidos.

We hope to win a lot of games.

Who hopes? We do. Who wins? We do.

Todos necesitan traer sus cuadernos.

Everyone needs to bring his or her notebook.

Who needs? Everyone. Who brings? Everyone.

English sentences often use an infinitive even when there is a change of subject. For example, you cannot translate the following sentence into

Spanish word for word: "<u>He</u> doesn't want <u>me</u> to go." It is better to think of this sentence as "He doesn't want that I go" because, in Spanish, you cannot use the infinitive when there are two different subjects in the sentence and the main verb is a subjunctive indicator.

One common expression used to express a wish is somewhat unusual because it is impersonal. The expression *ojalá* is one exception in which you use the subjunctive mood without *que*. An Arabic expression that means "may Allah grant that," *ojalá* is used in Spanish to mean "hopefully" or "if only." Because it is impersonal, there is no subject and it is technically not conjugated. It is always written in the same form and is always followed by the subjunctive mood even if there is no *que*.

Examples:

> *Ojalá que <u>traigas</u> las direcciones.*
> Hopefully, you will bring the address.
>
> *Ojalá <u>veamos</u> a su novio esta noche.*
> Hopefully, we will see your boyfriend tonight.
>
> *Ojalá que no <u>pierda</u> su pasaporte.*
> Hopefully, he will not lose his passport.

Emotion

When the first clause expresses an emotion about what is happening in the second clause, the verb in the second clause (after *que*) is in the subjunctive mood. Therefore, verbs that express emotion are subjunctive indicators. Many verbs of emotion are very similar to the verb *gustar*.

The Spanish versions of "it angers me" or "it disappoints him" use an impersonal sentence structure, which means the subject of the sentence is "it." For this reason, the verb stays in the *él* form. An indirect object (see Chapter 12), such as *le,* is used to reflect the individual who is feeling the emotion. The sample sentences below demonstrate how indirect objects other than *le* are used with these verbs. Notice that when the sentence is negative, the *no* precedes the indirect object and the verb following *que* is still in the subjunctive.

> *(le) conmueve que* = it moves (him) that
> *Les conmueve que su abuela <u>se mude</u> hoy.*
> It moves them that their grandmother is moving today.

(le) desilusiona que = it disappoints (him) that
No me desilusiona que tu equipo siempre pierda.
It does not disappoint me that your team always loses.

(le) emociona que = it thrills (him) that
Les emociona que su músico favorito toque.
It thrills them that their favorite musician is performing.

(le) encanta que = it delights (him) that
Nos encanta que ustedes nos visiten.
It delights us that you guys visit us.

(le) enfada que = it angers (him) that
¿Le enfada a Ud. que los políticos no le escuchen?
Does it anger you that the politicians do not listen to you?

(le) enoja que = it angers (him) that
Me enoja que los avaros tengan todo el dinero.
It angers me that the greedy ones have all the money.

(le) entristece que = it saddens (him) that
Le entristece que los pobres vivan en las calles.
It saddens her that the poor live in the streets.

(le) gusta que = it pleases (him) that
No me gusta que tu siempre olvides mi cumpleaños.
It does not please me that you always forget my birthday.

(le) hace feliz que = it makes (him) happy that
¿Les hace felices que yo pinte su casa?
Does it make them happy that I am painting their house?

(le) hace (emoción) que = it makes (him) (emotion) that
Nos hace feliz que no tengas ningún problema.
It makes us happy that you do not have any problem.

(le) irrita que = it irritates (him) that
Les irrita que sepas todo.
It irritates them that you know everything.

(le) molesta que = it bothers (him) that
A Rafael no le molesta que yo hable con su madre.
It does not bother Rafael that I speak with his mom.

(le) pone contento que = it makes (him) content that
*Las pone contentas que él les **dé** buenos consejos.*
It makes them content that he give them good advice.

(le) pone (emoción) que = it makes (him) (emotion) that
*Te pone triste que yo no **pueda** asistir a tu presentación.*
It makes you sad that I cannot attend your presentation.

(le) sorprende que = it surprises (him) that
*No me sorprende que tú **quieras** casarte con ella.*
It does not surprise me that you want to marry her.

Listed below are more subjunctive indicators that express emotion. Unlike the verbs above, these verbs must be conjugated in order to agree with the subject of the first clause. Notice that the verb following *que* must be in the subjunctive mood. The subjunctive indicator is bold and the verb that is conjugated in the subjunctive mood is underlined.

If the verb has *se* attached to the infinitive, it is reflexive. Reflexive verbs are reviewed in Chapter 12, but you may be able to remember reflexive pronouns after looking at the sample sentences.

alegrarse de que = to be happy that
*Me **alegro de que** Raquel **utilice** el idioma extranjero.*
I am happy that Raquel uses the foreign language.

enorgullecerse de que = to be proud that
*No **se enorgullecen de que** su hijo **tenga** problemas con la ley.*
They are not proud that their son has problems with the law.

estar encantado de que = to be delighted that
*Ellas **están encantadas de que** les **regalemos** una televisión.*
They are delighted that we are giving them a TV.

lamentar que = to regret that
*Toni **lamenta que** no yo **esquíe** cada día.*
Toni regrets that I do not ski every day.

sentir (e>ie) que = to regret that
*Constanza y Pilar **sienten que** tu libro **esté** roto.*
Constanza and Pilar regret that your book is ripped.

temer que = to fear that

¿Temes que tu hijo crea en monstruos?

Are you afraid that your son believes in monsters?

tener miedo de que = to be afraid that

Ellos no tienen miedo de que las corporaciones los roben.

They are not afraid that the corporations will rob them.

Impersonal expressions

There are many expressions in Spanish that are considered impersonal because they do not have a specific person as the subject. They are always conjugated in the *él* form because the subject is "it." These expressions often indicate some sort of opinion about the clause that follows *que*. Because the focus of the sentence is on the opinion being expressed rather than on the action of the verb that comes after *que*, that verb is in the subjunctive.

Notice in the examples that follow that the verb is already conjugated in the *él* form. Most of the expressions include *es* + adjective + *que*. With a few exceptions (which are explained later), any impersonal expression constructed using *es* + adjective + *que* will be followed by a verb in the subjunctive. It does not matter whether these expressions are affirmative or negative, sentences or questions.

In the sample sentences, the subjunctive indicator is bold and the verb that is conjugated in the subjunctive mood is underlined.

conviene que = it is advisable that

No conviene que visites sin llamar.

It is not advisable that you visit without calling.

más vale que = it is better that

Más vale que tus amigos te protejan.

It is better that your friends protect you.

puede ser que = it may be that

Puede ser que Rebeca no siga asistiendo a esa escuela.

It may be that Rebeca will not continue attending that school.

es bueno que = it is good that

No es bueno que Daniel gima cuando tiene tarea.

It is not good that Daniel whines when he has homework.

es difícil que = it is unlikely that
Es difícil que _devuelva_ *tu periódico.*
It is unlikely that he will return your magazine.

es dudoso que = it is doubtful that
Es dudoso que _almorcemos_ *hoy.*
It is doubtful that we will eat lunch today.

es fácil que = it is likely that
Es fácil que *ellos* _castiguen_ *al ladrón.*
It is likely that they will punish the thief.

es fantástico que = it is fantastic that
Es fantástico que _juegues_ *jai alai.*
It is fantastic that you play jai alai.

es hora de que = it is time that
*¿***Es hora de que** _salgamos_ *para el aeropuerto?*
Is it time that we leave for the airport?

es importante que = it is important that
Es importante que _abrace_ *a sus hijos.*
It is important that you hug your children.

es imposible que = it is impossible that
Es imposible que *la televisión no* _influya_ *en los niños.*
It is impossible that television does not influence children. **Note:** The double negation in Spanish "no and impossible" does not produce a change of the meaning to "possible," as in English.

es improbable que = it is unlikely that
Es improbable que *Susana* _se ahogue_ *porque ella nada bien.*
It is unlikely that Susan will drown because she swims well.

es increíble que = it is incredible that
Es increíble que _durmamos_ *tantas horas cada noche.*
It is incredible that we sleep so many hours each night.

es (una) lástima que = it is a shame that
Es una lástima que *Belinda* _se vista_ *tan mal.*
It is a shame that Belinda dresses so badly.

es malo que = it is bad that
Es malo que <u>contaminemos</u> *la naturaleza.*
It is bad that we pollute nature.

es mejor que = it is better that
Es mejor que <u>escojas</u> *algo muy cómodo.*
It is better that you choose something very comfortable.

es necesario que = it is necessary that
No **es necesario que** *me* <u>convenzan</u>.
It is not necessary that they convince me.

es posible que = it is possible that
Es posible que *yo* <u>tenga</u> *el periódico en casa.*
It is possible that I have the newspaper at home.

es preciso que = it is necessary that
Es preciso que *Uds.* <u>lleguen</u> *a tiempo.*
It is necessary that you arrive on time.

es preferible que = it is preferable that
Es preferible que *Manuela lo* <u>explique</u>.
It is preferable that Manuela explain it.

es ridículo que = it is ridiculous that
Es ridículo que *ella no* <u>sepa</u> *la dirección.*
It is ridiculous that she does not know the address.

es terrible que = it is terrible that
Es terrible que *los niños no* <u>se comuniquen</u> *con sus padres.*
It is terrible that kids do not communicate with their parents.

es triste que = it is sad that
Es triste que *la casa no* <u>valga</u> *más.*
It is sad that the house is not worth more.

An impersonal expression does not need to express doubt in order to be followed by the subjunctive, but the few impersonal expressions that completely eliminate doubt (**affirmative** expressions of certainty) are followed by the indicative. *Note:* Verbs that express certainty are subjunctive indicators only when used negatively; this will be discussed later in this chapter. Look carefully at the following sample sentences for each expression in this category. These affirmative expressions of certainty are not subjunctive indicators and no verb is conjugated in the subjunctive mood, so there is nothing bold or underlined in the sample sentences.

> *es claro que* = it is clear that
> *Es claro que el jugador le miente a su novia.*
> It is clear that the player lies to his girlfriend.

> *es cierto que* = it is certain that
> *Es cierto que no vivimos bastante.*
> It is certain that we do not live enough.

> *es evidente que* = it is evident that
> *Es evidente que la economía cambia.*
> It is evident that the economy changes.

> *es que* = it is that
> *Es que voy a perder mi vuelo si no me apresuro.*
> It is that I will miss my flight if I do not hurry.

> *es verdad que* = it is true that
> *Es verdad que tú mereces buenas notas.*
> It is true that you deserve good grades.

There is one expression that must be negative in order to indicate certainty and, therefore, requires you to use the indicative mood after *que*. In its affirmative form, it is listed with the subjunctive indicators, earlier in this chapter.

> *no es dudoso que* = it is not doubtful that
> *No es dudoso que Diana es la verdadera líder.*
> It is not doubtful Diana is the real leader.

Requests

The first group of subjunctive indicators that follow includes verbs that indicate some type of request or indirect command. The person who is the subject of the first clause requests that the subject of the second clause do something or not do something.

Because the action of the verb being requested may never occur, the verb is in the subjunctive mood. It makes no difference whether the sentences are affirmative or negative for this group of indicators. The verbs implying an indirect request are subjunctive indicators because they indicate that the verb in the clause that follows *que* must be in the subjunctive. The subjunctive indicator itself is used in the beginning of the sentence, so it is not conjugated in the subjunctive mood. It indicates that the verb in the second clause (after *que*) be conjugated in the subjunctive mood.

In the sample sentences, the subjunctive indicator is bold and the verb that is conjugated in the subjunctive mood is underlined. Pay attention to what the subjunctive conjugation looks like and the verb that was used in the beginning of the sentence that required the use of the present subjunctive after *que*.

> *aconsejar* = to advise, to warn
> *Ellos me **aconsejan** que yo trabaje más.*
> They advise me that I (should) work more.
>
> *aprobar (o>ue)* = to approve
> *Elena **aprueba** que mi familia tenga la fiesta.*
> Elena approves that my family have the party.
>
> *decirle (e>i)* = to tell
> *Estela te **dice** que hagas tu tarea.*
> Estela tells you to do your homework.
>
> *dejar* = to let, to allow
> *Mi padre no **deja** que yo conduzca solo.*
> My father does not permit that I drive alone.
>
> *empeñarse en* = to insist
> *Los maestros **se empeñan en** que sus estudiantes los oigan.*
> The teachers insist that their students listen to them.
>
> *exigir* = to demand
> *Yolanda **exije** que sus niños hagan sus quehaceres.*
> Yolanda demands that her children do their chores.
>
> *gustar* = to please
> *¿Te **gusta** que te llame de vez en cuando?*
> Do you like that I call you occasionally?
>
> *hacer* = to make
> *Emilio **hace** que nosotras vengamos a verlo.*
> Emilio makes us come to see him.

impedir (*e>i*) = to prevent, to impede
Sus problemas **impiden** *que Marco* <u>*tenga*</u> *éxito.*
His problems prevent Mark from being successful.

insistir en = to insist
El abogado **insiste en** *que ellos me* <u>*ayuden*</u>.
The lawyer insists that they help me.

mandar = to order, to demand
El jefe **manda** *que los empleados* <u>*lleguen*</u> *a tiempo.*
The boss demands that the employees arrive on time.

pedir (*e>i*) = to request
Silvia **pide** *que el camarero* <u>*traiga*</u> *un vaso de agua.*
Silvia requests that the waiter bring a glass of water.

permitir = to permit
El gerente no **permite** *que los empleados* <u>*lleguen*</u> *tarde.*
The manager does not permit that the employees arrive late.

preferir = to prefer
La esposa **prefiere** *que el esposo* <u>*cocine*</u> *la cena.*
The wife prefers that the husband cook dinner.

prohibir = to prohibit
La ley no **prohíbe** *que* <u>*fumen*</u> *cigarrillos.*
The law does not prohibit that they smoke cigarettes.

proponer = to propose
Berto **propone** *que Ernesto* <u>*trabaje*</u> *con él.*
Berto proposes that Ernesto work with him.

rezar = to pray
Lupe **reza para** *que su padre* <u>*se cuide*</u>.
Lupe prays that her father will be careful.

sugerir (*e>ie*) = to suggest
El doctor **sugiere** *que yo no* <u>*coma*</u> *tantos dulces.*
The doctor suggests that I do not eat so many sweets.

suplicar = to beg

*Los mendigos **suplican** que alguien les dé dinero.*

The mendicants beg that someone give them money.

For the above verbs to be subjunctive indicators, they must be followed by *que*. As you can see in the examples below, you use the infinitive after any of the above verbs if the sentence does not have *que*.

Examples:

Me gusta estudiar las ciencias sociales.

It pleases me to study the social sciences.

Prefieren comer verduras.

They prefer to eat vegetables.

Doubt

Although doubt is not the only reason for using the subjunctive after *que*, the elimination of doubt requires the use of the indicative mood after *que*. Therefore, the following verbs that express doubt are subjunctive indicators only if used affirmatively.

dudar = to doubt

*Sus padres **dudan** que ella ponga la mesa.*

Her parents doubt that she sets the table.

negar (e>ie) = to deny

*Leonora **niega** que Ana aborrezca sus clases.*

Leonora denies that Ana hates her classes.

When used negatively, these verbs eliminate doubt, and the verb after *que* must be in the indicative mood. Keep an eye out for negative words such as *nunca* or *nadie*. When used before the noun, these words make a sentence negative without using the word *no*.

Maribel no duda que yo me opongo a su plan.

Maribel does not doubt that I oppose her plan.

Nadie niega que sus planes nunca funcionan.

Nobody denies that her plans never work.

Remember, verbs that express certainty are subjunctive indicators only when used negatively. It is important to realize a cultural difference between English and Spanish speakers. When a Spanish speaker states that she thinks or believes something is true, she considers this a certainty and uses the indicative mood after *que*. An English speaker uses the verbs "to think" and "to believe" only when he does not know for certain. This basic difference is why the verbs *creer* and *pensar* are included in the list of verbs that express certainty and which must be negative in order to be subjunctive indicators.

In the sample sentences below, the negative word is bold because it is part of the subjunctive indicator and the verb that is conjugated in the subjunctive mood is underlined.

> *no creer que* = not to believe that
> **Nunca creen que** *ella* <u>*se despierte*</u> *a las cinco.*
> They never believe that she wakes up at five.
>
> *no decir que* = not to say that
> *Loli* **no dice que** *su hermano* <u>*tenga*</u> *que venir con nosotras.*
> Loli is not saying that her brother has to come with us.
>
> *no pensar que* = not to think that
> *José* **no piensa que** <u>*vaya*</u> *a llover.*
> José does not think that it is going to rain.
>
> *no saber que* = not to know that
> *Yo* **no sé que** *Uds.* <u>*lleguen*</u> *a tiempo.*
> I do not know that you will arrive on time.

Notice in the following sample sentences that these verbs are followed by the indicative mood when used affirmatively.

> *Crees que la vida es una fiesta.*
> You believe that life is a party.
>
> *Me dicen que esta pulsera cuesta dos mil euros.*
> They tell me that this bracelet costs two thousand euros.
>
> *A veces pienso que Soledad no quiere tener amigos.*
> Sometimes I think that Soledad does not want any friends.
>
> *Sabemos que nuestro perro nos entiende.*
> We know that our dog understands us.

Another type of doubt that causes the subjunctive to be used is when there is some doubt about the existence of the second clause's subject. How can the verb of the second clause occur if the subject doing the verb may not even exist? This type of subjunctive situation requires some thought as well as cultural understanding because the Spanish language reflects a cultural tendency to "believe it when I see it." An English speaker is probably certain that she can find what she wants when she states, "I'm looking for a hotel that has a view of the sea." To the Spanish speaker, the fact that the sentence begins with "I'm looking for" indicates that what follows technically may not exist, or at least that the speaker is unsure as to which hotel he will find.

This type of sentence always uses the conjunction *que,* and the subject after *que* is always what is being looked for or what is needed in the first clause. When something mentioned in the first clause is used as the subject of the second clause, it is called an **antecedent.** When the existence of the antecedent is unknown, the subjunctive is used. You may have heard the term "unknown antecedent." This refers to a sentence in which there is no certainty of the existence of the person(s) or things(s) that would be the subject of the clause after *que.*

Whether or not a verb is a subjunctive indicator because it establishes some doubt about the existence of the subject of the clause after *que* depends on whether the first clause is affirmative or negative, and on whether it is a sentence or a question. For this reason, there are several examples for each verb in the sections that follow. Pay attention to the bold and underlined verbs in the examples. Think about how the existence of the subject of the second clause depends on whether it is a sentence or a question, and also on whether it is affirmative or negative; look to see if the verb is in the subjunctive (that is, underlined) for each example.

One of the most common verbs of this type is the word *hay* (*haber*). Because *hay* does not get conjugated, it is considered idiomatic and is an important expression to learn. *Hay* is used to indicate the existence of people or things both singular and plural.

> *hay* (followed by something singular) = there is
> **Hay** *un abogado que <u>habla</u> español aquí.*
> There is a lawyer that speaks Spanish here.
>
> *hay* (followed by something plural) = there are
> **Hay** *muchos abogados que <u>hablan</u> español aquí.*
> There are many lawyers that speak Spanish here.

Below, when *hay* is used in a question, it is bold because it questions the existence of what follows.

> *¿hay?* = is there?
>
> *¿**Hay** un abogado que <u>hable</u> español aquí?*
>
> ¿hay? = are there?
>
> *¿**Hay** muchos abogados que <u>hablen</u> español aquí?*

Hopefully, you noticed that the verb *hablar* (after *que*) is in the subjunctive when *hay* is used as a question, but is in the indicative when *hay* is used in an affirmative statement. What happens to the verb that follows *que* if *hay* is used in a negative statement? While considering the examples, notice the necessary double negative in Spanish.

> *no hay* = there is not
>
> *No **hay** ningún abogado que <u>hable</u> español aquí.*

Hay in its negative form creates a sentence in which the subject of the second clause does not exist; therefore, the verb that goes with the nonexistent subject should be in the subjunctive mood. The same thing is true for the following verbs.

> *Tener* (to have)
>
> *¿**Tienes** un libro que <u>enseñe</u> francés?*
>
> Do you have a book that teaches French?
>
> *No **tengo** ningún diccionario que <u>incluya</u> esa palabra.*
>
> I do not have any dictionary that includes that word.

Tener used negatively or as a question in the first clause requires the subjunctive mood in the clause that follows *que*. Notice in the example below that, when *tener* is used affirmatively in the first clause, it requires the indicative mood in the second clause. The same applies to *conocer*.

> *Tiene un novio que llama cada noche.*
>
> She has a boyfriend that calls every night.
>
> *Conocer* (to know, to be acquainted with)
>
> *¿**Conoces** a un médico que les <u>dé</u> dulces a los niños?*
>
> Do you know a doctor that gives sweets to kids?
>
> *No **conozco** a nadie que <u>viva</u> en una cueva.*
>
> I do not know anyone that lives in a cave.

Conoce a un hombre simpático que vive en Guadix.
He knows a nice man that lives in Guadix.

A verb in the first clause that expresses a need, or the search for something or someone, requires the subjunctive after *que* even when the sentence is affirmative. This is because Spanish speakers never assume that a thing or person exists. If a definite article follows the verb, the verb is no longer a subjunctive indicator because it refers to a very specific, known entity. The next few examples make this more clear.

Buscar (to look for)
Ella **busca** *una secretaria que sepa escribir a máquina.*
She is looking for a secretary that knows how to type.

Yo busco a la secretaria que escribió a máquina ese ensayo.
I am looking for the secretary that typed that essay.

Necesitar (to need)
Necesito *un disco compacto que tenga canciones para bailar.*
I need a CD that has dance songs.

Necesito el disco compacto que tiene mi canción favorita.
I need the CD that has my favorite song.

Querer (to want)
Queremos *una boda que impresione a todos nuestros amigos.*
We want a wedding that impresses all our friends.

Miguel quiere a la profesora que siempre da buenas notas.
Miguel wants the teacher that always gives good grades.

Desear (to want)
Mercedes **desea** *un puesto que ofrezca muchas oportunidades.*
Mercedes wants a job that offers many opportunities.

Ana desea el puesto que acaba de ver en el periódico.
Ana wants the job that she just saw in the newspaper.

There is a second kind of doubt to consider as a subjunctive indicator. When there is doubt as to whether or not the action of the verb in the second clause will take place, that verb is in the subjunctive. This type of sentence has a different kind of subjunctive indicator, a conjunction. A **conjunction** (see Chapter 13) is a word or phrase that joins two clauses together. So far, all of the subjunctive indicators you have seen in this chapter have been a verb or expression in the first clause followed by the conjunction *que*. There are other conjunctions however, that will be discussed later, that join clauses in a way that indicates the need for the subjunctive in the second clause.

When the conjunction that joins two clauses indicates that the action of the verb in the second clause has not yet occurred and, therefore, may never occur, the verb after the conjunction is in the subjunctive. Luckily, these conjunctions all include the word *que,* so you can still look for the verb after *que* to conjugate in the subjunctive. When the word *que* is missing from these conjunctions, they become prepositions and are followed by an infinitive rather than a subjunctive conjugation. The verb in the first clause does not have to be any of the above listed subjunctive indicators. Always use the subjunctive for the verb that follows any of the conjunctions below:

a menos que = unless

*Vamos al Caribe este otoño **a menos que** un huracán destruya la playa.*
We are going to the Caribbean this fall unless a hurricane destroys the beach.

a fin (de) que = so that

*Los padres castigan a sus hijos **a fin de que** obedezcan las reglas.*
Parents punish their kids so that they obey the rules.

antes (de) que = before

*Tienes que practicar mucho **antes de que** ganes el campeonato.*
You have to practice a lot before you win the championship.

para que = so that

*Ella quiere adelgazar **para que** su novio la vea bonita.*
She wants to lose weight so that her boyfriend sees her pretty.

por más que = no matter how much that

*Yo no te diré **por más que** pidas mi número.*
I will not tell you no matter how much you request my number.

sin que = without (that)

*No salimos **sin que** hagamos nuestros quehaceres.*
We do not leave without doing our chores.

en caso de que = in case that

*Llevo mi móbil **en caso de que** haya una emergencia.*
I carry my cellphone in case there is an emergency.

con tal que = provided that
*Lola puede entrar **con tal que** finja ser miembro.*
Lola can enter provided that she pretend to be a member.

There are also some conjunctions that will always be followed by the indicative because their meaning indicates a certainty of the occurrence of the verb that follows. Conjugate the verb in the indicative mood if it follows one of the conjunctions listed below.

No word is in bold below because these conjunctions are *always* followed by the indicative. No verb is underlined because there is no verb in the subjunctive in the sample sentences.

ahora que = now that
El viento no es tan fuerte ahora que la ventana está cerrada.
The wind is not as strong now that the window is closed.

desde que = since (a time when something happened)
Las torres han sido una maravilla desde que las construyeron.
The towers have been a marvel since they built them.

porque = because
El pollo cruza la calle porque quiere llegar al otro lado.
The chicken crosses the street because he wants to arrive at the other side.

puesto que = since (because)
Yo siempre compro los regalos puesto que nunca olvido un cumpleaños.
I always buy the gifts since I never forget a birthday.

ya que = now that
Tú puedes visitarme más a menudo ya que vives más cerca.
You can visit me more often now that you live more close by.

Conjunctions that determine mood by the tense of the first clause

Conjunctions are subjunctive indicators when they indicate that the action of the clause that follows has not yet occurred. There are a few conjunctions that require the indicative if the verb after *que* is in a past tense because the action of the verb has already happened. If, however, the action of the verb after *que* has not yet occurred, this verb is in the present subjunctive.

They are only subjunctive indicators, however, if the verb in the first clause is in the present tense, is in the future tense, or is a command. There are two examples for each conjunction. Look carefully at the bold words and the underlined verbs to determine when the conjunction is a subjunctive indicator, and consider how the tense of the first verb influences whether or not the second verb has occurred and whether or not the subjunctive is used. Some of the following conjunctions do not include the word *que,* but they still are conjunctions.

después de que = after

*El concierto empezará **después de que** el guitarrista <u>llegue</u>.*
The concert will begin after the guitarist arrives.

El concierto empezó después de que el guitarrista llegó.
The concert began after the guitarist arrived.

hasta que = until

*No contaron los pollitos **hasta que** <u>nacieron</u>.*
They did not count the chicks until they were born (hatched).

No comieron los pollos hasta que los cocinaron bien.
They did not eat the chickens until they cooked them well.

luego que = as soon as

*Tú tendrás tu coche **luego que** yo <u>reciba</u> tu dinero.*
You will have your car as soon as I receive your money.

Tú obtuviste tu coche luego que recibí tu dinero.
You got your car as soon as I received your money.

cuando = when

*Llámame **cuando** <u>llegues</u> a casa.*
Call me when you arrive at home.

Tú no me llamaste cuando llegaste a casa.
You did not call me when you arrived home.

en cuanto = as soon as

*Jerónimo comprará un coche **en cuanto** <u>se gradúe</u>.*
Jeronimo will buy a car as soon as he graduates.

Jerónimo compró un coche en cuanto se graduó.
Jeronimo bought a car as soon as he graduated.

tan pronto como = as soon as

*Comeremos **tan pronto como** traiga la comida.*

We will eat as soon as he brings the food.

Comimos tan pronto como trajo la comida.

We ate as soon as he brought the food.

The most important thing about the subjunctive mood is to think constantly about the reasons behind the indicators so that you do not have to try to memorize so much. It is better to understand each of the subjunctive situations and the reasons the subjunctive is used. You will never memorize all of the verbs and phrases that could be subjunctive indicators, but you can recognize whether a new verb or expression would fit into one of the categories that represent the reasons for using the subjunctive.

Chapter Checkout

Decide whether the indicative or subjunctive is appropriate and write the correct form of the verb in parentheses in the blank.

1. *El concierto _____ después de que el guitarrista llegó. (empezar)*
2. *Ella _____ una secretaria que sepa escribir a máquina. (buscar)*
3. *Es verdad que tú _____ buenas notas. (merecer)*
4. *Ojalá que ella no _____ su pasaporte. (perder)*
5. *Nos encanta que ustedes nos _____. (visitar)*
6. *Tú puedes visitarme más a menudo ya que _____ más cerca. (vivir)*

Answers: 1. *empezó* **2.** *busca* **3.** *mereces* **4.** *pierda* **5.** *visiten* **6.** *vives*

Chapter 9
THE IMPERATIVE

Chapter Check-In

❏ Using your knowledge of the subjunctive to create command forms

❏ Creating affirmative *tú* commands

❏ Using commands with pronouns

The imperative, or command, form is used to tell someone to do something. The verb conjugation is in a command form when the understood recipient of the command is "you." When an English command is given, the "you" is almost never stated; Spanish speakers, however, commonly place the subject pronoun for "you" (*tú, Ud., or Uds.*) after the command form of the verb.

> Set the table, please.
> *Pon **tú** la mesa, por favor.*
>
> Do not do your homework in class.
> *No hagan **Uds.** su tarea en clase.*
>
> Repeat the verbs.
> *Repita **Ud.** los verbos.*
>
> Swim until five.
> *Nada **tú** hasta las cinco.*

Because there are three different ways to say "you" in Spanish, there are three different types of commands: *tú, usted* and *ustedes.* You must consider how you would address the person you are commanding and use the appropriate command form for *tú, Ud., or Uds.* For the *Ud.* and *Uds.* commands, you use the same form whether you are telling the person(s) to do or *not* to do something. For the *tú* commands, however, a different form is used for the negative than for the affirmative command.

Affirmative *Tú* Commands

The subjunctive mood is used to express the affirmative and negative commands of the *Ud.*, *Uds.*, and *nosotros* forms, and only the negative commands of the *tú* and *vosotros* forms. The affirmative *tú* commands are not based on the subjunctive. There is however, a list of verbs that are irregular in the affirmative *tú* command form that you must learn.

Regular verbs

The most unusual type of command is the form used when you wish to give an affirmative command to someone you would address as *tú*. Oddly enough, the form of the verb used for an affirmative *tú* command looks exactly like the present tense *él* form of the verb: *not* the present subjunctive but rather the present indicative, and *not* the *tú* form but the *él* form. For this reason, it is common to use the pronoun *tú* after the command so you can tell the difference between "he does something," and "you, do something." For example:

> *Llama cada día.*
> He calls every day.
> *Llama tú cada día.*
> (You) Call every day.

If you remember how to create the present tense *él* form of the verb in the indicative mood, you can create the affirmative *tú* command form. If a verb undergoes a stem change in the present tense, the command form will undergo the same stem change. Notice that the subject pronoun may or may not follow a command form.

> *Produce más comida ahora.*
> Produce more food now.
> *Cuenta tú el dinero antes de salir.*
> Count the money before leaving.
> *Almuerza durante el descanso.*
> Eat lunch during the break.

Irregular affirmative *tú* commands

There are a few affirmative *tú* commands that are not like the present tense *él* form of the verb; these are considered irregular. Learn the irregular affirmative *tú* commands for the seven basic verbs in Table 9-1.

Table 9-1   Irregular Affirmative *Tú* Command Forms

Infinitive	Affirmative Tú Command	Translation
tener	ten	have
poner	pon	put
salir	sal	leave
venir	ven	come
hacer	haz	make or do
decir	di	say or tell
ser	sé	be
ir	ve	go

Because the *tú* command for *ser* is the same as the present tense *yo* form of the verb *saber,* you must consider the context of the sentence in order to determine which of the two is intended. In the following examples, notice how using a subject pronoun clarifies these identical forms with completely different meanings.

> *Sé tú médico porque así ganarás mucho dinero.*
>
> Be a doctor because you will earn a lot of money. (affirmative *tú* command, *ser*)
>
> *Yo sé que los médicos ganan mucho.*
>
> I know that doctors earn a lot. (present tense *yo* form, *saber*)

If you tell someone whom you address as *tú* not to do something, it is a negative command and, thus, you must use a different form. Only the *tú* and the *vosotros* commands have different forms for the negative and the affirmative. For *Ud.* and *Uds.* commands, the same form is used for negative and affirmative commands.

Command Forms Using the Subjunctive

Affirmative and negative *Ud.* and *Uds.* commands and negative *tú* and *vosotros* commands are created by using the appropriate present-tense subjunctive conjugation form. To create these commands, remember the mantra: "form of *yo,* drop the *-o,* add the opposite ending." If necessary, go back to Chapter 7 and review the subjunctive because affirmative and negative *Ud.* and *Uds.* commands as well as negative *tú* and *vosotros* commands are simply the subjunctive forms. The affirmative *tú* command forms of sample verbs are included in Table 9-2, so that you remember that, although the negative *tú* command is simply the subjunctive *tú* form, the subjunctive is not used when a *tú* command is affirmative.

Table 9-2   Sample Verbs in Command Forms

Infinitive	Neg. Ud. Command	Affirm. Ud. Command	Neg. Uds. Command	Affirm. Uds. Command	Neg. Tú Command	Affirm. Tú Command
trabajar (to work)	no trabaje	trabaje	no trabajen	trabajen	no trabajes	trabaja
vender (to sell)	no venda	venda	no vendan	vendan	no vendas	vende
vivir (to live)	no viva	viva	no vivan	vivan	no vivas	vive
perder (to lose)	no pierda	pierda	no pierdan	pierdan	no pierdas	pierde
repetir (to repeat)	no repita	repita	no repitan	repitan	no repitas	repite
rogar (to beg)	no ruegue	ruegue	no rueguen	rueguen	no ruegues	ruega
practicar (to practice)	no practique	practique	no practiquen	practiquen	no practiques	practica
comenzar (to begin)	no comience	comience	no comiencen	comiencen	no comiences	comienza

Table 9-3   Command Forms of Common -go Verbs

Infinitive	Neg. Ud. Command	Affirm. Ud. Command	Neg. Uds. Command	Affirm. Uds. Command	Neg. Tú Command	Affirm. Tú Command
decir (to say)	no diga	diga	no digan	digan	no digas	di
tener (to have)	no tenga	tenga	no tengan	tengan	no tengas	ten
poner (to put)	no ponga	ponga	no pongan	pongan	no pongas	pon
salir (to leave)	no salga	salga	no salgan	salgan	no salgas	sal
venir (to come)	no venga	venga	no vengan	vengan	no vengas	ven

All the issues of the present subjunctive are reflected in the command forms. If a verb undergoes a stem change in the present tense, the command form will undergo the same stem change. If a verb undergoes a spelling change in the present tense, the command form will undergo the same spelling change. These kinds of verbs include those that end in *-go* or *-zco*.

Table 9-3 includes all the command forms for several *-go* verbs. Notice that the *-go* verbs all have irregular affirmative *tú* command forms.

Spelling changes

In Chapter 7, you learned a list of common verbs that end in *-car*, *-gar*, or *-zar* that change spelling in the subjunctive and, therefore, affects all the command forms except the *tú* and *vosotros* affirmative, as demonstrated below.

If a verb ends in *-car*, change the *c* to *qu* in all command forms except the *tú* affirmative. Table 9-4 offers some sample verbs to help you remember this type of verb. An extensive list of the most common *-car* verbs is in Chapter 7.

If a verb ends in *-gar*, change the *g* to *gu* in all command forms except the *tú* affirmative. Look carefully at the sample *-gar* verbs in Table 9-5. Chapter 7 has an extensive list of the most common *-gar* verbs.

If a verb ends in *-zar*, change the *z* to *c* in all command forms except the *tú* affirmative. The command forms of a few verbs from the list in Chapter 7 are provided in Table 9-6.

Verbs that end in a vowel + *-cer* are called *-zco* verbs in the present tense. The command forms for this kind of verbs are illustrated in Table 9-7.

Table 9-4 Command Forms of Common -car Verbs

Infinitive	Neg. Ud. Command	Affirm. Ud. Command	Neg. Uds. Command	Affirm. Uds. Command	Neg. Tú Command	Affirm. Tú Command
buscar (to look for)	no busque	busque	no busquen	busquen	no busques	busca
explicar (to explain)	no explique	explique	no expliquen	expliquen	no expliques	explica
indicar (to indicate)	no indique	indique	no indiquen	indiquen	no indiques	indica
sacar (to take)	no saque	saque	no saquen	saquen	no saques	saca
tocar (to touch)	no toque	toque	no toquen	toquen	no toques	toca

Table 9-5 Command Forms of Common -gar Verbs

Infinitive	Neg. Ud. Command	Affirm. Ud. Command	Neg. Uds. Command	Affirm. Uds. Command	Neg. Tú Command	Affirm. Tú Command
cargar (to load)	no cargue	cargue	no carguen	carguen	no cargues	carga
entregar (to deliver, to hand over)	no entregue	entregue	no entreguen	entreguen	no entregues	entrega
jugar (to play)	no juegue	juegue	no jueguen	jueguen	no juegues	juega
llegar (to arrive)	no llegue	llegue	no lleguen	lleguen	no llegues	llega

Table 9-6   Command Forms of Common *-zar* Verbs

Infinitive	Neg. Ud. Command	Affirm. Ud. Command	Neg. Uds. Command	Affirm. Uds. Command	Neg. Tú Command	Affirm. Tú Command
abrazar (to hug)	no abrace	abrace	no abracen	abracen	no abraces	abraza
comenzar (to begin)	no comience	comience	no comiencen	comiencen	no comiences	comienza
organizar (to organize)	no organice	organice	no organicen	organicen	no organices	organiza
realizar (to realize)	no realice	realice	no realicen	realicen	no realices	realiza

Table 9-7   Command Forms of Common Verbs Ending in a Vowel Plus *-cer*

Infinitive	Neg. Ud. Command	Affirm. Ud. Command	Neg. Uds. Command	Affirm. Uds. Command	Neg. Tú Command	Affirm. Tú Command
desaparecer (to disappear)	no desaparezca	desaparezca	no desaparezcan	desaparezcan	no desaparezcas	desaparece
obedecer (to obey)	no obedezca	obedezca	no obedezcan	obedezcan	no obedezcas	obedece
ofrecer (to offer)	no ofrezca	ofrezca	no ofrezcan	ofrezcan	no ofrezcas	ofrece

A verb that ends in a consonant + -*cer* or -*cir* has a *yo* form ending in -*zo*. The command forms for these types of verbs are demonstrated in Table 9-8.

A verb that ends in -*gir* reflects the present subjunctive -*ja* endings, as you can see in the examples in Table 9-9.

Notice in Table 9-10 that verbs that end in -*uir* have a *y* in front of the command endings.

The above rule does not apply to verbs that end in -*guir* (such as *seguir*), whose *yo* form ends in -*go* because the *u* in the infinitive is only present to attain the hard *g* sound.

In Table 9-11, you can see a stem change in all command forms of *conseguir* (to get). This verb is like *seguir* and all its prefix verbs. Notice that the *u* from the infinitive disappears in all command forms except the affirmative *tú*.

If a verb is really irregular in the present tense subjunctive, the *Ud., Uds.,* and negative *tú* command forms will reflect the same irregularity. Table 9-12 is a list of all the truly irregular command forms.

Table 9-8 Command Forms of Common Verbs Ending in a Consonant Plus -cer or -cir

Infinitive	Neg. Ud. Command	Affirm. Ud. Command	Neg. Uds. Command	Affirm. Uds. Command	Neg. Tú Command	Affirm. Tú Command
esparcir (to scatter)	no esparza	esparza	no esparzan	esparzan	no esparzas	esparce
vencer (to conquer)	no venza	venza	no venzan	venzan	no venzas	vence

Table 9-9 Command Forms of Common -gir and -ger Verbs

Infinitive	Neg. Ud. Command	Affirm. Ud. Command	Neg. Uds. Command	Affirm. Uds. Command	Neg. Tú Command	Affirm. Tú Command
corregir (to correct)	no corrija	corrija	no corrijan	corrijan	no corrijas	corrige
escoger (to choose)	no escoja	escoja	no escojan	escojan	no escojas	escoge
dirigir (to direct)	no dirija	dirija	no dirijan	dirijan	no dirijas	dirige
proteger (to protect)	no proteja	proteja	no protejan	protejan	no protejas	protege

Table 9-10   Command Forms of Common -uir Verbs

Infinitive	Neg. Ud. Command	Affirm. Ud. Command	Neg. Uds. Command	Affirm. Uds. Command	Neg. Tú Command	Affirm. Tú Command
contribuir (to contribute)	no contribuya	contribuya	no contribuyan	contribuyan	no contribuyas	contribuye
destruir (to destroy)	no destruya	destruya	no destruyan	destruyan	no destruyas	destruye
huir (to run away, to flee)	no huya	huya	no huyan	huyan	no huyas	huye
incluir (to include)	no incluya	incluya	no incluyan	incluyan	no incluyas	incluye

Table 9-11   Command Forms of Conseguir

Infinitive	Neg. Ud. Command	Affirm. Ud. Command	Neg. Uds. Command	Affirm. Uds. Command	Neg. Tú Command	Affirm. Tú Command
conseguir (to get)	no consiga	consiga	no consigan	consigan	no consigas	consigue

Table 9-12   Truly Irregular Command Forms

Infinitive	Neg. Ud. Command	Affirm. Ud. Command	Neg. Uds. Command	Affirm. Uds. Command	Neg. Tú Command	Affirm. Tú Command
dar (to give)	no dé	dé	no den	den	no des	da
estar (to be)	no esté	esté	no estén	estén	no estés	está
ir (to go)	no vaya	vaya	no vayan	vayan	no vayas	ve
ser (to be)	no sea	sea	no sean	sean	no seas	sé
saber (to know)	no sepa	sepa	no sepan	sepan	no sepas	sabe

Nosotros ("Let's") Commands

The present tense subjunctive *nosotros/nosotras* form is used to give a command addressed to a group that includes the speaker. To create an affirmative command such as this in English, you place "let's" in front of the verb:

> Let's dance the tango.
> Let's attend the concert this Saturday.

To make a negative command of this type in English, you use "let's not":

> Let's not forget to buy the tickets this time.
> Let's not put them on the credit card.

Spanish speakers simply use the "we" form of the subjunctive to indicate "let's":

> *Bailemos el tango.*
> *Asistamos al concierto este sábado.*

The negative command is formed in the same way, but with a *no* or other negative word placed in front.

> *No olvidemos comprar las entradas esta vez.*
> *No las pongamos en la tarjeta de crédito.*

One exception to the above rule is the verb *ir,* whose subjunctive form is used only for the negative *nosotros/nosotras* command. The affirmative *nosotros/nosotras* command is the indicative form: *vamos.*

> *Vamos a la fiesta esta noche.*
> Let's go to the party tonight.

> *Tengo prisa. No vayamos al centro comercial primero.*
> I'm in a hurry. Let's not go to the mall first.

To learn some rules that apply only to *nosotros/nosotras* commands, see the "Using Pronouns with Commands" section later in this chapter.

The affirmative *nosotros/nosotras* command form of a reflexive verb attaches the reflexive pronoun *nos* to the end of the subjunctive *nosotros/nosotras* form of the verb. This creates a tongue twister, so Spanish speakers drop the *s* that would have preceded the *nos.*

> *Sentémonos en la primera fila.*
> Let's sit in the first row.

> *Vistámonos como piratas este año.*
> Let's dress as pirates this year.

Casémonos en Jamaica en la playa.

Let's get married in Jamaica on the beach.

Even though the affirmative *nosotros/nosotras* command form of *ir* is irregular, it is still necessary to drop the *s* in front of the pronoun *nos*.

Vámonos para el aeropuerto.

Let's leave for the airport.

However, because the negative command requires the pronoun to precede the subjunctive *nosotros/nosotras* form, there is no need to drop any letters in this case.

No nos olvidemos del horno cuando salgamos.

Let's not forget about the oven when we leave.

No nos durmamos durante su presentación.

Let's not fall asleep during his presentation.

Vosotros Commands

A *vosotros/vosotras* command is used to order a group of people whom you would individually address in the *tú* form. The *vosotros/vosotras* command forms are used mainly in Spain, so you may not encounter them frequently. Even those who use *vosotros* commands understand you perfectly well if you use *ustedes* rather than *vosotros*. If the *vosotros* commands scare you, just be prepared to recognize them—you can always get away with the *Uds.* commands with any group.

The affirmative form of *vosotros/vosotras* commands is completely different from the negative form. To create an affirmative *vosotros/vosotras* command, replace the -*r* at the end of the infinitive with a -*d*.

Contestad las preguntas, niños.

Bebed refrescos.

Servid los postres.

If a verb is reflexive and the pronoun *os* is attached, the -*d* is dropped. This will only happen with affirmative commands because the pronoun precedes the negative command form and because negative *vosotros/vosotras* commands are nothing like affirmative commands.

Bañaos vosotros por la mañana.

A negative *vosotros/vosotras* command is simply the present subjunctive conjugation for *vosotros/vosotras*. To make a negative *vosotros/vosotras* command, drop the -*o* ending of the present tense *yo* form and add the indicative *vosotros/vosotras* ending normally used for the opposite kind of infinitive: Use -*éis* for an -*ar* verb and -*áis* for an -*er* or -*ir* verb. The endings listed in Table 9-13 are added to the *yo* form of the verb (minus the -*o*).

Table 9-13   Endings for Negative *Vosotros* Commands

Infinitive	Negative Vosotros Command Ending
-ar	no -éis
-er	no -áis
-ir	no -áis

A few common verbs are used in negative *vosotros/vosotras* command forms below:

bailar	*No bailéis vosotros.*
comer	*No comáis la torta.*
pedir	*No pidáis comida muy cara en este restaurante.*
hacer	*No hagáis la tarea en la mesa.*

Using Pronouns with Commands

Reflexive, indirect object, and direct object pronouns must be attached to the end of an affirmative command. (See Chapter 12 for a discussion of pronouns.) Remember the acronym RID because, if more than one of these pronouns are used together, they will consistently be used in that order. When you attach even one pronoun to the end of an affirmative command, you must add an accent mark to the command form in order to maintain the correct stress. The written accent mark is placed on what was the next-to-the-last syllable before you attached any pronoun.

> *Julio, tu hermano necesita una chaqueta. Cómprasela para su cumpleaños, por favor.*
>
> Julio, your brother needs a jacket. Buy it for him for his birthday, please.
>
> *Levántate ahora mismo.*
>
> Get (yourself) up right now.

If the command is negative, the pronouns are placed in front of the command form (but after the *no* or other negative word).

No se me quejen del hotel.

Do not complain to me about the hotel.

Nunca nos diga mentiras.

Never tell us lies.

Table 9-14 provides the command forms of several reflexive verbs. The placement of the reflexive pronouns in the chart also indicates where any indirect or direct object pronoun would be placed with affirmative and negative commands. Because reflexive pronouns are used below, notice that *te* is the pronoun used for both negative and affirmative *tú* commands, and that *se* is the pronoun used for the *Ud.* and *Uds.* forms. Learn where the pronoun is placed in each negative and affirmative form, and pay close attention to written accent marks.

Table 9-14   Command Forms of Reflexive Verbs

Infinitive	Neg. Ud. Command	Affirm. Ud. Command	Neg. Uds. Command	Affirm. Uds. Command	Neg. Tú Command	Affirm. Tú Command
lavarse (to wash oneself)	*no se lave*	*lávese*	*no se laven*	*lávense*	*no te laves*	*lávate*
caerse (to fall, to fall down)	*no se caiga*	*caígase*	*no se caigan*	*caíganse*	*no te caigas*	*cáete*
sentarse (to sit down)	*no se siente*	*siéntese*	*no se sienten*	*siéntense*	*no te sientes*	*siéntate*
dormirse (to fall asleep)	*no se duerma*	*duérmase*	*no se duerman*	*duérmanse*	*no te duermas*	*duérmete*

Chapter Checkout

For the following verbs, write the command forms in the following order: negative *Ud.*, affirmative *Ud.*, negative *Uds.*, affirmative *Uds.*, negative *tú*, affirmative *tú*. Remember that the affirmative *tú* command is the strangest form.

1. *comenzar*

2. *morirse*

3. *vestirse*

4. *tener*

5. *ser*

For the following verbs, write the affirmative and negative *vosotros/vosotras* command forms, then the affirmative and negative *nosotros/nosotras* command forms.

6. *venir*

7. *salir*

8. *sentarse*

Answers:

1. *no comience, comience; no comiencen, comiencen; no comiences, comienza*
2. *no se muera, muérase; no se mueran, muéranse; no te mueras, muérete*
3. *no se vista, vístase; no se vistan, vístanse; no te vistas, vístete* **4.** *no tenga, tenga; no tengan, tengan; no tengas, ten* **5.** *no sea, sea; no sean, sean; no seas, sé*
6. *venid, no vengáis; vengamos, no vengamos* **7.** *salid, no salgáis; salgamos, no salgamos* **8.** *sentaos, no os sentéis; sentémonos, no nos sentemos*

Chapter 10

ADJECTIVES AND COMPARISONS

Chapter Check-In

❑ Modifying nouns with adjectives of the correct gender and number

❑ Placing adjectives correctly in a sentence

❑ Writing comparisons using adjectives

Spanish adjectives are tricky for English speakers because they reflect the gender and number of the noun they modify. The placement of adjectives is also different and adjectives are used to create comparisons differently in Spanish. This chapter will simplify all the issues posed by adjectives and comparisons.

Basic Review of Adjectives

Adjectives are used to describe or modify nouns or pronouns. There are different types of adjectives that indicate possession, demonstrate distance, and make comparisons. This chapter reviews how to use Spanish adjectives. You must remember how to create the appropriate form of an adjective to match the number and gender of the noun it describes and how to place the adjective correctly in a sentence. A Spanish adjective often follows the noun it modifies (describes), but there are some circumstances in Spanish sentences in which the adjective must be placed before the noun.

Correct gender

In vocabulary lists and in dictionaries, adjectives are always listed in the singular masculine form. In this form, most adjectives end in *-o,* but there are a few that end in *-e* or a consonant.

If an adjective ends in *-o* in its singular masculine form, the final *-o* will change to *-a* when it is used to describe a feminine noun. In the examples below, the definite article is included to remind you of the gender of the noun; you must know the gender of the noun in order to use the adjective correctly.

el novio guapo	the attractive boyfriend
la novia guapa	the attractive girlfriend
el coche blanco	the white car
la casa blanca	the white house
el libro divertido	the amusing book
la novela divertida	the amusing novel

Many commonly used adjectives end in *-e*. Adjectives that end in *-e* do not change endings for feminine nouns.

el tío inteligente	the intelligent uncle
la tía inteligente	the intelligent aunt
el estadio enorme	the enormous stadium
la montaña enorme	the enormous mountain
la realidad triste	the sad reality
el cuento triste	the sad story

Adjectives that end in a consonant do not change endings to indicate gender.

el cantante popular	the popular singer
la música popular	popular music
el dilema difícil	the difficult dilemma
la situación difícil	the difficult situation
el cielo azul	the blue sky
la camisa azul	the blue shirt

The exceptions to the above rule are adjectives of nationality. Adjectives of nationality that end in *-o* behave like any other adjective: The *-o* changes to *-a* if the adjective describes a feminine noun. Notice in the examples below that you need not capitalize Spanish adjectives of nationality.

el hombre mexicano	the Mexican man
la mujer mexicana	the Mexican woman

el muchacho cubano	the Cuban boy
la muchacha cubana	the Cuban girl

Adjectives of nationality that end in *-e* also behave like other adjectives, except that the same form is used for both masculine and feminine nouns.

el padre costarricense	the Costa Rican father
la madre costarricense	the Costa Rican mother
el lago canadiense	the Canadian lake
la carretera canadiense	the Canadian highway

Adjectives of nationality that end in a consonant follow specific rules. Unlike other adjectives, you must add the letter *a* after the consonant at the end of an adjective of nationality in order to use it with a feminine noun.

el edificio español	the Spanish building
la oficina española	the Spanish office

Adding a syllable to the end of a word alters where the stress of the word naturally falls. If an adjective of nationality has an accent mark on the last syllable, the accent mark will disappear when you add *-a* to the feminine form.

el actor inglés	the English actor
la actriz inglesa	the English actress
el río japonés	the Japanese river
la ciudad japonesa	the Japanese city
el dulce francés	the French candy
la comida francesa	the French food

Using the plural forms of adjectives

When a noun is plural, any adjective that modifies it must also be in a plural form. In addition, the definite article *el* becomes *los* and *la* becomes *las* when the noun is plural. The plural forms of adjectives are created the same way as the plural forms of nouns.

If an adjective ends in a vowel, add *-s* to make it plural.

los árboles verdes	the green trees
las hierbas verdes	the green grass
los pueblos blancos	the white villages
las montañas blancas	the white mountains

If an adjective ends in a consonant, add *-es* to make it plural.

los dilemas difíciles	difficult dilemmas
las situaciones difíciles	difficult situations
los jóvenes populares	the popular teenagers
las animadoras populares	the popular cheerleaders

When you add *-es* to pluralize, remember that "*z* changes to *c* when followed by *e.*"

el señor andaluz	the Andalusian gentleman
los señores andaluces	the Andalusian gentlemen

Placement of adjectives in a sentence

In a Spanish sentence, an adjective is generally placed after the noun it modifies, but some types of adjectives must be placed in front of a noun.

Adjectives that indicate quantity are placed in front of the nouns they quantify. This includes all numbers and any adjectives that indicate amount. Some common adjectives of quantity are listed below.

mucho, mucha	much
muchos, muchas	many
poco	little, few
bastante	enough
suficiente	enough
alguno, alguna, algunos, algunas	some

Apocopated is a grammatical term used to indicate that something is shortened. Some adjectives are called "apocopated" because their endings are cut short in specific circumstances. The adjectives listed below lose the final *-o* when immediately followed by a singular masculine noun. These adjectives are usually placed in front of a noun; you should drop the final *-o* of the adjective only if that noun is singular and masculine, as in the examples below.

bueno	good
la buena alumna	the good student (feminine)
el buen alumno	the good student (masculine)
malo	bad
la mala escritora	the bad writer (feminine)
el mal escritor	the bad writer (masculine)

primero	first
la primera nieta	the first granddaughter
el primer nieto	the first grandson
tercero	third
la tercera reina	the third queen
el tercer rey	the third king
uno	one
una abogada	one (a) lawyer (feminine)
un abogado	one (a) lawyer (masculine)
alguno	some
alguna amiga	some friend (feminine)
algún amigo	some friend (masculine)

Although the above adjectives drop the *-o* only in front of a singular masculine noun, one adjective is shortened in front of any singular noun: The adjective *grande* can be used in front of a noun or after it. It is unique because *grande* shortens to *gran* when placed before any singular noun, regardless of gender, and it has the meaning of "great."

el gran líder	the great leader
la gran fachada	the great facade

When *grande* is placed after the noun, the full form is used and the meaning of the adjective changes to "large" rather than "great."

el piano grande	the large piano
la ciudad grande	the large city

Certain other adjectives also change meaning depending on where they are placed in the sentence.

el antiguo director	the former principal
el director antiguo	the elderly principal
la pobre mujer	the poor woman (unfortunate)
la mujer pobre	the poor woman (impoverished)
diferentes opiniones	various opinions
opiniones diferentes	different opinions
la nueva motocicleta	the new motorcycle (new to you)
la motocicleta nueva	the brand-new motorcycle

Possessive Adjectives

Possessive adjectives indicate ownership. Although they express the owners of the nouns they modify, they must match the gender and number of the nouns they describe, not the gender and number of the owners.

There are two kinds of possessive adjectives: The shorter forms are usually placed in front of the noun, and the longer forms follow the noun. The former are listed in Table 10-1.

Table 10-1   Possessive Adjectives (When in Front of a Noun)

Person	Possessive Adj.	Person	Possessive Adj.
yo	*mi, mis*	*nosotros/nosotras*	*nuestro, nuestra, nuestros, nuestras*
tú	*tu, tus*	*vosotros/vosotras*	*vuestro, vuestra, vuestros, vuestras*
él/ella/Ud.	*su, sus*	*ellos/ellas/Uds.*	*su, sus*

Remember that the possessive adjective must match the noun being owned, not the owner. Once you decide to use the adjective *su*, only make it plural if it is in front of a plural noun—no matter how many people own the noun. If a family owns a car, "their car" is written *su coche*. If a man owns many cars, "his cars" is written *sus coches*.

Table 10-2 can help you understand the Spanish equivalents of English possessive adjectives.

Table 10-2   Possessive Adjectives in English

Person	Possessive Adj.
my	*mi* or *mis*
your (if you = *tú*)	*tu* or *tus*
your (if you = *Ud.* or *Uds.*)	*su* or *sus*
your (if you = *vosotros* or *vosotras*)	*vuestro, vuestra, vuestros,* or *vuestras*
his	*su* or *sus*
her	*su* or *sus*
our (if we = *nosotros* or *nosotras*)	*nuestro, nuestra, nuestros,* or *nuestras*

The pronoun *su* is used to mean his, her, their, and your. The pronouns *él, ella,* and *Ud.* share the same conjugated form of the verb as well as the same possessive adjective. If you (*Ud.*) own a book, "your book" is written *su libro.* If you (*tú*) own a book, "your book" is written *tu libro.* Notice that the subject pronoun *tú* has an accent and means "you." The possessive adjective *tu* has no accent and means "your." There are four forms of *nuestro* and *vuestro* because they end in -*o* and, thus, must change to match the number and gender of the nouns they modify.

The long form of a Spanish possessive adjective is used when it is placed after the noun. In Table 10-3, notice that all the long forms of possessive adjectives have gender endings to match the nouns they modify. Use the correct gender and number of the possessive adjective to match the noun it follows.

Table 10-3   Long Form of Possessive Adjectives

Person	Possessive Adj.	Person	Possessive Adj.
yo	mío, mía, míos, mías	nosotros/nosotras	nuestro, nuestra, nuestros, nuestras
tú	tuyo, tuya, tuyos, tuyas	vosotros/vosotras	vuestro, vuestra, vuestros, vuestras
él/ella/Ud.	suyo, suya, suyos, suyas	ellos/ellas/Uds.	suyo, suya, suyos, suyas

In English, the possessive changes when it follows a form of "to be" (such as, "is" or "are"). For example, "<u>my</u> book" becomes "the book is <u>mine</u>." In Spanish, the long form of a possessive adjective is used after the linking verbs *ser* or *estar* or when an article precedes the noun being modified.

<u>mi</u> pupitre (short)	<u>my</u> desk
el pupitre <u>mío</u> (long)	<u>my</u> desk
El pupitre es <u>mío</u>. (long, after a form of *ser*)	The desk is <u>mine</u>.
<u>tus</u> pruebas malas (short)	<u>your</u> bad quizzes
las pruebas malas <u>tuyas</u> (long)	<u>your</u> bad quizzes
Las pruebas malas son <u>tuyas</u>. (long, after a form of *ser*)	The bad quizzes are <u>yours</u>.
<u>nuestro</u> horario (short)	<u>our</u> schedule
el horario <u>nuestro</u> (long)	<u>our</u> schedule
El horario es <u>nuestro</u>. (long, after a form of *ser*)	The schedule is <u>ours</u>.

sus canciones (short)	<u>his</u> songs/<u>her</u> songs/<u>their</u> songs/<u>your</u> (formal) songs
las canciones <u>suyas</u> (long)	<u>his</u> songs/<u>her</u> songs/<u>their</u> songs/<u>your</u> (formal) songs
Las canciones son <u>suyas</u>. (long, after a form of *ser*)	The songs are <u>his</u>./The songs are <u>hers</u>./The songs are <u>theirs</u>./The songs are <u>yours</u> (formal).

Did you notice that the *nosotros/nosotras* and *vosotros/vosotras* do not have a short and/or a long form?

The following examples highlight the difference in how the two types of possessive adjectives, which are basically equivalent, are used. The longer form puts a little more emphasis on the possessor than on the object possessed.

mi barrio = el barrio mío	my neighborhood
tu vecina = la vecina tuya	your neighbor
nuestro despacho = el despacho nuestro	our office
vuestra piscina = la piscina vuestra	your (plural) swimming pool
su habitación = la habitación suya	his, her, their, or your (formal) room

Demonstrative Adjectives

Demonstrative adjectives are aptly named because they demonstrate the distance between the noun being modified and the speaker of the sentence. To indicate that the noun being modified is "here," English uses the words "this" (singular) and "these" (plural). To indicate that something is "there," the demonstrative adjectives are "that" (singular) and "those" (plural). So, in English, there are only two possible distances ("here" and "there") and there are two different forms for singular nouns (this, that) and plural nouns (these, those).

Another concept of distance is the amount of time that has passed. For example:

Esta camiseta que llevo hoy es muy cómoda.

This T-shirt that I am wearing today is very comfortable.

Esa camisa que llevaba ayer era de lana.

That shirt that I was wearing yesterday was wool.

Because Spanish indicates the gender as well as the number of the noun being modified by an adjective, demonstrative adjectives have masculine and feminine forms. The Spanish word for "this" has a feminine form (*esta*) and a masculine form (*este*). There are also feminine and masculine forms of the equivalent of "these" (*estos* and *estas*). The words for "that" (*ese* and *esa*) and "those" (*esos* and *esas*) also indicate gender and number and are just like the words for "this" except that they lack the letter *t*. Chant the following words like a mantra to remember:

> The Spanish words for "this" and "these" both have *t*s. "That" and "those" don't.

Examine the sample sentences below, then reread the phrase above. Understanding it will help you differentiate between the demonstrative adjectives later.

Este video es interesante.	This video is interesting.
Esta película es muy romántica.	This movie is very romantic.
Estos apartamentos tienen buenas vistas.	These apartments have good views.
Estas paredes son muy altas.	These walls are very tall.
Ese traje es negro.	That suit is black.
Esa falda es azul.	That skirt is blue.
Esos maestros son muy exigentes.	Those teachers are very demanding.
Esas reglas de la clase me molestan mucho.	Those rules in class bother me a lot.

Unlike the English language, which—as discussed earlier—only has two demonstrative distances, the Spanish language differentiates between three distances: "here," "there," and "far away." If you want to indicate that a noun is "way over there," use the singular demonstrative adjectives *aquel* (masculine) or *aquella* (feminine) or the plural demonstrative adjectives *aquellos* (masculine) or *aquellas* (feminine). Because English does not have three demonstrative distances, there is no English equivalent to these words; for this book's purposes, these words are translated as "that (noun) way over there" or "those (nouns) way over there." The following sentences illustrate this concept.

Aquel país tiene muchos problemas.	That country (way over there) has many problems.
Aquella nación es pobre.	That nation (way over there) is poor.

Aquellos políticos gastan todos los impuestos.	Those politicians (way over there) spend all the taxes.
Aquellas familias necesitan comida.	Those families (way over there) need food.

To indicate the three different distances in the Spanish language, you must learn three important words. If you see one of these in a sentence, it is a good clue as to which demonstrative adjective is appropriate to use in the sentence. Table 10-4 demonstrates which type of demonstrative adjective should be used with each distance word.

Table 10-4   The Three Distances and Demonstratives

Spanish Distance	English Equivalent	Demonstratives
aquí	here	*este, esta, estos,* or *estas*
allí	there	*ese, esa, esos,* or *esas*
allá	way over there (far away)	*aquel, aquella, aquellos,* or *aquellas*

Table 10-5 organizes all the demonstrative adjectives by gender and number. Consistently, the singular feminine forms and plural masculine and plural feminine forms of all the demonstrative adjectives have "normal" endings (*-a, -os,* and *-as*). The singular masculine forms are the ones that break the pattern with *este, ese,* and *aquel.*

This is important to know because in Chapter 12 you will learn about demonstrative pronouns, which have a form that looks like what you would expect for the singular masculine form of demonstrative adjectives. Also notice that demonstrative adjectives do not have any accent marks. If you see similar words with accents, they are demonstrative pronouns, which replace nouns rather than modify them.

Table 10-5   Demonstrative Adjectives

Singular	Masculine	Feminine	Plural	Masculine	Feminine
this	*este*	*esta*	these	*estos*	*estas*
that	*ese*	*esa*	those	*esos*	*esas*
that (way over there)	*aquel*	*aquella*	those (way over there)	*aquellos*	*aquellas*

Comparisons

When an adjective has only one syllable, the English language creates a special form of the adjective to compare one noun to another: By adding the suffix -er to an adjective, you imply "more." In a complete sentence, this comparative form of the adjective is followed by the word "than."

> Mario is tall. Shelly is taller than Mario.
>
> I am smart. You are smarter than I.

However, when an adjective is more than one syllable, you must use the adverbs "more" or "less," followed by the adjective and the word "than," to create a comparison.

> Lisa is intelligent. Erin is more intelligent than Lisa.
>
> Danny is annoying. Paul is less annoying than Danny.

All comparisons in Spanish are created like the longer adjectives above. The basic adjective form is used with a similar sentence structure to express a comparison. The adverb *más* means "more" and *menos* means "less." The formula to indicate comparison is constructed by using these two modifiers followed by an adjective, then the conjunction *que,* as illustrated below. Notice that the adjective is used to reflect the gender and number of the first noun being compared.

> (1st noun) *es más* (adjective) *que* (2nd noun)
>
> (1st noun) is more (adjective) than (2nd noun) **or** (1st noun) is (adjective + *er*) than (2nd noun)
>
> *Marta es más alta que Marco.*
>
> Marta is more tall than Marco **or** Marta is taller than Marco.
>
> (1st noun) *es menos* (adjective) *que* (2nd noun)
>
> (1st noun) is less (adjective) than (2nd noun)
>
> *Memo y Cristóbal son menos prácticos que sus hermanas.*
>
> Memo and Cristóbal are less practical than their sisters.

One important exception to the comparative formulas is when the second noun is a number. In these types of sentences, there is often a verb other than *ser,* and the *que* is replaced by *de,* as you can see in the examples below.

> *Zobeida tiene más de 30 pares de zapatos.*
>
> Zobeida has more than 30 pairs of shoes.
>
> *Yo necesito menos de 10 voluntarios para tener éxito.*
>
> I need less than 10 volunteers to be successful.

Sometimes, the point of a comparison is to indicate that the two nouns are the same.

> (1st noun) *es tan* (adjective) *como* (2nd noun)
> (1st noun) is as (adjective) as (2nd noun)
> *La criada es tan importante como el abogado.*
> The maid is as important as the lawyer.
>
> *Tus amigos son tan importantes como tu profesión.*
> Your friends are as important as your work.

A few adjectives in Spanish have irregular comparative and superlative forms. Rather than using *más* or *menos* with the basic adjective, the irregular form is used.

bueno (good)	*mejor* (better)
malo (bad)	*peor* (worse)
grande (big, age-wise)	*mayor* (bigger, older)
viejo (old)	*mayor* (older)
pequeño (little, age-wise)	*menor* (younger)
joven (young)	*menor* (younger)

Superlatives

In high school, students often select "senior superlatives" such as "best smile," "nicest," or "most likely to succeed." If an adjective has only one syllable, the superlative form is created by adding the suffix *-est*. Notice that superlatives usually include the definite article "the."

big	the biggest
hot	the hottest

With longer adjectives and when you want to express "least," there is no special adjective form. In these cases, the adverb "most" or "least" is placed in front of the adjective.

interesting	the least interesting
beautiful	the most beautiful

The Spanish language uses a formula to create superlatives that includes the words *más* or *menos,* similar to the comparatives above. To make these adverbs indicate the absolute extremes "most" and "least" (rather than "more" or "less"), the appropriate definite article (*el, la, los,* or *las*) is used.

Este libro es <u>el más</u> aburrido que he leído.
This is the most boring book that I have read.

Esa revista es <u>la más</u> interesante en la tienda.
That magazine is the most interesting in the store.

When a comparison is followed by a prepositional phrase that limits it to a certain group, English uses "in" but Spanish uses *de.*

Catalina es <u>la menos</u> interesada de la clase.
Catalina is the least interested one in the class.

Granada es <u>la ciudad más</u> bonita de España.
Granada is the most beautiful city in Spain.

In Spanish, there is a type of superlative adjective form that makes that adjective even more extreme. When the Spanish suffix *-ísimo* added to an adjective, it has the same effect as placing the word "very" in front of an English adjective. Like any adjective ending in *-o,* these superlatives have four forms to match the gender and number of the nouns they modify. Notice in the examples below that an adjective that ends in *-go* will change to *gu* in front of the *-ísimo* ending. Also, a *-co* ending changes to *qu* and a final *-z* changes to *c.*

lindo (pretty)	*lindísimo* (very pretty)
alto (tall)	*altísimo* (very tall)
rico (rich)	*riquísimo* (very rich)
largo (long)	*larguísimo* (very long)
feliz (happy)	*felicísimo* (very happy)

Chapter Checkout

In the blank provided, write the correct form of the adjective listed in parentheses. The adjective will always be provided in its singular masculine form; you may or may not have to change it in order to match the gender of the noun it modifies.

1. *Esa madre es _____. (español)*
2. *La novela _____ está en mi habitación. (interesante)*
3. *Hablamos alemán en _____ familia. (nuestro)*
4. *_____ muchachas viven aquí. (este)*
5. *Los hombres _____ juegan al fútbol. (popular)*

Use the appropriate comparison or superlative formula to translate the following English sentences into Spanish.

6. Juana is taller than Juan.

7. Virginia is the best in the class.

8. Daniela is very thin.

Answers: 1. *española* **2.** *interesante* **3.** *nuestra* **4.** *estas* **5.** *populares* **6.** *Juana es más alta que Juan.* **7.** *Virginia es la mejor de la clase.* **8.** *Daniela es delgadísima.*

Chapter 11

PREPOSITIONS

Chapter Check-In

❑ Using simple prepositions

❑ Determining which preposition is appropriate for idiomatic expressions

❑ Understanding when to use a preposition with a verb

Prepositions link together the different parts of a sentence and show the relationship between these parts. Prepositions do not, however, translate well from English to Spanish and vice versa. They are problematic because you must understand when each preposition is appropriate, and you cannot simply replace a Spanish preposition with an English equivalent.

Simple Prepositions

Simple prepositions, the most common of which are *a, en, de, con, para,* and *por,* are called "simple" because they consist of one word. Other than that there is nothing simple about them, because it is impossible to translate any of them to one English word. Instead, you must understand the situations in which you each preposition. The sample sentences that follow can help you better understand when a particular preposition can be used.

The preposition *a*

The preposition *a* has several purposes. Usually, it indicates motion toward a place or thing. In these cases, the preposition *a* means "to," "toward," or "at."

> *Fuiste a la pizarra.*
> You went to the chalkboard.

Simón llegó a su dormitorio muy tarde.

Simón arrived at his bedroom very late.

Jimena regresó a la escuela este lunes.

Jimena returned to school this Monday.

The preposition *a* is also used to label a direct object when it refers to a person. You must use the "personal *a*" in front of the direct object if the direct object refers to any person or persons, or a beloved animal that is treated like a person. The personal *a* is simply one usage of the preposition *a*, but because this usage does not have an English equivalent, it will not appear in the English translation of the examples below.

Necesito llamar a Manuela también.

I need to call Manuela also.

¿A quién invitas tú?

Whom are you inviting?

The preposition *a* is also used in front of an indirect object (see Chapter 12) to clarify to whom the indirect object pronoun refers. Because indirect objects are used with certain verbs like *gustar*, this clarification is very important. Consider the following examples:

Alicia le dio todo su dinero <u>al</u> plomero.

Alicia gave all her money to the plumber.

<u>A</u> Mariana y Daniela les gusta ese museo.

Mariana and Daniela like that museum.

When there is no indirect object pronoun in the sentence, the preposition *para* may be used instead of *a* to introduce the recipient of the direct object. Compare the examples below.

Belita <u>les</u> compró un buen regalo a sus padres.

Belita bought her parents a good gift.

Belita compró un buen regalo <u>para</u> sus padres.

Belita bought a good gift for her parents.

Several verbs are followed by the preposition *a* and an infinitive. The most common example of this is when a conjugated form of the verb *ir* (to go) is followed by *a* + infinitive. Notice in the examples that follow that the English version is usually stated using the present progressive ("someone is going to do something"); in Spanish, the present tense of *ir* is used ("someone goes to do something"). In both languages, this type of sentence can be used to indicate that something will happen in the future without using the future tense conjugation of the verb.

Vamos a asistir a un concierto de hip-hop esta noche.
We are going to attend a hip-hop concert tonight.

Chico y Mercedes van a casarse.
Chico and Mercedes are going to get married.

Another use of the preposition *a* is to indicate the manner in which something is done. Unfortunately, not all expressions indicating the manner of doing something use this preposition, so you have to learn which pronoun to use with each phrase. A few idiomatic expressions of manner that require the preposition *a* are included in the examples below. A more extensive list of idiomatic expressions using prepositions is included in Idiomatic Expressions (visit www.cliffsnotes.com/extras). Unfortunately, the correct preposition for each idiomatic expression must be memorized, so focus on the specific preposition used for each expression because it may not be the same as the English equivalent.

No puedes firmar a lápiz porque es un documento oficial.
You cannot sign in pencil because it is an official document.

Para hacer el camping allí tienes que llegar a pie.
In order to camp there, you have to arrive on foot.

Me encanta montar a caballo en la playa.
I love to ride on horseback along the beach.

Note: Not all expressions that describe a manner of doing something are created using the preposition *a.* Some use the prepositions *en* or *de,* and each must be learned individually. The most common idiomatic expressions including prepositions are included later in this chapter.

The preposition *a* also is used to identify a specific point of time, like the English time expression "at (hour) o'clock." To indicate what time something occurred or will occur, the preposition *a* is followed by the definite article *la* or *las* followed by a number.

Empezó a llover a la una.
It began to rain at one o'clock.

¿A qué hora terminarán? Terminaremos a las cuatro.
At what hour will you finish? We'll finish at four.

Any time the pronoun *a* is followed by the definite article *el,* the contraction *al* must be used. This contraction does not occur with the other definite articles, nor does it occur with the pronoun *él.*

> *Mis primos van al centro comercial esta noche.*
> My cousins are going to the mall tonight.

> *Ojalá vayamos a la playa este fin de semana.*
> Hopefully, we'll go to the beach this weekend.

> *Vicente iba a las presentaciones cada día.*
> Vicente went to the presentations every day.

> *Yo le di mi entrada a él.*
> I gave my ticket to him.

The preposition *de*

The simple English prepositions "of," "from," and "by," as well as a few compound prepositions, are all translated in specific situations to the Spanish preposition *de,* one of the most ubiquitous prepositions in Spanish because it is used with so many expressions and has various meanings. The preposition *de* is appropriate in several situations, which are explained below with sample sentences and English translations.

The preposition *de* is used to indicate origin.

> *El coche de la marca Mercedes viene de Alemania.*
> A Mercedes car comes from Germany.

> *La nueva ingeniera en mi compañía es de Colombia.*
> The new engineer in my company is from Colombia.

Possession is indicated in Spanish by using *de* because there are no apostrophes in Spanish. In English, the owner of the item comes first, but in Spanish, the item that is possessed comes first, followed by *de* and the person who owns it.

> *Los amigos de Adela son locos.*
> Adela's friends are crazy.

The preposition *de* also is placed in front of the question word *quién* to inquire about the possessor of something. This Spanish expression *de quién* is comparable to the English question word "whose."

> *¿De quién es la moto?*
> Whose motorcycle is it?

Es la moto de Nacho.

It's Nacho's motorcycle.

You may see the preposition *de* used to express a married woman's official last name. If a girl named Julia Flores marries Virgilio García, she may be called Julia Flores de García. This tradition is not quite as common as it once was, though, as many women no longer choose to use *de* as part of their official married name.

The preposition *de* also can indicate motion away from some place. A few verbs that are typically followed by *de* because they indicate movement away from somewhere are *venir, salir,* and *llegar.*

Cuando llegué de Los Ángeles, ya había aprendido español.

When I arrived from Los Angeles, I already had learned Spanish.

¿Saliste de la reunión para asistir a un concierto?

You left the meeting to attend a concert?

Use the preposition *de* to indicate the contents of something or the material of which it is made.

La bolsa de manzanas es muy cara.

The bag of apples is very expensive.

Notice in the example below that the Spanish equivalent of the word "made" can be understood and not stated.

El suéter es de lana.

The sweater is made of wool.

The preposition *de* is used between two nouns when one modifies the other. In English, it is common to use a noun as an adjective by simply placing it in front of what it modifies. For example, in the expression "soccer game," the noun "soccer" modifies another noun, "game." In Spanish, the noun that is being described comes first, followed by the preposition *de* and the noun that describes it. *Un partido de fútbol* is literally translated as "a game of soccer" but is Spanish for "a soccer game."

Siempre escucho mi disco compacto de Shakira.

I always listen to my Shakira CD.

Lupita asiste a sus clases de negocios después del trabajo.

Lupita attends her business classes after work.

The preposition *de* contracts with the definite article *el* like the preposition *a*.

> *Habla así porque viene del norte.*
>
> He talks like that because he comes from the north.

Remember that these contractions do not occur with the other definite articles or with the pronoun *él*.

> *La vista de la montaña es lindísima.*
>
> The view of the mountain is very beautiful.

> *No acepto ningún dinero de él.*
>
> I do not accept any money from him.

The preposition *en*

There are many reasons for using the preposition *en*. *En* can, for instance, indicate "in" when referring to a location—a situation in which many English speakers use the pronoun "at." For example, a person works in a restaurant, not at a restaurant, so the Spanish language, which is more literal, uses the preposition *en* to indicate this concept.

> *Mis amigos trabajan en Toro Bravo.*
>
> My friends work at Toro Bravo.

> *Nos reunimos todos los días en el centro comercial.*
>
> We meet every day at the mall.

You can also use *en* to express the time required for the completion of a task. In this case, *en* sounds right to an English speaker because in the English equivalent the preposition "in" sounds similar.

> *Debes terminar la tarea en 20 minutos.*
>
> You should finish your homework in 20 minutes.

> *Volveré en cinco meses.*
>
> I will return in five months.

In some specific expressions, *en* is used to indicate the means by which something is done. Focus on the fact that the necessary preposition for these expressions is *en* because there is no way to predict whether each expression of manner is *en* or *a* other than memorization.

> *Te dije que lo hicieras en broma.*
>
> I told you to do it jokingly.

Margarita nunca habla en serio.

Margarita never speaks seriously.

In some circumstances, Spanish requires the preposition *en* where English uses the preposition "on."

Ellos pusieron los libros en la mesa.

They put the books on the table.

Sometimes, although the preposition "on" is used in English, no preposition is used in Spanish. This occurs when you refer to days of the week. To state that something occurs "on Friday" in Spanish, you would use the definite article *el* as in *el viernes.* If you want to say that something happens on Mondays in general, the plural form of the definite article is used: *Los domingos* means "on Sundays" or "every Sunday." *Los fines de semanas* means "on weekends."

Patricio nunca trabaja los sábados.

Patricio never works on Saturday.

Uds. tienen un examen el jueves.

You guys have a test on Thursday.

The preposition *con*

The preposition *con* indicates accompaniment, as in the English use of "with."

Su esposo llegó con su hija.

Her husband arrived with their daughter.

Nunca saldré con un borracho.

I will never go out with a drunk.

Me gusta el café con leche.

I like coffee with milk.

Con is another preposition that can indicate the means by which something is done. You must memorize which expressions of manner require the use of the preposition *con. Con* may be followed by a noun or by a verb in its infinitive form.

Cierra la puerta con llave.

Lock the door.

Ella tendrá éxito con ese libro.

She will be successful with that book.

Spanish also uses the preposition *con* to express surprise at what has been accomplished under certain circumstances. In this usage, you can translate *con* as the English expression "in spite of."

> *Con todo su dinero, ella todavía está triste.*
> With (in spite of) all her money, she is still sad.

> *Todavía no tengo dinero con todo lo que gano.*
> I still have no money in spite of all I earn.

Con can be used instead of *de* to indicate the contents of a container.

> *Tenemos una bolsa con tamales.*
> We have a bag of tamales.

> *El cesto con ropa está lleno.*
> The basket of clothing is full.

Por and *para*

Two Spanish prepositions are always explained together because they are easily confused by English speakers. A number of English prepositions are translated as *por* or *para,* but the word that you would use in English does not determine which of the two prepositions you use in Spanish. You must consider what relationship is being expressed and use the appropriate preposition.

It is helpful to have a memory device to remember the reasons for using *para.* The acronym **P.R.O.D.D.S.** represents the first letter of each of the situations that call for the use of the preposition *para.*

Purpose	**D**estination
Recipient	**D**eadline
Opinion	**S**tandard

Para is used in front of an infinitive to express the **purpose** of doing something. This can be expressed in English by using the phrase "in order to." Note, in English, it is not necessary to use any preposition in such expressions, and sometimes the preposition "to" is used. Even if the English sentence does not use a preposition, the Spanish equivalent requires the preposition *para* to express the purpose of doing something.

> *Pablo estudia mucho para recibir buenas notas.*
> Pablo studies a lot in order to receive good grades.

Cecilia viaja para experimentar una vida diferente.
Cecilia travels in order to experience a different life.

Enrique no come carne para no enfermarse.
Enrique does not eat meat for health reasons.

Sometimes, English uses the preposition "for" followed by a gerund to express the purpose "for doing" something. Remember that a verb that immediately follows a preposition in Spanish will always be in its infinitive form.

Esa agua no es para beber.
That water is not for drinking.

The intended **recipient** of an object is indicated with the preposition *para.*

Jaime llevó la caja para su abuela.
Jaime carried the box for his grandmother.

José compró un regalo para mí.
José bought a gift for me.

The exception to this rule is the recipient of an emotion, which is expressed by the use of *por,* not *para.*

Tito no tiene nada salvo rencor por su enemigo.
Tito does not have anything but hatred for his enemy.

Siento mucho amor por mi abuela.
I feel much love for my grandmother.

Para is also used to indicate the person whose personal **opinion** is being expressed.

Para el líder, los derechos humanos no son importantes.
To the leader, human rights are not important.

Las corporaciones son importantes para el presidente.
The corporations are important to the president.

Para is used to indicate the **destination** of something both in a real, physical sense and in a figurative, metaphorical sense.

Las alfombras son para el comedor.
The rugs are for the dining room.

Salimos para Jamaica mañana.

We are leaving for Jamaica tomorrow.

Para is used to indicate a **deadline** or due date.

Tendrás que entregar el proyecto para el lunes que viene.

You will have to hand in the project next Monday.

Debemos terminar nuestros ejercicios para las diez.

We should finish our exercises by ten o'clock.

In Spanish, *para* also is used to express that something is contrary to the standard. The **standard** is what is considered "normal." To express that something strays from the norm, the preposition "for" is used in an expression such as "She is very cool <u>for</u> a teacher." In other words, she is not all that cool, it is just that she is cooler than what is considered typical for a teacher.

Su hijo sabe mucho para ser un niño.

His son knows a lot for a child.

Para ser taxista, él conduce muy despacio.

For a taxi driver, he drives very slowly.

The reasons for using *por* can easily be remembered with the acronym **D.E.E.M.M.S.**

Duration	**M**otivation
Emotions	**M**eans
Exchange	**S**ubstitution

Although this acronym is a great way to memorize the reasons for using the preposition *por*, you must first understand what the acronym means. The situations in which *por* is appropriate are explained below.

Por is used to express the **duration** of time, or the length of time something lasts. In English, this is usually done by using the preposition "for."

Vivimos en Puerto Rico por dos años.

We lived in Puerto Rico for two years.

¡Por dos horas busqué mis llaves!

I looked for my keys for two hours!

As mentioned earlier, the recipient of an **emotion** is expressed by using the preposition *por*. Remember that *para* (described earlier in the chapter) is used for the recipient of anything other than emotion.

Su amor no es por mí.

His love is not for me.

Los jóvenes casi nunca muestran su cariño por sus padres.

Teenagers almost never show their affection for their parents.

Por is used to express when one thing is **exchanged** for another. This includes cash transactions as well as bartering.

Timoteo cortaría el césped por 30 dólares.

Timoteo would cut the grass for 30 dollars.

Me cobraron demasiado dinero por las joyas.

They charged me too much money for the jewels.

When you thank someone, you exchange words of gratitude for something that has been given to you or done for you. For this reason, *por* is used after *gracias* or the verb *agradecer* (to thank).

Muchas gracias por tu ayuda.

Thanks a lot for your help.

Estoy muy agradecida por toda su amabilidad.

I am very grateful for all your kindness.

Por is used to express the **motivation** behind something. If you find it difficult to differentiate between motivation (which is expressed with *por*) and purpose (which is expressed with *para*) decide whether the idea could be expressed using the compound preposition "due to." If that is what you are trying to say, use the Spanish preposition *por*. Motivation is the cause rather than the goal. The preposition *para* is used to express the idea of "in order to."

Tengo muchas muestras de champú por mi viaje de negocios.

I have many samples of shampoo due to my business trip.

Tengo muchas muestras de champú para el viaje.

I have many samples of shampoo for the trip.

Nevertheless, a few verbs are consistently followed by the preposition *por* to indicate motive even though you would not say "due to" in English. *Andar, caminar, ir, regresar, volver,* and verbs of motion similar to these are followed by *por* when the purpose or motive is provided.

Ellos caminan al supermercado por el agua.

They walk to the supermarket for water.

Ricardo volvió por la ropa que olvidó.
Ricardo returned for the clothing he forgot.

There are basically two ways in which *por* is used to express **means:** It is used to express a means of communication or means of transportation. Listed below are some typical expressions with *por* indicating means.

por autobús	by bus
por avión	by plane
por barco	by boat
por computadora	by computer
por correo	by mail
por correo electrónico	by e-mail
por escrito	in writing
por fax	by fax
por ferrocarril	by train
por medio de	by means of
por móbil	by cellphone
por teléfono	by phone

Although it is rarely a good idea to translate an English preposition to a Spanish preposition, you should use *por* anytime the idea expresses "through," "by," or "along" to indicate movement within an area.

Viajamos por los pueblos blancos de la Costa del Sol
We travel through the whitewashed villages of the Costa del Sol.

Paseo por las orillas del río.
I walk along the banks of the river.

Ella continúa por la calle oscura.
She continues along the dark street.

Another reason for using *por* is to express **substitution.** The best way to know that the preposition is indicating substitution is to determine whether the idea could be expressed with the English "in place of" or "instead of." If these expressions sound good, the preposition is indicating a substitution, which requires the use of *por.* Compare the pairs of sentences below.

Irene compró el regalo por su hermana. Su hermana está enferma y no puede ir de compras.
Irene bought the gift for (in place of) her sister. Her sister is ill and cannot go shopping.

Irene compró el regalo para su hermana. Es el cumpleaños de su hermana.
Irene bought the gift for her sister. It is her sister's birthday.

Rebeca canta para Enriqueta. A Enriqueta le gusta escuchar sus canciones.
Rebeca sings for Enriqueta. Enriqueta likes to listen to her songs.

Rebeca canta por Enriqueta. Enriqueta tiene laringitis y no puede cantar.
Rebeca sings in place of Enriqueta. Enriqueta has laryngitis and cannot sing.

Because both the acronyms to help you remember *por* and *para* include reasons that start with the letter **D,** you need to remember which one goes with which. Because the preposition *por* has only one **D** reason, remember that *por* is used to express duration; then you can just remember that the other two **D** reasons (destination and deadline) require the use of *para*.

Compound Prepositions

A preposition that is composed of more than one word is called a compound preposition. The last word of a compound preposition is always one of the simple prepositions, so compound prepositions are easy to recognize. You will notice that many of the following compound prepositions are formed with a directional word and the simple preposition *de*. Remember that if a directional word is used without *de,* it is no longer considered a preposition.

a partir de	from (time or date) on, starting (time or date)
al lado de	next to
a lo largo de	along
a través de	through
a espaldas de	behind
a fines de	at the end
abajo de	underneath
adentro de	inside (of)
afuera de	outside (of)
alrededor de	around
antes de	before
arriba de	above
cerca de	near
debajo de	under

delante de	before (space), in front of
dentro de	in, within, inside of
después de	after (time or order)
detrás de	behind, after
en vez de	instead of
en lugar de	in place of
encima de	on top of, above
enfrente de	in front of
frente a	opposite, facing
fuera de	outside of
junto a	close to, next to
lejos de	far from

Idiomatic usage

One of the most frustrating aspects of learning a foreign language is that often you can look up every word individually, but when you put them together they make no sense. When a group of words has a meaning separate from the individual words of which it is composed, it is called an **idiomatic expression.** Most idiomatic expressions include at least one preposition. It is important to learn to use the correct preposition in an idiomatic expression because a different preposition can completely change the meaning of the expression.

A lot of idiomatic expressions include the preposition *por.* You must memorize each expression because none logically follows any of the rules for using *por.* The following is a list of important idiomatic expressions that include the preposition *por.* For other idiomatic expressions, see Idiomatic Expressions (www.cliffsnotes.com/extras).

por supuesto	of course, naturally
por lo visto	apparently
por un lado	on one hand
por otro (lado)	on the other (hand)
por ejemplo	for example
por lo demás	furthermore
por lo menos	at least
por lo mismo	for that very reason
por lo que a mí me toca	as far as I am concerned

poner en ridículo	to make someone look ridiculous
por desgracia	unfortunately
por mi parte	as far as I am concerned
por último	finally
por poco	almost
por completo	completely
por lo contrario	on the contrary
por otra parte	on the other hand
por consecuencia	consequently
por consiguiente	accordingly
por lo tanto	consequently
por culpa de	by fault of
por motivo de	on account of
por allá	around there, that way
por aquí	around here, this way
por todos lados	all over, everywhere
por todas partes	on all sides, all over, everywhere
por dentro y por fuera	inside and outside
por ahora	for now
por aquel entonces	at that time
por esa epoca	at that time
por lo pronto	for the time being
por separado	separately
por la mañana	in the morning
por la tarde	in the afternoon
por la noche	at night

Here are some idiomatic expressions using the preposition *para*:

para siempre	forever
para nada	no way (not for anything)
para que	so that

Here are some idiomatic expressions using the preposition *a*:

a caballo	on horseback
a fines de	at the end of
a la antigua	in the old fashioned way

a lo (adjective)	in the (adjective) style
a la orilla de	at the edge of
a lo sumo	at the most

Any verb can be used after the preposition *a* + *el* (*al*) in its infinitive form to mean "upon (verb)-ing."

| *al entrar* | upon entering |
| *al terminar* | upon finishing |

The following list contains idiomatic expressions using the preposition *con:*

con cariño	affectionately, caringly
con énfasis	emphatically
con cuidado	cautiously
con gusto	with pleasure
con permiso	excuse me (when passing)
con razón	with reason (correct)

Here are some idiomatic expressions using the preposition *de:*

de corazón	sincerely
de acuerdo	in agreement
de hoy en adelante	from today on
de mal en peor	from bad to worse
de modo que	so that
de pie	upright, standing

The following list presents idiomatic expressions using the preposition *en:*

en avión	by plane
en cambio	in exchange
en efecto	in fact
en voz alta	in a loud voice (out loud)
en voz baja	in a soft voice
en la actualidad	nowadays
en realidad	in reality

Here are some idiomatic expressions using the preposition *sin:*

sin embargo	nevertheless
sin ton ni son	without rhyme or reason
sin más ni más	without further ado

Verbs with prepositions

Another idiomatic usage of prepositions is with verbs. Certain Spanish verbs require that a specific preposition always follow any form of the verb. After the preposition, there may be a noun or another verb. If a verb follows the preposition, it must be in the infinitive form, regardless of how the English equivalent is stated. In English, the second verb will often be in its infinitive form, as in Spanish; sometimes, however, the second verb is in its gerund form, with the -*ing* ending (for example, "He limits himself to watching the games because of his injury" or "She risks losing everything").

Acertar a (in the third list, below) is a good example because there are two ways to translate it. *Él acierta a terminar su tarea* can be translated as "He manages to finish his homework" or as "He succeeds in finishing his homework"; in both English phrases, when translated back into Spanish, the verb that follows a form of *acertar a* will be in its infinitive form.

The verbs below are always followed by the preposition that follows in the list, even though English might use a different preposition.

Here is a list of verbs followed by the preposition *por:*

comenzar por	to begin by
preocuparse por	to be worried about
interesarse por	to be interested in
estar por	to be inclined to

Below is an example of a verb followed by the preposition *para:*

estar para	to be about to

This list contains verbs followed by the preposition *a:*

acercarse a	to get close to
acertar (e>ie) a + infinitive	to manage to, to succeed in
acudir a	to turn to
animar a + *infinitive*	to encourage to
aprender a + infinitive	to learn + infinitive
asistir a	to attend (a function)
atreverse a	to dare to
ayudar a + infinitive	to help + infinitive
comenzar (e>ie) a + infinitive	to begin + infinitive
cuidar a	to care for, take care of (someone)

decidirse a + infinitive	to decide + infinitive
dedicarse a	to dedicate oneself to
echarse a	to begin
empezar (e>ie) a + infinitive	to begin + infinitive
enseñar a + infinitive	to teach + infinitive
forzar (o>ue) a + infinitive	to force + infinitive
inspirar a + infinitive	to inspire + infinitive
invitar a	to invite to
negarse (e>ie) a + infinitive	to refuse + infinitive
ponerse a	to begin to
probar (o>ue) a + infinitive	to try + infinitive
resignarse a	to resign oneself to
sonar (o>ue) a	to sound like (something)
subir a	to climb, to go up, or to get on (something)
volver a	to do (something) again

This list contains verbs followed by the preposition *de:*

acabar de + infinitive	to have just (past tense)
acordarse de	to agree about
alegrarse de	to be happy about
avergonzarse (o>ue) de	to be ashamed of
cansarse de	to get tired of
cuidar de	to care for (something)
deber de	to feel obliged to
dejar de + infinitive	to stop (gerund)
depender de	to depend on
disfrutar de	to enjoy
enamorarse de	to be in love with
encargarse de	to take charge of
gozar de	to enjoy
informarse de	to become aware of
marcharse de	to leave
morir (o>ue) de	to die of (literally)
morirse (o>ue) de	to die of (figuratively)

olvidarse de	to forget about
parar de + infinitive	to stop (gerund)
pensar (e>ie) de	to think of, to have an opinion of
probar (o>ue) de	to sample, to try out
quejarse de	to complain about
reírse de	to laugh about
salir de	to go away from (somewhere)
servir de	to be useful as
sufrir de	to suffer from
tratar de + infinitive	to try + infinitive

The following list contains verbs followed by the preposition *en:*

caber en	to fit in (something)
consentir (e>ie) en + infinitive	to consent to + infinitive
consistir en	to consist of
convertir (se) (e>ie) en	to become, to change into
empeñarse en	to insist on
equivocarse en	to make a mistake about
fijarse en	to pay attention to
insistir en	to insist on
molestarse en + infinitive	to take the trouble + infinitive
montar(se) en	to ride
parar(se) en	to stop at, to stay in
pensar en	to think about (a topic not an opinion)
quedar en	to agree on
tardar en	to delay in
trabajar en	to work on, to work at

This list contains verbs followed by the preposition *con:*

casarse con	to marry
conformarse con	to conform to, to make do with
contar (o>ue) con	to count on
dar con	to happen upon
encontrarse (o>ue) con	to meet up with, to run into
enfadarse con	to get angry at

enojarse con	to get angry at
equivocarse con	to be mistaken about
preocuparse con	to worry about
salir con	to go out with, to date
soñar con	to dream of
tropezar con	to bump into

To help you learn which preposition follows each of the verbs in the lists above, put all the verbs that must be followed by a specific pronoun on one color of flashcard and those followed by another preposition on a different color; in this way, your brain will subliminally register the color and help you remember the appropriate preposition. When you quiz yourself, rewrite both sets of verbs on all white cards to see if you can remember which preposition goes with each verb, as well as to see whether you understand what the verb expression means.

Verbs Followed by Prepositions in English but Not in Spanish

Some expressions in English require a verb to be followed by a preposition. You often do not notice the preposition when you speak English, but you will incorrectly think you need to provide a Spanish equivalent when you translate these expressions. For the English expressions below, the Spanish translation includes a verb that is not followed by any preposition.

to be grateful for	*agradecer*
to turn off	*apagar*
to go down	*bajar*
to look for	*buscar*
to fall down	*caerse*
to heat up	*calentar (e>ie)*
to hang up	*colgar (o>ue)*
to be acquainted with	*conocer*
to cut off, to cut out	*cortar*
to hand over	*entregar*
to wrap up	*envolver (o>ue)*
to listen to	*escuchar*
to wait for, to hope for	*esperar*

to look at	*mirar*
to pay for	*pagar*
to take off	*quitar*
to know how to	*saber*
to take out	*sacar*
to go out	*salir*

After the difficulties presented by *por* and *para*, it should be refreshing to learn that some simple prepositions can be translated to a simple English equivalent. The most common truly simple prepositions are listed below.

ante	before, in the presence of
bajo	under
contra	against
desde	from (as in since)
después de	after
durante	during
entre	among
entre	between
excepto	except
hacia	toward
hasta	as far as, even up to; until
mediante	by means of
menos	except
salvo	except
según	according to
sin	without
sobre	about, concerning (topic); above, on, over, on top of (physically)
tras	after; behind

Use with infinitive

Remember that any time a preposition is immediately followed by a verb, that verb will be in its infinitive form. This is not always true in English, so there will be times when it will not "sound right" to use an infinitive, but there are no exceptions to the Spanish rule: A verb must be in its infinitive form if it immediately follows a preposition.

Los jóvenes aprenden a esquiar.
The teenagers are learning to ski.

Yoli está cansada de prestar atención.
Yoli is tired of paying attention.

Es imposible terminar sin empezar.
It is impossible to finish without beginning.

Chapter Checkout

For the following sentences, decide whether a preposition is necessary to fill in the blank. If so, write the correct preposition; if not, leave it blank.

1. *Los franceses aprenden _____ hablar el inglés muy bien.*
2. *El abogado debe notificarte _____ escrito.*
3. *La policía busca _____ la niña por todas partes.*
4. *Siempre he soñado _____ viajar a España.*
5. *Eduardo es muy alto _____ un niño de tres años.*

Answers: 1. *a* 2. *por* 3. *a* 4. *con* 5. *para*

Chapter 12

PRONOUNS

Chapter Check-In

❏ Understanding the cases of pronouns and the different parts of speech pronouns replace

❏ Learning the pronoun charts

❏ Placing pronouns correctly within a sentence

Pronouns do the same thing in Spanish as they do in English: replace a noun and its modifiers. The challenge is that you must learn to analyze a sentence and determine what role each noun plays in order to know what kind of pronoun must be used to replace it. A noun can play several different roles in the sentence. It can be the subject, the direct object, the indirect object, the object of a preposition, or a predicate nominative. Pronouns come in cases, and you have to consider which case of pronoun is appropriate, as well as how much information is being replaced by the pronoun.

Object Pronouns

Once you understand the subject pronouns, you're ready to learn another case of pronouns called the "object case." In English, object pronouns are used when the noun being replaced is the indirect object, the direct object, or the object of a preposition in the sentence. The Spanish language, however, has three separate cases of object pronouns: one to replace an indirect object, another to replace a direct object, and a third to replace the object of a preposition (the latter is known as *pronombres tónicos*).

Because you must determine which of the object pronouns to use in Spanish, you must learn to identify the indirect and direct object in a sentence.

To determine which pronoun to use to replace a noun, you must first determine what role the noun is playing in the sentence. There is actually a very simple way to systematically identify the role of any noun in any sentence. It's a four-step process, and the steps must be taken in the following order:

1. To find the subject of the sentence, determine the action of the sentence. That action word is the verb of your sentence.

2. Ask yourself who or what is responsible for the action. The noun that answers that question is the subject of your sentence.

3. Then ask yourself who or what is being "verb-ed"? The answer to that question is the direct object of the sentence. The direct object does not do anything, it is just receiving the action of the verb. You may not have a direct object, but if there is a direct object, there's a chance that there may also be an indirect object. If that is the case, proceed to Step 4.

4. To identify the indirect object of the sentence, determine to whom, or for whom or what, is the direct object being "verb-ed"? Replace the word "verb-ed" with the verb of the sentence to determine the direct object of the sentence.

It is much easier to understand this system with an example or two. Remember that every sentence must have a subject and a verb, but not every sentence will have a direct object and/or indirect object. To analyze the following sentences, use the above steps in the correct order. Practice in English first:

> Jerónimo buys Maricarmen diamonds.

1. What is the action of the sentence? The verb is "buys."
2. Who or what is responsible for buying? The subject is "Jerónimo."
3. Who or what is being bought? The direct object is "diamonds."
4. For whom are the diamonds bought? The indirect object is "Maricarmen."

Now try to identify the verb, subject, direct object, and indirect object in the following sentence:

> Mercedes sends a card to Ariana.

1. What is the action of the sentence? The verb is "sends."
2. Who or what is responsible for sending? The subject is "Mercedes."
3. Who or what is being sent? The direct object is "a card."
4. To whom is the card sent? The indirect object is "Ariana."

Direct object pronouns

If the noun you want to replace with a pronoun is serving as the direct object of the sentence, you must select the appropriate pronoun from the direct object case of pronouns. In Table 12-1, the Spanish direct object pronouns are listed in the same order the subject pronouns were presented in Chapter 2. To determine which pronoun is appropriate, consider what pronoun you would have used if you were using a subject pronoun and select the direct object pronoun from the same spot in the chart below.

Table 12-1   Direct Object Pronoun Chart

	Singular	*Plural*
First person	*me*	*nos*
Second person	*te*	*vos*
Third person (masculine)	*lo*	*os*
Third person (feminine)	*la*	*las*

Because all nouns have a gender in Spanish, there is no need for a neutral pronoun like the English word "it." The direct object pronoun *lo* literally translates as "him," but, when used to replace a masculine noun that is an object, *lo* is translated as "it." The direct object pronoun *la* means "her" but also means "it" when replacing a feminine noun that is an object. Just remember that *lo, la, los,* and *las* refer to both people and things.

Lo and *la* are also the direct object pronouns for *Ud.,* so you must consider the gender of the singular "you" that you are replacing with a pronoun. *Los* and *las* are also the direct object pronouns for *ustedes* and will reflect the gender of the group of people that the plural "you" refers to.

It is especially confusing that the direct object pronouns *la, los,* and *las* look exactly like the definite articles *la, los,* and *las.* Just remember that when one of these words isn't followed by a noun, it is probably replacing one.

A direct object in English always follows the verb, even when the direct object is a pronoun. In Spanish, a direct object follows a conjugated form of a verb <u>except</u> when you turn the direct object into a pronoun. When you do this, the direct object pronoun is moved in front of the conjugated form of the verb. If the sentence is negative, the *no* or other negative word will precede the direct object pronoun. Watch what happens in the following pairs of sample sentences. The direct object is underlined in each sentence; in the second sentence, the direct object has been changed to a direct object pronoun and moved directly in front of the verb.

Mateo invita a Gabriela. (Mateo invites Gabriela.)

Mateo la invita. (Mateo invites her.)

Maya escribe un libro. (Maya writes a book.)

Maya lo escribe. (Maya writes it.)

Anita mira a Martin. (Anita looks at Martin.)

Anita lo mira. (Anita looks at him.)

El jefe no invita a las mujeres. (The boss doesn't invite the women.)

El jefe no las invita. (The boss doesn't invite them.)

Benjamín tiene los discos. (Benjamin has the records.)

Benjamín los tiene. (Benjamin has them.)

The above examples are all simple one-verb sentences. In more complex sentences, direct object pronouns can be in different places (see the "Pronoun Placement" section, later in this chapter).

Indirect object pronouns

Not every sentence has a direct object pronoun, but if it does, there's a good chance that it also has an indirect object. Except with specific exceptions presented later in this chapter, a sentence cannot have an indirect object unless it has a direct object.

Table 12-2 lists the indirect object pronouns in the same order as the subject and direct object pronouns earlier in this chapter.

Table 12-2   Indirect Object Pronoun Chart

	Singular	*Plural*
First person	*me*	*nos*
Second person	*te*	*os*
Third person	*le*	*les*

Most of the Spanish indirect object pronouns look exactly like direct object pronouns except for the third person. The indirect object pronoun for the masculine "him" and the feminine "her" are exactly the same: The pronoun *le* is used as the indirect object pronoun for both genders.

Because the pronoun *le* is not very clear, a clarification can be placed either at the beginning of the sentence or after the verb to indicate the gender or even the specific person. To create a clarification, the preposition *a* is followed by a subject pronoun. Depending on the context, *a él, a ella,* or *a usted* can be used to clarify the pronoun *le,* or any noun can be used after the preposition *a* to specify exactly who is the indirect object.

> *Salvador le da el libro a María.*
> Salvador gives the book to María.

The pronoun *les* has the same problem, so if it is necessary to clarify the gender, do so by adding *a ellos, a ellas,* or *a ustedes.* It is common for the indirect object pronoun to be clarified by the actual noun that the indirect object replaces. Unlike the direct object, however, the indirect object pronoun is used even when the noun is stated.

> *Santino les causó problemas a Mario y Andrea.*
> Santino caused Mario and Andrea problems.

> *Stacy nos escribe que la universidad es perfecta.*
> Stacy writes to us that the university is perfect.

Whenever a sentence has both an indirect object and direct object pronoun, the indirect object is first and both follow the subject pronoun if stated. If the sentence is negative, the negative word is placed between the subject pronoun and the object pronouns.

> *Ella nos la vendió cuando terminó su obra.*
> She sold us it when she finished her painting.

> *Sharkey no me lo dijo.*
> Sharkey didn't tell me it.

When there are two object pronouns together (indirect and direct) in the third person (*le, la, lo, los, las*), the indirect object pronoun *le* or *les* changes to *se.*

> *El artista mostró la pintura a los estudiantes.* (The artist showed the painting to the students.)
> *El artista la mostró a los estudiantes.* (The artist showed it to the students.)
> *El artista les mostró la pintura.* (The artist showed them the painting.)
> *El artista se la mostró (a ellos).* (The artist showed them it.)

The following verbs are used idiomatically with an indirect object. As an example, let's look at *gustar* (*me gusta, te gusta, le gusta,* and so on). The form of the verb depends on what follows. Generally, the third person singular (*él*) form of the verb is used if followed by an infinitive or something singular. The third person plural is used when followed by something plural. Because these verbs are used with an indirect object, they're listed in the *él* form with various indirect object pronouns. They are listed in the present tense but can be used in any tense.

me aburre	it bores me
te agrada	it pleases you
le basta	it's enough for him (her, you)
nos cae bien	it goes well for us
les concierne	it concerns them
me complace	it pleases me
les conviene	it is better for them
me duele	it pains me
me disgusta	it disgusts me
te distrae	it distracts you
te encanta	it charms you
le extraña	it's strange to you (her, him)
nos (hace) falta	it's lacking for us
les fascina	it fascinates them
me fastidia	it annoys (bothers) me
te gusta	it pleases you
le hace daño	it does harm to him (her, you)
les importa	it's important to them
me interesa	it interests me
les inquieta	it upsets them
te molesta	it bothers you
le parece	it seems to her (him, you)
me place	it pleases me
le preocupa	it worries him (her, you)
les queda	it remains for them
me sobra	it is extra for me
te sorprende	it surprises you
le toca	it's your (his, her) turn

Reflexive Pronouns

The one time that it is not necessary to decide whether the pronoun is replacing a direct object or an indirect object is when a verb is reflexive. A reflexive pronoun is used when the subject of the sentence is both the agent of and the recipient of the action of the verb. The closest equivalent in English would be to use "myself," "yourself," "himself," "herself," "ourselves," or "themselves" after a verb. Another use of the reflexive is to indicate that the members of a plural subject do something to each other (this is called "reciprocity").

To memorize the reflexive pronouns and their purposes, try singing the following to the tune of "Three Blind Mice":

> *Me, te, se,*
>
> *nos, os, se:*
>
> These are the pronouns *reflexivos.*
>
> You use them when the action reflects back on the subject,
> or to show reciprocity:
>
> I love you and you love me.
>
> *Me, te se,*
>
> *nos, os, se.*

A reflexive verb has -*se* attached to the end of its infinitive form and, when conjugated, will use the appropriate reflexive pronoun in front of any conjugated form of the verb. Table 12-3, demonstrates which reflexive pronoun is appropriate for each subject pronoun.

Table 12-3   Reflexive Pronouns with Subject Pronouns

yo me __	*nosotros/nosotras nos* __
tú te __	*vosotros/vosotras os* __
él se __	*ellos se* __
ella se __	*ellas se* __
usted se __	*ustedes se* __

In Spanish, a reflexive verb always has a reflexive pronoun whether or not the subject pronoun is used. The reflexive pronoun is placed in the sentence in exactly the same way as a direct object pronoun or an indirect object pronoun. If a reflexive pronoun is used in conjunction with a direct object pronoun or an indirect object pronoun, the reflexive pronoun is always first. The order of object pronouns in a sentence is easily remembered with the acronym **RID** (Reflexive, Indirect, Direct). Although all three pronouns are never used together, whichever object pronouns are in a sentence will follow the order RID (see the "Pronoun Placement" section, later in this chapter).

> *Yo me lo prometí que visitaría a Marruecos otra vez.*
> I promised it to myself that I would visit Morrocco again.

> *Te la pusiste (la falda).*
> You wore it (the skirt).

When a reflexive verb is conjugated in any tense, the *-se* is removed from the infinitive form and the appropriate reflexive pronoun is used to reflect the subject of the sentence. Notice in Table 12-3 that the reflexive pronouns are similar to direct object pronouns and indirect object pronouns, but they are even easier to learn because the third person reflexive pronoun is always *se*. The blank represents where the conjugated form of the verb goes.

Some verbs are always reflexive, but any verb that can have an indirect object or direct object can be used as a reflexive verb if the object is the same as the subject. The term "reflexive" indicates that the subject of the sentence both causes and receives the action of the verb. For example, the verb *bañar* means "to bathe something or someone else," but the reflexive verb *bañarse* means "to bathe oneself." A strange quirk of the English language is that reflexives are occasionally stated with an expression using "take." For example, "she bathes herself" is equivalent to "she takes a bath." The only way to express this in Spanish is to use the reflexive. Table 12-4, the conjugation chart for the reflexive verb *bañarse,* shows which reflexive pronoun goes in front of each conjugated form of the verb.

Table 12-4   Present Tense Conjugation of the Reflexive Verb *Bañarse*

yo me baño	*nosotros/nosotras nos bañamos*
tú te bañas	*vosotros/vosotras os bañáis*
él se baña	*ellos se bañan*
ella se baña	*ellas se bañan*
usted se baña	*ustedes se bañan*

When the plural subjects have reflexive pronouns, there are actually two possible interpretations. As you learned in the song above, reflexive pronouns can indicate reciprocity. That means that the people represented by the plural subject do the action of the verb to each other. Sometimes, it is obvious that the reflexive pronoun is being used to indicate reciprocity:

> *Ellos se casaron el 21 de mayo.*
>
> They married each other on May 21.

Technically, the sentence could be stating that they married themselves, but logic allows us to assume that reciprocity is indicated. The other use of the reflexive can also be assumed in a sentence:

> *Nosotros nos bañamos todas las mañanas.*
>
> We take a bath (bathe ourselves) each morning.

It is possible but not probable that we bathe each other. When a reflexive verb has a plural subject, there will be two possible translations, but the context of the sentence should give away the correct interpretation. This problem does not occur when the subject is singular because it is impossible to have reciprocity with only one person.

Common reflexive verbs

Some verbs are always reflexive, some verbs have a completely different meaning when they are reflexive, and some are simply used reflexively to indicate that the action of the verb is being done by the subject to the subject. The following lists of the different kinds of reflexive verbs provide a great opportunity to improve your vocabulary as well as your understanding of the different kinds of reflexive verbs.

The verbs in the following list can be used as reflexive verbs to indicate that the action of the verb is being done to oneself. You will notice that it is common in English to use the expression "get" to indicate that something is being done to oneself. For example "to get tired" or "to get dressed" is the same as saying "to tire oneself" or "to dress oneself."

acostar (o>ue)	to put (someone) to bed
acostarse (o>ue)	to go to bed
afeitar	to shave (someone else)
afeitarse	to shave (oneself)
arreglar	to arrange, to fix
arreglarse	to get fixed up (to arrange oneself)

bañar	to bathe someone
bañarse	to bathe oneself, to take a bath
cansar	to tire (someone)
cansarse	to get tired
cortar	to cut
cortarse	to cut oneself
cepillar	to brush (someone else's or a pet's hair or teeth)
cepillarse	to brush (one's own hair or teeth)
despedir	to fire, to dismiss
despedirse	to say goodbye (to dismiss oneself)
despertar (e>ie)	to wake up (someone)
despertarse (e>ie)	to awake
divertir (e>ie)	to amuse
divertirse (e>ie)	to have fun (to amuse oneself)
enfermar	to make sick
enfermarse	to get sick
lastimar	to hurt
lastimarse	to get hurt
lavar	to wash (someone else or something)
lavarse	to wash oneself
levantar	to raise up (something)
levantarse	to get up, to stand (oneself) up
llamar	to call (someone)
llamarse	to be called, to call oneself
maquillar	to apply makeup (to someone)
maquillarse	to put on one's makeup
peinar	to comb (someone else's) hair
peinarse	to comb (one's own) hair
poner	to put
ponerse	to put something on oneself
vestir (e>i)	to dress (someone else)
vestirse (e>i)	to get dressed

Many reflexive verbs indicate that one is doing something to one's own body. Because the reflexive pronoun already indicates that the subject of the sentence is doing the action of the verb to him- or herself, it is considered repetitive to use a possessive adjective in front of the body parts in question. Thus, use the appropriate definite article in front of the body part rather than a possessive adjective:

> *Yo me peino dos veces al día.*
> I comb my hair twice a day.
>
> *Lolita se lava las manos antes de comer.*
> Lolita washes her hands before eating.

Linguistically, Spanish speakers take responsibility for their own emotions because many verbs indicating emotions are used reflexively. It is almost as if a person "bores himself" or "angers herself." The English translations of these kinds of emotion verbs often begin with the expressions "to get" or "to become." These same verbs can be used without the reflexive pronoun when the action of the verb is being done to someone else.

aburrir	to bore (someone)
aburrirse	to get bored
alegrar	to make (someone) happy
alegrarse	to become happy
animar	to encourage (someone)
animarse	to get motivated
asustar	to frighten (someone)
asustarse	to get scared
calmar	to calm (someone) down
calmarse	to stop worrying
enfadar	to anger (someone)
enfadarse	to get mad
enojar	to anger (someone)
enojarse	to get mad
entusiasmar	to thrill, to excite
entusiasmarse	to get excited
exasperar	to make (someone) lose patience
exasperarse	to lose patience

molestar	to annoy
molestarse	to get annoyed
ofender	to offend
ofenderse	to be offended
preocupar	to worry (someone)
preocuparse	to get worried
sorprender	to surprise (someone)
sorprenderse	to be surprised
tranquilizar	to calm (someone) down
tranquilizarse	to stop worrying

Many reflexive verbs have only slightly different meanings from their non-reflexive versions. Sometimes you have to think about it, but they make sense. For example, *parar* means "to stop" and *pararse* means "to stand," which is what happens after you stop yourself.

acercar	to bring (something) closer
acercarse	to approach
alejar	to move (something) away
alejarse de	to move away from
colocar	to place (something)
colocarse	to get a job, to place oneself
correr	to run, race, flow
correrse	to move over to make room
decidir	to decide
decidirse (a)	to make up one's mind
detener	to stop (someone or something), to bring to a halt
detenerse	to stop (yourself), to come to a halt
instalar	to install, to put in
instalarse	to install oneself, to move in
ir	to go
irse	to leave, to go away
levantar	to lift up
levantarse	to get up
parar	to stop

pararse	to stand
perder	to lose (something)
perderse	to get lost
probar (o>ue)	to try, taste
probarse (o>ue)	to try on
quedar	to be remaining, to be left over
quedarse	to stay, to remain
quitar	to remove
quitarse	to take something off (oneself)
reunir	to join, to gather
reunirse	to have a meeting (with)
tirar	to throw (something)
tirarse	to throw oneself, to jump, to lie down

Some verbs are simply always reflexive. The list that follows includes verbs that are used reflexively even though there is no logical reason for a reflexive usage. The reflexive pronoun must be used because it is part of the idiomatic expression—and not because someone is doing something to him- or herself, nor for any reciprocation reason.

Many of these verbs are generally followed by a specific preposition. This preposition follows the infinitive in the list below. If more than one preposition can be used, the second option is in parentheses.

acordarse de (o>ue)	to remember
apoderarse de	to take possession (of)
apresurarse a	to hurry to
aprovecharse de	to take advantage (of)
apuntarse a (para)	to register, to sign up (for)
arrepentirse de (e>ie)	to regret
atreverse a	to dare to
ausentarse de	to be out, to be absent
burlarse de	to make fun of, to laugh at (not yourself)
casarse con	to marry, to get married
comprometerse	to get engaged
desayunarse	to eat breakfast

desmayarse	to faint
divorciarse	to get divorced
echarse	to lie down
escaparse	to escape
empeñarse en	to insist on
enamorarse de	to fall in love with
enterarse de	to find out about
fiarse de	to trust
figurarse	to imagine
fijarse en	to notice
inclinarse	to bend over
jactarse de	to brag about
moverse (o>ue)	to move
mudarse	to move (change residence)
negarse a (de) (e>ie)	to refuse to
ocuparse de	to take care of
olvidarse de	to forget
oponerse a	to oppose
parecerse a	to resemble
pasearse	to take a stroll
portarse + adverb	to behave + verb + -ly
quejarse de	to complain about
recostarse (o>ue)	to lie down
reírse de (e>i)	to laugh at (about)
sentirse (e>ie)	to feel
suicidarse	to commit suicide
tratarse de	to be a matter of

Sometimes, a verb is used reflexively to indicate that the action of the verb happened without the active participation of the subject:

caerse	to fall down
morirse (o>ue)	to die
dormirse (o>ue)	to fall asleep

Pronouns Used after a Preposition

A pronoun that follows a preposition is called the object of a preposition; in English, these pronouns are the same as any other object (indirect or direct) pronoun. In Spanish, however, there is a special case of pronouns that must be used whenever replacing a noun that follows a preposition. The pronouns in Table 12-5 are formally called *pronombres tónicos,* but it is easier to think of this case as the "prepositional pronouns." Notice that the pronouns used after a preposition are exactly like subject pronouns, with the exceptions of *mí* and *ti.* Also notice that *mí* has an accent mark, but *ti* does not.

Table 12-5   Object of a Preposition Pronoun Chart

	Singular	*Plural*
First person	*mí*	*nosotros/nosotras*
Second person	*ti*	*vosotros/vosotras*
Third person (masculine)	*él*	*ellos*
Third person (feminine)	*ella*	*ellas*
Third person (formal "you")	*usted*	*ustedes*

As you'll notice in the examples below, these pronouns may sound strange to the ears of an English speaker because the pronouns used after a preposition sound like direct and indirect object pronouns in English and like subject pronouns in Spanish (except for *mí* and *ti*).

La clase de álgebra es mejor para ella.
The algebra class is best for her.

Quiero viajar con ellos porque ellos conocen bien la nación.
I want to travel with them because they know the nation well.

Elena nos invita a nosotros porque somos buenos amigos.
She invites us because we are good friends.

When the preposition *con* is followed by the pronoun *mí,* the two words join to become a single word: *conmigo.* Note that the accent mark disappears from *mí* when *-go* is added. *Conmigo* is translated as "with me" and must be used whenever *con* is followed by *mí.* The same thing happens when *con* is followed by *ti: Contigo* means "with you" and must be used whenever the preposition *con* is followed by *ti.*

Alejandro debe explorar <u>conmigo</u> porque yo conozco todas las cuevas de Guadix.

Alejandro should explore <u>with me</u> because I know all the caves of Guadix.

Memo no quiere bailar <u>contigo</u>. Él desea bailar <u>conmigo</u>.

Memo doesn't want to dance <u>with you</u>. He wants to dance <u>with me</u>.

Demonstrative Pronouns

Demonstrative adjectives are placed in front of a noun to indicate the proximity of the noun to the speaker (see Chapter 10). A demonstrative pronoun is basically the same as a demonstrative adjective but is used to replace a noun rather than modify it. If the noun is understood rather than stated, you must use a demonstrative pronoun rather than a demonstrative adjective. Demonstrative pronouns and demonstrative adjectives are so similar that you can't hear the difference in spoken Spanish because the only difference between them is a written accent mark to differentiate the parts of speech.

In English, it is common to say "this one" or "these ones." Technically, the word "this" or "these" should be used alone to replace a noun, so the words "one" or "ones" are unnecessary and incorrect. In Spanish, the appropriate demonstrative pronoun is used alone to replace a noun:

Do you need that knife? No, I can use this (one).

¿Necesitas ese cuchillo? No, puedo usar éste.

The demonstrative pronouns in Table 12-6 are exactly like demonstrative adjectives except that each has an accent.

Table 12-6   Demonstrative Pronoun Chart

Singular	Masculine	Feminine	Plural	Masculine	Feminine
this	*éste*	*ésta*	these	*éstos*	*éstas*
that	*ése*	*ésa*	those	*ésos*	*ésas*
that (way over there)	*aquél*	*aquélla*	those (way over there)	*aquéllos*	*aquéllas*

When a demonstrative pronoun refers to an idea, a situation, or a concept, the appropriate neutral demonstrative pronoun is used. Because demonstrative pronouns do not replace a specific noun, they do not need to represent any gender and there is only one form. Notice in Table 12-7 that the neutral pronouns are the only demonstrative pronouns that do not have accent marks.

Table 12-7   Neutral Demonstrative Pronoun Chart

this	*esto*
that	*eso*
that (far away/long ago)	*aquello*

> *La venganza; <u>eso</u> es el problema.*
> Revenge; that is the problem.
>
> *<u>Eso</u> es su motivación.*
> That is her motivation.
>
> *<u>Esto</u> no me gusta.*
> I don't like it (an idea, thought, issue).

Possessive Pronouns

Possessive adjectives have two forms. The long form is used with a definite article to make a possessive pronoun. This form is used whenever the noun is being replaced rather than modified.

Possessive pronouns match the gender and number of the noun they replace, not the gender and number of the possessor of the noun. The possessive pronouns are usually listed in a chart similar to a conjugation chart (see Table 12-8).

The chart below shows how the possessive pronoun is based on the long form of the possessive adjective with a definite article. When there is no stated noun, the long form of the possessive adjective becomes a possessive pronoun. The possessive pronoun and the article that precedes it reflect the gender of the unstated but understood noun that is possessed.

Table 12-8   Possessive Pronoun Generation

Possessive Adjectives with a Noun	Possessive Pronouns with a Noun	Possessive Pronouns
mi libro (my book)	*el libro mío*	*el mío* (mine)
tu pluma (your pen)	*la pluma tuya*	*la tuya* (yours)
nuestro amigo (our friend)	*el amigo nuestro*	*el nuestro* (ours)
vuestra hermana (your sister)	*la hermana vuestra*	*la vuestra* (yours)
su madre (his/her/their/ your mother)	*la madre suya*	*la suya* (his/hers/ theirs/yours)

The order of the possessive pronouns in Table 12-9 reflects the order of the subject pronouns that would refer to the owner. For example, if the owner is *yo*, the possessive pronoun is either *el mío, la mía, los míos*, or *las mías*. The number (plural or singular) of the possessive pronoun matches the noun being owned, not the owner. Once you decide to use the possessive pronoun *el suyo*, for example, you only make it plural if it is in front of a plural noun. It doesn't matter how many people own the noun.

Table 12-9   Possessive Pronoun Chart

Persona o cosa poseída en singular y plural	
el mío, la mía, los míos, las mías	*el nuestro, la nuestra, los nuestros, las nuestras*
el tuyo, la tuya, los tuyos, las tuyas	*el vuestro, la vuestra, los vuestros, las vuestras*
el suyo, la suya, los suyos, las suyas	*el suyo, la suya, los suyos, las suyas*

A common usage of this version of possessive pronoun is after a form of the linking verbs *ser* or *estar*. Notice that the English possessive is different when it follows a form of "to be" ("is" or "are"). For example, "<u>my</u> book" becomes "the book is <u>mine</u>."

> *el libro <u>mío</u>* (<u>my</u> book)
> *El libro es <u>mío</u>.* (The book is <u>mine</u>.)
>
> *las fotografías bonitas <u>tuyas</u>* (<u>your</u> pretty pictures)
> *Las fotografías bonitas son tuyas.* (The pretty pictures are <u>yours</u>.)

la casa nuestra (our house)

La casa es nuestra. (The house is ours.)

las niñas suyas (his/her/their/your [formal] girls)

Las niñas son suyas. (The girls are his/hers/theirs/yours.)

Pronoun Placement

An "object of a preposition" pronoun is by definition placed after a preposition, but the other two types of object pronouns and the reflexive pronouns all go in the same place. Because it is common to use more than one of these pronouns at a time, you must know what order to follow:

A **R**eflexive pronoun is in front of an **I**ndirect object pronoun, and a **D**irect object is the last pronoun.

Use the memory device **RID** (Reflexive, Indirect, Direct) to remember the order of object pronouns in a sentence. You may have a reflexive pronoun and a direct object or an indirect object and a direct object, but rarely will all three be used together.

Note: When two object pronouns begin with the letter *l,* the first object pronoun is changed to *se.* This is not a reflexive pronoun although it looks like it. (See the section on indirect object pronouns earlier in this chapter.)

Every sentence must have at least one verb. If there is only one conjugated verb in the sentence, the RID pronouns must be placed in front of the conjugated verb (unless it is a command). In many cases there will be a conjugated verb used with an infinitive or present participle. The good news is that you can consistently place the RID pronouns in front of the conjugated verb no matter how many other verb forms are in the sentence.

La señora Gómez enseña las lecciones. (Mrs. Gomez teaches the lessons.)

La señora Gómez las enseña. (Mrs. Gomez teaches them.)

La señora Gómez se las enseña a los estudiantes. (Mrs. Gomez teaches them to the students.)

Victor no va a traer los regalos a la fiesta. (Victor isn't going to bring the gifts to the party.)

Victor no los va a traer a la fiesta. (Victor isn't going to bring them to the party.)

Victor no se los va a traer a la fiesta a los recién casados. (Victor isn't going to bring them for the newlyweds to the party.)

Orlando lleva a los novios. (Octavio takes the fiances.)

Orlando los lleva. (Octavio takes them.)

When the conjugated verb is followed by an infinitive, the RID pronouns may still be placed in front of the conjugated verb or they may be attached to the infinitive. They may not, however, be split up. If there is more than one RID pronoun, the pronouns stay together wherever you choose to place them.

Daniela la quiere llamar. (Daniela wants to call her.)

Daniela quiere llamarla. (Daniela wants to call her.)

Yoruba lo necesita mejorar. (Yoruba needs to improve it.)

Yoruba necesita mejorarlo. (Yoruba needs to improve it.)

RID pronouns may be attached to the present participle or placed in front of the conjugated verb. When a sentence is in the present progressive tense, there will be a conjugated form of *estar* and the present participle form of the verb. RID pronouns may be placed in front of the conjugated form of *estar* or attached to the end of the verb in the present participle form (ending in *-iendo* or *-ando*). This will mess up the natural stress, so you must add an accent mark to the vowel preceding *-ndo* when you attach any RID pronouns. If you choose to place the object pronouns in front of the conjugated form of *estar,* you can avoid using a written accent mark.

Juan la está llamando. (Juan is calling her.)

Juan está llamándola. (Juan is calling her.)

Other verbs that may be followed by the present participle include *ir, quedar, correr, andar, seguir, continuar,* and other verbs of motion.

Because RID pronouns may be attached to the present participle form of the verb, many mistakenly do the same with a past participle. RID pronouns are never attached to a past participle; they go in front of the conjugated form of *haber,* which will precede the past participle to create the perfect tenses:

Guada lo ha practicado toda la noche.

Guada has practiced it all night.

RID pronouns must be attached to affirmative commands. The addition of even one RID pronoun to the end of a command messes up the natural stress, so you must add an accent mark to what would be the next-to-last syllable before adding any pronoun to the end:

Báñate. (Take a bath.)

Levántense. (Get up [you guys].)

Although it is necessary to attach RID pronouns to the end of an affirmative command, the opposite is true if the command is negative. You must place any RID pronouns in front of a negative command:

No me lo digas. (Don't tell me that.)

Nunca me lo digas. (Never tell me that.)

Relative Pronouns

Relative pronouns refer to an antecedent in the main clause of the sentence and serve to introduce the subordinate clause. They do not have a written accent.

Que is used to refer to people or things. After the prepositions *a, con,* and *de,* it can only be used to refer to things:

El viaje que he reservado es para relajarme.

The trip that I have reserved is for me to relax.

El niño que habla es mi sobrino.

The boy that's speaking is my nephew.

La oficina en la que trabajamos no tiene aire acondicionador.

The office in which we work doesn't have an air conditioner.

Quien is used after the prepositions *a, de, en,* and *con* to refer only to people. As you can see in the first example below, this includes the personal *a.* Because it is not a question word, there is no accent:

Llamé a mi viejo vecino a quien extraño mucho.

I called my old neighbor whom I miss a lot.

El hombre de quien hablas es mi tío.

The man of whom you speak is my uncle.

Quien also can be used in place of *que* to refer to people if the clause is between commas:

Ese bombero, quien acaba de entrar, es un héroe.

That firefighter, who just entered, is a hero.

Los cantantes, quienes ganaron premios, van a una fiesta privada.

The singers, who won awards, are going to a private party.

The relative pronouns below refer to people or things and are especially used after some prepositions of more than one syllable:

el cual, los cuales, la cual, las cuales

el que, los que, la que, las que

Relative pronouns are also used to avoid confusion between two antecedents. They agree in number and gender with the antecedent:

Los edificios, cerca de los cuales robaron esa tienda, necesitan más seguridad.

Los edificios, cerca de los que robaron esa tienda, necesitan más seguridad.

The buildings, near which they robbed that store, need more security.

Mi cuñado, el cual vive en Barcelona, siempre visita el Parque Güell.

Mi cuñado, el que vive en Barcelona, siempre visita el Parque Güell.

My brother-in-law, who lives in Barcelona, always visits Güell Park.

El que, los que, la que, and *las que* can be used instead of *quien* (*quienes*) as the subject of the sentence:

El que no hace ejercicios no tiene buena salud.

Quien no hace ejercicios no tiene buena salud.

He that doesn't exercise doesn't have good health.

Los que persisten tienen éxito.

Quienes persisten tienen éxito.

Those that persevere have success.

Lo que and *lo cual* are neutral expressions that refer to an already expressed idea or concept:

El huracán no destruyó nuestro hotel, lo cual nos alegra.

El huracán no destruyó nuestro hotel, lo que nos alegra.

The hurricane didn't destroy our hotel, which makes us happy.

El equipo no ha ganado ningún partido, lo cual nos entristece.

El equipo no ha ganado ningún partido, lo que nos entristece.

The team hasn't won a game, which makes us sad.

When an idea or concept is implicit, understood, or previously mentioned, only *lo que* is used. In this case, *lo que* usually serves as the subject at the beginning of the sentence.

Lo que me gusta es su sonrisa.

What I like is his smile.

Lo que ellos quieren es mejorar el mundo.

What they want is to improve the world.

Cuyo, cuya, cuyos, and *cuyas* are used as possessive adjectives and must agree in gender and number with the object being possessed, not with the possessor. These will be used either within commas or following a preposition:

Las niñas, cuyos discos ya son famosos, tienen siete años.

The girls, whose records are already famous, are seven years old.

La policía, cuyas acciones salvaron a la víctima, recibió una medalla de honor.

The policewoman, whose actions saved the victim, received a bravery medal.

Sometimes, the adverbs *como, donde, cuanto,* and *cuando* are used instead of the relative pronouns:

¿Te impresiona la manera en que ella juega al fútbol?

¿Te impresiona la manera como ella juega al fútbol?

Are you impressed by the manner in which she plays soccer?

Ese es el gimnasio en el que yo hago ejercicios.

Ese es el gimnasio donde yo hago ejercicios.

That is the gym where (in which) I exercise.

Durante el tiempo en que ella trabajaba allí, ganaba mucho dinero.

Durante el tiempo cuando ella trabajaba allí, ganaba mucho dinero.

During the time she worked there, she earned a lot of money.

Chapter Checkout

1. What subject pronoun in Spanish is third person singular (masculine)?
2. What pronoun would replace the underlined word in the following sentence? *Ella le da <u>regalos</u> a su madre.*
3. Where do you place RID pronouns when using a negative command?
4. Conjugate the verb with the appropriate pronoun: *Martina y Juan _____ el sábado pasado.* (*casarse*)
5. Conjugate the verb in present tense with the appropriate reflexive pronoun: *Paulina ___ en la silla.* (*sentarse*)

Answers: 1. *él* **2.** *los* **3.** You place RID pronouns in front of the command form. **4.** *se casaron* **5.** *se sienta*

Chapter 13

PASSIVE VOICE, CONJUNCTIONS, AND MORE SENTENCE VARIATIONS

Chapter Check-In

❑ Passive voice versus active voice

❑ Using conjunctions to build longer sentences

❑ Writing negative sentences

❑ Asking questions

❑ Creating exclamations

There are many variations to the basic sentence structure of subject + verb + object. To exceed the elementary level of language usage, you must be prepared to understand and write negative sentences and sentences in the passive voice, as well as to ask questions. Also, you can express the relationship between thoughts in more complex sentences by using conjunctions to join two clauses.

Using the Passive Voice

The passive voice is used when the subject of the sentence is unimportant, unknown, or refers to a generalized subject. In the passive voice, the thing that receives the action of the verb comes first, followed by the verb "to be" and the past participle of the main verb. If the actual "subject" of the sentence is stated, it is called "the agent," and it follows the word "by." Consider the following examples of the passive voice in English:

The jewels were found by the explorers.

The game is won by the team that works hardest.

In English, it is recommended that you avoid the passive voice and write sentences in the active voice when writing any formal essay. In reality, the passive voice is quite common in English, both in spoken and written form.

You can tell a sentence is in the active voice if the subject of the sentence is actually doing the action of the verb rather than receiving the action of the verb. If the above examples of the passive voice were written in the active voice, they would read:

> The explorers found the jewels.
> The team that works hardest wins the game.

Passive voice created by *ser* and a past participle

In Spanish, the passive voice is both a commonly used and perfectly acceptable sentence structure. You will find it expressed in two forms. The easiest of the two forms to understand is created exactly as in English: The object or person receiving the action of the verb is followed by a form of the verb *ser* and a past participle. If the person doing the action of the verb (the agent) is stated, it follows the preposition *por:*

> *Las joyas fueron encontradas por los exploradores.*
> *El partido es ganado por el equipo que se esfuerza más.*

There are a few important details to notice in the above examples. The verb *ser* must be conjugated to go with the subject that precedes it. The subject of a sentence written in the passive voice would be the direct object of a sentence written in the active voice. For example:

Active voice: The politician writes the laws. *El político escribe las leyes.*

subject = the politician (*el político*)

Passive voice: The laws are written by the politician. *Las leyes son escritas por el político.*

subject = the laws (*las leyes*)

The past participle in a passive voice sentence would be the main verb in an active voice sentence. Because the past participle follows the verb *ser,* it is technically acting like an adjective. Therefore, you must change the ending of the past participle to match the noun it modifies, which is always the subject of a passive voice sentence (placed in front of *ser*). In the following examples, the ending of the past participle and the noun that it modifies are both underlined:

> *Las <u>casas</u> son pintad<u>as</u> por mis empleados.* (The houses are painted by my employees.)

Los regalos fueron dados para su día del santo. (The gifts were given for her saint's day.)

Sometimes, the person doing the action of the verb is not important, so the agent is not mentioned (as in the second example above).

Passive voice created by *se*

Spanish has another type of passive voice that doesn't exist in the English language. English speakers often use the pronoun "they" when referring to everyone in general (for example, "They sell books in that store"). While this sentence could be used when talking about one specific group of individuals, it is also a way to generalize. The passive voice can also be used to generalize (for example, "Books are sold in that store"). When the subject is not stated and the sentence is in the passive voice, it is understood to be an unknown or generalized subject. For this reason, the Spanish construction that is used to express this idea is considered another type of passive voice.

This type of sentence is created in Spanish by using the reflexive pronoun *se* followed by the verb to express the idea that "one does it" or "they do it" or "you (in general) do it." The best way to understand this construction is through examples:

Se venden libros en esa tienda.

They sell books in that store.

Books are sold in that store.

Se toma mucho café en Sudamérica.

They drink a lot of coffee in South America.

A lot of coffee is drunk in South America.

Se puede evitar muchos problemas dándole mantenimiento al coche.

One can avoid many problems by maintaining one's car.

Many problems can be avoided by maintaining one's car.

Se encuentran muchos problemas cuando hay una guerra.

One encounters many problems when there is a war.

Many problems are encountered when there is a war.

A few details are necessary to effectively build a sentence by using the reflexive pronoun to make a sentence passive. First of all, notice that the verb is conjugated in the third person singular (*él*) form or the third person plural (*ellos*) form. The one you use depends on the noun that follows the verb. If the noun is singular, the verb is in the *él* form. If the noun that follows the verb is plural, the *ellos* form of the verb is used.

Passive voice created by *hay que*

Another pseudo-passive voice construction is created by using the word *hay*, followed by *que*, followed by an infinitive. For example:

Hay que apoyar a los músicos latinos.

This is a highly idiomatic sentence structure that follows no rules and has no English equivalent. This sentence can be translated into English as, "One must support Latin musicians," or, "Latin musicians must be supported."

Conjunctions

A conjunction joins two phrases (basically two sentences) together. The most common conjunctions are discussed in this section. In some cases, an explanation is necessary because English conjunctions don't always have exact Spanish equivalents.

Pero and *mas*

The conjunction *pero* joins two independent clauses and means "but" (as in "however"):

Quieren asistir al concierto de Orishas <u>pero</u> no pueden viajar a Francia.
They want to attend the Orishas concert <u>but</u> they can't travel to France.

The conjunction *mas* means "but" (as in "other than"). *Mas* is a synonym of *pero*. However, when the word "but" is used to indicate an exception to the norm, the word *mas que* is used:

No compraría un nuevo coche <u>mas</u> lo necesito tanto.
I wouldn't buy a new car <u>but</u> I need it so much.

Nadie <u>mas que</u> Luis quiere asistir al concierto de Ranchero.
Nobody <u>but</u> Luis wants to attend the Ranchero concert.

Sino

The conjunction *sino* means "but rather" and is only used when the first part of the sentence is negative and the second part contradicts the first:

Shakira no canta su nueva canción en inglés <u>sino</u> en español.
Shakira doesn't sing her new song in English <u>but rather</u> in Spanish.

If a verb immediately follows *sino,* it must be in the infinitive form:

> *No queremos trabajar <u>sino</u> escaparnos a la playa.*
>
> We don't want to work <u>but rather</u> escape to the beach.

If a clause that includes a subject and a conjugated verb follows *sino,* you must use *sino que:*

> *Tú no hiciste tus quehaceres <u>sino que</u> jugaste juegos de video.*
>
> You didn't do your chores <u>but rather</u> you played video games.

Another time *sino* is necessary is in the Spanish equivalent of the expression "not only . . . but also," which is *no solamente . . . sino también:*

> *<u>No solamente</u> los niños <u>sino también</u> los padres querrán ver la nueva película de Disney.*
>
> <u>Not only</u> the kids <u>but also</u> the parents will want to see the new Disney flick.

O and *y*

The conjunction *o* means "or" and is used to join two singular nouns; the subject (made up of the two nouns) is considered singular, and the verb is in singular form:

> *Juan <u>o</u> Carlos baila el flamenco hoy.*
>
> Juan <u>or</u> Carlos dances the flamenco today.

Above, the verb *baila* is in the *él* form because only one of the possible subjects is doing the action of the verb. If the nouns joined by *o* are both plural, however, the plural form of the verb is used:

> *Mis vecinos <u>o</u> mis amigos cuidan a mis perros cuando viajo.*
>
> My neighbors <u>or</u> my friends care for my dogs when I travel.

O changes to *u* when it precedes a word that begins with *o* or *ho:*

> *No sé si su vuelo llega a Miami u Orlando.*
>
> I don't know if his flight arrives in Miami or Orlando.

> *¿Debo decir buenos días u hola?*
>
> Should I say good morning or hello?

The conjunction *y* means "and." It is used to create a compound subject; thus, the verb is in a plural form.

> *Memo <u>y</u> Amberina bailan bien la salsa.*
>
> Memo <u>and</u> Amberina dance the salsa well.

Above, the verb *bailan* is in the *ellos* form because the conjunction *y* creates a compound verb.

Y changes to *e* when it precedes a word that begins with *i* or *hi:*

> *Lilia e Ignacio se casan este junio.*
> Lilia <u>and</u> Ignacio are getting married this June.

> *No hay nada mejor que agua e hielo cuando tiene sed.*
> There is nothing better than water <u>and</u> ice when you're thirsty.

In a negative sentence, the conjunction *ni* is used as the translation for the English words "neither" and "nor." Contrary to the English rule, in Spanish the verb with two subjects joined by *ni . . . ni* requires the plural conjugation.

> <u>*Ni*</u> *Julia* <u>*ni*</u> *Manolo entienden la lección.*
> <u>Neither</u> Julia <u>nor</u> Manolo understands the lesson.

Subordinate conjunctions

Subordinate conjunctions are followed by a dependent clause. Although they are not always followed by the subjunctive, you have already seen some of these as subjunctive indicators in Chapter 7.

Some common subordinate conjunctions include the following:

> *a condición que* (under the condition that)
>
> *a fin (de) que* (so that)
>
> *a menos que* (unless)
>
> *a no ser que* (unless)
>
> *a que* (in order that)
>
> *antes (de) que* (before)
>
> *como si* (as if [followed by past subjunctive])
>
> *con tal (de) que* (provided that)
>
> *en caso de que* (in case that)
>
> *para que* (so that)
>
> *por más que* (no matter how much that)
>
> *sin que* (without [that])

Some conjunctions are always followed by the indicative because their meaning indicates a certainty of the occurrence of the verb that follows:

ahora que (now that)

debido a que (due to the fact that)

desde que (since [a time when something happened])

mientras (whereas)

porque (because)

puesto que (since [because])

ya que (now that)

The following subordinate conjunctions may be followed by either the indicative or subjunctive:

a pesar de que (in spite of the fact that)

aun cuando (even if, although)

así que (so that)

cuando (when)

de manera que (so that)

de modo que (so that)

después (de) que (after)

en cuanto (as soon as)

hasta que (until)

luego que (as soon as)

mientras que (while)

salvo que (unless)

si (if)

siempre que (provided that)

tan pronto como (as soon as)

When followed by the subjunctive, the conjunction *aunque* is translated as "even if" because there is no certainty that the clause that follows will occur:

La amará para siempre <u>aunque</u> ella se case con otro hombre.

He will love her forever <u>even if</u> she marries another man.

When followed by the indicative, *aunque* is translated as "even though" because the indication is that the clause that follows will definitely occur:

> *J.Lo no se casará con él <u>aunque</u> él escribió esa canción sobre ella.*
>
> J.Lo will not marry him <u>even though</u> he wrote that song about her.

The conjunctions *así que, de modo que,* and *de manera que* mean "so that" and may be followed by either the indicative or the subjunctive. If the action of the main clause has not yet occurred, the verb of the second clause is in the subjunctive. The first two examples that follow show the indicative tense. The third example shows the subjunctive.

> *Enviamos muchas cartas <u>así que</u> recibiremos algo en el correo.*
>
> We send many letters <u>so that</u> we'll receive something in the mail.

> *Ahorran su dinero ahora <u>de modo que</u> tendrán una jubilación con muchas opciones.*
>
> They save their money now <u>so that</u> they'll have a retirement with many opportunities.

> *Alberto rompió la carta <u>de manera que</u> nunca pudiera arreglarla.*
>
> Alberto tore the letter <u>so that</u> he could never fix it.

The conjunction *como* means "in the same way as," "like," "as," or "since":

> *Te amo <u>como</u> amo a mi hermano.*
>
> I love you <u>in the same way as</u> my brother.

> *Él se comporta <u>como</u> el diablo.*
>
> He acts <u>like</u> the devil.

> *Queremos un carro grande <u>de manera que</u> todos quepamos.*
>
> We want a big car <u>so that</u> we can all fit.

> *<u>Como</u> tienes 15 años, ya puedes conducir con la licencia en este estado.*
>
> <u>Since</u> you're 15 years old, you can drive with a driver's license in this state.

When the second clause expresses the purpose for the action of the first clause, use the conjunction *para que.* The verb following *para que* is in the subjunctive:

> *Ana estudia mucho <u>para que</u> sus padres se sientan orgullosos de ella.*
>
> Ana studies a lot <u>so that</u> her parents are proud of her.

When the second clause indicates the reason behind the first clause, use the conjunction *porque*. If a question includes the words *por qué*, the answer uses the conjunction *porque:*

> *¿Por qué trajiste esa maleta contigo? La traje porque tengo que salir para Chicago.*
>
> Why did you bring that suitcase with you? I brought it <u>because</u> I have to leave for Chicago.

In Spanish, there are several ways to indicate an underlying reason in the way English does with the word "since." *Puesto que* is generally used between two clauses when the second clause provides a reason for the first:

> *No vamos al parque puesto que llueve mucho.*
>
> We're not going to the park <u>since</u> it's raining so much.

Ya que can precede an introductory clause that provides the reason for the second clause. When *ya que* is between two clauses, the second one provides the reason for the first. Notice in the examples below that a comma is necessary when the conjunction precedes the introductory clause:

> *Ya que llegaste temprano, podemos tomar el próximo autobús.*
>
> <u>Since</u> you arrived early, we can take the next bus.
>
> *Podemos tomar el próximo autobús ya que llegaste temprano.*
>
> We can take the next bus <u>since</u> you arrived early.

Correlative conjunctions

Correlative conjunctions are used together surrounding other words in a sentence. The correlative conjunctions in Spanish include:

> *ni . . . ni* (neither . . . nor)
>
> *o . . . o* (either . . . or)
>
> *ya . . . ya* (whether . . . or [sometimes . . . sometimes])
>
> *así . . . como* (both . . . and)
>
> *no sólo . . . sino también* (not only . . . but also)
>
> *no bien . . . cuando* (no sooner . . . than)
>
> *tanto . . . como* (as much . . . as)
>
> *apenas . . . cuando* (scarcely . . . when)

Here are some other conjunctive phrases:

aun (even)

empero (notwithstanding)

sin embargo (nevertheless)

entretanto que (meanwhile)

mas bien que (rather than)

mientras tanto (meanwhile)

ni siquiera (not even)

no obstante (not withstanding)

Negatives

A Spanish sentence utilizes multiple negative words in one sentence, and there must be a negative word in front of the verb for a clause to be negative. If no other negative word precedes the verb, the word *no* is placed (preceding any RID pronouns; see Chapter 12) in front of the conjugated verb.

The use of the following affirmative words and their negative counterparts is explained below.

Affirmatives	Negatives
sí (yes)	*no* (no)
alguien (somebody)	*nadie* (nobody)
algo (something)	*nada* (nothing)
también (also)	*tampoco* (neither)
con (with)	*sin* (without)
o . . . o (either . . . or)	*ni . . . ni* (neither . . . nor)
siempre (always)	*nunca, jamás* (never)
alguno (algún, alguna, algunos, algunas) (some)	*ninguno (ningún, ninguna, ningunos, ningunas)* (none, not any)

Alguno is used in front of the preposition *de* to mean "any" or "some." When this word directly precedes a singular masculine noun, it shortens to *algún*. The other forms follow typical gender and number patterns and precede the nouns they modify:

> <u>*Alguno*</u> *(de ellos) vendrá a la fiesta. Ella comprará* <u>*algún*</u> *bolso.*
>
> Any (one of them) will come to the party. She will buy a bag (any kind).

Algunos problemas son imposibles de resolver. Algunas veces es difícil continuar.

Some problems are impossible to resolve. Sometimes it's difficult to continue.

When a sentence is negative, *ninguno* is used to mean "none" when preceding the preposition *de* or when used alone to replace a noun. When immediately preceding a masculine noun, it shortens to *ningún;* the other forms show the gender and number of the noun they precede:

No tengo ningún problema. No me dan ninguna libertad.

I don't have any problem. They don't give me any freedom.

Algo means something and *nada* means nothing. When a sentence is negative, *nada* must be used rather than *algo* — even when the English sentence would use "something." *Nada* can also be used as an adverb that has the effect of a negative intensifier. In this case, it means "not at all":

Tú no has dormido nada — no puedes conducir.

You haven't slept at all — you can't drive.

Lolita no trabaja nada.

Lolita doesn't work at all.

When *algo* is used in a similar fashion, it means "somewhat":

Ese proyecto es algo complicado.

That project is somewhat complicated.

Estoy algo preocupada.

I'm somewhat concerned.

Questions

Question words can be tricky because Spanish and English do not use them in exactly the same way. This section explains the difficulties of Spanish question words. (See Chapter 2 for more-in-depth coverage).

Cuál and *qué*

Cuál and *qué* can both be translated as "what" or "which," but they are not interchangeable. Each must be used in specific situations to elicit specific information. When *cuál* refers to more than one item, it must be *cuáles*.

Qué is always used in front of any noun or verb (except *ser* and *preferir*) to mean "which" or "what":

¿Qué vacaciones planeas?

What vacation are you planning?

¿Qué libro quieres leer?

Which book do you want to read?

Both *qué* and *cuál* may be used with the verb *ser,* but each elicits a different type of answer. When *qué* is used in front of *ser,* it requests an explanation or a definition; *cuál* is used with *ser* to request a specific example:

> Question: *¿Qué es la dirección?* (asks for an explanation of the word *dirección*)
>
> Answer: *La dirección es el número y nombre de la calle, la ciudad y el estado y el código postal.*
>
> Question: *¿Cuál es la dirección?* (asks for a specific address)
>
> Answer: *La dirección es 322 Altavista Lane, Sante Fe, New Mexico.*

Prepositions in questions

In Spanish, you may not end a sentence in a preposition, so the question word "where" must have any preposition in front of it, rather than at the end of the sentence. It is quite common to end a question about origin with a preposition in English: "Where is he from?" for example. The Spanish equivalent of, "Where is he from?" must be stated, "From where is he?" (*¿De dónde es él?*).

The same is true for the preposition *a* (which means "to"). Sometimes, this preposition is not stated in an English sentence, but any time the question asks where a noun is headed (such as "Where are you going to?"), the word *dónde* must have *a* in front of or attached to it (*¿A dónde vas tú?* or *¿Adónde vas tú?*).

In Chapter 10, you learned the distinct uses for the prepositions *por* and *para.* One reason for using *por* is to express "due to" or "because of." When a question is asking for a response that will provide the reason behind something, *por qué* is used because it asks "why?" (as in "due to what reason?").

> *¿Por qué conduces el coche de tu hermano?*
>
> Why (due to what reason) are you driving your brother's car?

One reason for using *para* is to indicate the purpose for doing something. When the question "why" is asking, "For what purpose?" use the question phrase *para qué:*

> *¿Para qué sirve esta herramienta? Sirve para arreglar las botellas.*
> For what does this tool serve? It serves to fix the bottles.

> *¿Para qué estudia Emi? Ella estudia para pasar su examen.*
> Why is Emi studying? She is studying to pass her exam.

The personal *a* is used when the direct or indirect object of a sentence is a word that refers to a person.

> *¿A quién tiró la pelota?*
> To whom did he [she, formal you] throw the ball?

> *¿A quién llamaste tú?*
> Whom did you call?

To indicate the possessor of an item in Spanish, the item is followed by the preposition *de* and the owner. To request this information, *de* is followed by the question words *quién* or *quiénes,* depending on whether you expect the owner to be one person or more. The English equivalents are "Whose?" or "Of whom?":

> *¿De quién es el Pontiac azul en el aparcamiento?*
> Whose is the blue Pontiac in the parking lot?

> *¿De quiénes son esos coches en la esquina?*
> Of whom are those cars on the corner? (assuming the answer is more than one person)

The good news is that the question words *cuándo* (when?) and *cómo* (how?) are basically used the same in Spanish as in English.

Exclamations

Exclamations are expressions of surprise or amazement that usually start with a question word but are not questions (such as, "How beautiful!" or, "What a nice guy!"). The specific question word used in a Spanish exclamation depends on the part of speech of the word that follows it. Notice in all the examples below that the question words still carry accents even though they are no longer asking questions.

Qué

Qué is used in front of nouns, adjectives, and adverbs to mean "how" or "what a":

> *¡Qué interesantes son ellos!* (adjective)
> How interesting they are!

> *¡Qué rápidamente pasa la vida!* (adverb)
> How quickly life passes!

> *¡Qué atleta es mi sobrina!* (noun)
> What an athlete my niece is!

Cuánto

If the noun is quantifiable, an adapted form of the word *cuánto* may precede it to express surprise at the amount:

> *¡Cuánto dinero gasté durante mi vacación!*
> How much money I spent during my vacation!

> *¡Cuántos problemas tenemos!*
> How many problems we have!

Cuánto may also be used in front of a verb to express surprise at how much someone is doing that verb. When followed by a verb, *cuánto* must end in *-o:*

> *¡Cuánto bailaste anoche!*
> How much you danced last night!

Cómo

Cómo may also precede a verb to express surprise at the manner in which the verb was done:

> *¡Cómo celebramos durante la fiesta!*
> How we celebrated during the party!

> *¡Cómo canta el pájaro!*
> How the bird sings!

Chapter Checkout

In the blank provided, write the correct exclamation word.

1. ¡_____ *interesante es este programa!*

2. ¡_____ *canta Domingo! Un pájaro no canta mejor.*

3. ¡_____ *bien bailan esos flamenqueros!*

Switch the order of each sentence to convert it to the passive voice, maintaining the same verb tense.

4. *Todos amaban a la princesa.*

5. *Los oficiales encontraron al ladrón.*

6. *Nosotros conducimos el Mercedes.*

Write the correct Spanish conjunction to represent the English word in the sentence.

7. *Juana* (and) *Inez son amigas.*

8. *Salvador quiere ir* (but) *no puede.*

9. *A él no le gusta esta guitarra* (but) *ese piano.*

Write the negative sentence below in Spanish.

10. She never gives anyone anything.

Answers: 1. *Qué* **2.** *Cómo* **3.** *Qué* **4.** *La princesa era amada por todos.* **5.** *El ladrón fue encontrado por los oficiales.* **6.** *El Mercedes es conducido por nosotros.* **7.** *e* **8.** *pero* **9.** *sino* **10.** *Ella nunca le da nada a nadie.*

Chapter 14

PAST SUBJUNCTIVE AND SEQUENCE OF TENSES

Chapter Check-In

❑ Creating the past subjunctive verb forms

❑ Determining whether the present or past subjunctive is appropriate

❑ Reviewing subjunctive indicators with past tense examples

❑ Utilizing past subjunctive formulas

There is another subjunctive tense to use when the subjunctive is necessary but the sentence is in a past tense. Technically, it is called the **imperfect subjunctive,** but that title is unnecessarily confusing. There is only one way to put the subjunctive in the past tense, and because it's based on the preterit tense, it's more fitting to call it the "past subjunctive." Before you can learn how the past subjunctive is used in sentences, however, you must first learn to create the forms.

Verb Rules for Forming the Past Subjunctive

All verbs, without exception, follow the same rules for forming the past subjunctive; thus, the past subjunctive tense has no irregular verbs. Although that sounds simple, there is one difficulty: The first rule is to start with the third person plural form of the preterit. There are a plethora of verbs that are irregular in the preterit, but once you've remembered the *ellos* form, you can easily turn the preterit into the past subjunctive.

All verbs end in *-ron* in the third person preterit form. Remove the *-ron* and add the endings in Table 14-1.

Table 14-1   Past Subjunctive Verb Endings

Subject	Ending	Subject	Ending
yo	-ra	nosotros/nosotras	(accented vowel) + -ramos
tú	-ras	vosotros/vosotras	-rais
él	-ra	ellos	-ran
ella	-ra	ellas	-ran
usted	-ra	ustedes	-ran

Notice that the vowel in front of the *nosotros/nosotras* ending must have an accent mark. As you can see in the *tener* example in Table 14-2, that is *é* for some verbs. And as you can see in Table 14-3, *á* may be the accented vowel in front of some *nosotros/nosotras* endings.

The verb *tener* in Table 14-2 serves as a good example because it shows how different a verb can look in the past subjunctive due to the fact that the *ellos* preterit form often has little in common with the infinitive form.

Table 14-2   Past Subjunctive of the Verb *Tener*

Subject	Verb	Subject	Verb
yo	tuviera	nosotros/nosotras	tuviéramos
tú	tuvieras	vosotros/vosotras	tuvierais
él	tuviera	ellos	tuvieran
ella	tuviera	ellas	tuvieran
usted	tuviera	ustedes	tuvieran

Remember the following rule:

Preterit *ellos* form: *tuvieron* minus the *-ron* = *tuvie-*

Table 14-3   Past Subjunctive of the Verb *Hablar*

Subject	Verb	Subject	Verb
yo	hablara	nosotros/nosotras	habláramos
tú	hablaras	vosotros/vosotras	hablarais
él	hablara	ellos	hablaran

Subject	Verb	Subject	Verb
ella	hablara	ellas	hablaran
usted	hablara	ustedes	hablaran

Remember the following rule:

Preterit *ellos* form: *hablaron* minus the *-ron* = *habla-*

There is another set of endings, which is less frequently used, that can be used instead of the *-ra/-ras/-ramos/-rais/-ran* endings to create the past subjunctive. In Table 14-4, notice that the letters *-se* replace *-ra* in every form. To use these endings, you must also use the *ellos* form of the preterit minus the *-ron* ending. There is no special reason why you would have to use the *-se* endings because they are exactly the same as the *-ra* endings; just be prepared to understand what they mean when you hear or see them.

Table 14-4   The Other Past Subjunctive Endings

Subject	Ending	Subject	Ending
yo	-se	nosotros/nosotras	(accented vowel) + -semos
tú	-ses	vosotros/vosotras	-seis
él	-se	ellos	-sen
ella	-se	ellas	-sen
usted	-se	ustedes	-sen

Table 14-5   The Verb *Tener* Using the Other Past Subjunctive Endings

Subject	Verb	Subject	Verb
yo	tuviese	nosotros/nosotras	tuviésemos
tú	tuvieses	vosotros/vosotras	tuvieseis
él	tuviese	ellos	tuviesen
ella	tuviese	ellas	tuviesen
usted	tuviese	ustedes	tuviesen

Remember the following rule:

Preterit *ellos* form: *tuvieron* minus the *-ron* = *tuvie-*

Table 14-6   The Verb *Hablar* Using the Other Past Subjunctive Endings

Subject	Verb	Subject	Verb
yo	hablase	nosotros/nosotras	hablásemos
tú	hablases	vosotros/vosotras	hablaseis
él	hablase	ellos	hablasen
ella	hablase	ellas	hablasen
usted	hablase	ustedes	hablasen

There are so many irregularities in the preterit tense that it is necessary to review the preterit tense (see Chapter 4) with a special focus on the third person plural (*ellos*) form.

Sequence of Tenses

Once you have mastered the construction of the past subjunctive, the next step is to understand when to use it. In Chapters 7 and 8, you learned the logic behind the use of the present subjunctive and were introduced to a number of "subjunctive indicators" that represent each of the reasons for using the subjunctive. The same indicators are used to predict the need for the past subjunctive.

When the sentence is in a past tense and there is a reason to use the subjunctive, you must use the past subjunctive. In other words, when there is a subjunctive indicator in front of the *que,* and the verb in front of the *que* is in a past tense, the verb that follows the *que* is conjugated in the past subjunctive.

The term "sequence of tenses" is used for the rules governing the use of the correct subjunctive tense. There are three tenses that are considered past tenses: the preterit, the imperfect, and the conditional. Once you can identify that the subjunctive is appropriate for the sentence, the sequence of tenses is utilized. There are only two simple subjunctive tenses, past and present. The tense of the verb before *que* determines whether you use the present subjunctive or the past subjunctive after *que*.

The sequence of tenses for subjunctive sentences declares that the past subjunctive must be used in the second clause if the verb in the first clause is in either the preterit, the imperfect, or the conditional. Remember that the present subjunctive is used in the second clause if the verb in the first clause is in the present or future tense or if it is a command.

The chart below is important to memorize in order to determine which of the two subjunctive tenses is appropriate; this chart, however, can be used only if you have already determined that the subjunctive mood is necessary because of the presence of a subjunctive indicator.

Tense of the First Verb		Tense of the Second Verb
Present		
Future	*que*	Present Subjunctive
Command		
Conditional		
Preterit	*que*	Past Subjunctive
Imperfect		

Subjunctive Indicators

You have already practiced using the present subjunctive in the previous chapters of this book without realizing it; all the sample sentences in Chapters 7 and 8 had a verb in the first clause conjugated in either the present or future tense or in a command form.

You also learned to determine when the subjunctive mood is appropriate by using a list of indicators representing the various reasons behind the use of the subjunctive. Below are examples of each of the subjunctive indicators in sentences with the verb in the first clause in the preterit, the imperfect, or the conditional tense, which requires that the verb following *que* be in the past subjunctive mood.

Remember, the past subjunctive is used after verbs that indicate volition, desire, or an indirect command. Because it is so important to know the subjunctive indicators, the following list presents a sample sentence of each for you to review. The subjunctive indicator is in bold print for easy recognition. A variety of regular and irregular verbs will be in the subjunctive after *que*. The verb that is conjugated in the subjunctive mood is <u>underlined</u> so that you pay close attention to how verbs are conjugated in the past subjunctive.

*Ella me **aconsejaba** que underline{estudiara} más.*
She used to advise me that I should study more.

*El padre de Marcos no **aprobó** que underline{condujera} el coche.*
Marcos' father didn't approve that he drove the car.

*Ellas te **dijeron** que underline{hicieras} tu tarea.*
They told you to do your homework.
(They told you that you should have done your homework.)

*Mis padres no **dejaron** que yo underline{viajara} a El Salvador.*
My parents didn't permit me to travel to El Salvador.

*Los profesores **se empeñaban** en que sus estudiantes los underline{escucharan}.*
The teachers insisted that their students listen to them.

*Yo **exigí** que mis colegas underline{se reunieran} conmigo inmediatamente.*
I demanded that my colleagues meet with me immediately.

*Me **gustaba** que las presentaciones underline{fueran} interesantes.*
I liked that the presentations were interesting.

*El jefe **hacía** que underline{trabajáramos} los sábados . . .*
The boss would make us work on Saturdays but . . .

*Un árbol **impidió** que ella underline{condujera} por la calle.*
A tree impeded that she drive along the street.

*Las revolucionarias **insistieron** que el presidente underline{viniera}.*
The revolutionaries insisted that the president come.

*El líder **mandó** que los soldados underline{lucharan} en la batalla.*
The leader ordered that the soldiers fight in the battle.

*Yoli **pidió** que el mozo underline{trajera} las tapas.*
Yoli requested that the waiter bring tapas.

*Shakira no **permitía** que nadie underline{tradujera} la letra de sus canciones al inglés.*
Shakira didn't permit anyone to translate her lyrics to English.

*Jorge **prefería** que Juana underline{fuera} con él al Caribe.*
Jorge would prefer that Juana go with him to the Caribbean.

*La ley **prohibía** que los ciudadanos underline{fumaran} cigarrillos.*
The law prohibited that the citizens smoke cigarettes.

*Yo **propuse** que tú y yo <u>nos casáramos</u>.*
I proposed that we get married.

*Los peregrinos **rogaban** para que Dios <u>bendijera</u> su viaje.*
The pilgrims prayed so that God would bless their voyage.

*La madrastra **sugirió** que sus hijas <u>se probaran</u> el zapato de cristal.*
The stepmother suggested that her daughters try on the crystal shoe.

***Suplicamos** para que los pobres <u>tuvieran</u> comida.*
We prayed that the poor would have food.

*Ella no **deseaba** que yo la <u>llamara</u>.*
She didn't want me to call her.

*Celia **esperaba** que le <u>dieran</u> el premio.*
Celia hoped that they'd give her the prize.

***Necesitábamos** que tú <u>supieras</u> las respuestas.*
We needed you to know the answers.

*Carlos no **quería** que su hija <u>tocara</u> el tambor.*
Carlos didn't want his daughter to play the drums.

Ojalá

One exception where you will need to use the subjunctive mood with or without *que* is with the expression *ojalá*. The Arabic expression *ojalá* means "may Allah grant that" and is used in Spanish to express "hopefully, I wish, God grant" or "if only." Because *ojalá* is impersonal, there is no subject and it is technically not conjugated. It is the most consistent subjunctive indicator in the language and should always be followed by the subjunctive mood—even if there is no *que*.

When the past subjunctive follows *ojalá*, there are two possible meanings. The first indicates hope about something that occurred in the past without the outcome known to the speaker:

***Ojalá** <u>ganáramos</u> el partido.*
We wish we might win the game.

***Ojalá** que no <u>perdieran</u> mucho dinero en el casino.*
If only they wouldn't lose much money in the casino.

The past subjunctive is also used after *ojalá* to indicate that the statement is obviously contrary to fact, or to refer to a hypothetical situation.

Ojalá yo fuera su jefe!
I wish I were his boss!

Ojalá que tuvieras las direcciones.
If only you had the directions.

Introductory clauses that show emotion

Another group of subjunctive indicators are introductory clauses that express emotion. The following examples include a subjunctive indicator in a past tense (in bold) and the verb after *que* in the past subjunctive (underlined).

*Les **conmovía** que su hijo quisiera acompañarlos a la oficina.*
It moved them that their son wanted to accompany them to the office.

*¿No **te desilusionó** que no hubiera Papá Noel en realidad?*
Didn't it disappoint you that there really was no Santa Claus?

*Le **emocionaba** que su novio le trajera flores de vez en cuando.*
It thrilled her that her boyfriend brought her flowers from time to time.

*Le **encantó** a ella que su ciudad favorita no hubiera cambiado.*
It delighted her that her favorite city hadn't changed.

*Me **sorprendió** que tú quisieras ese coche.*
It surprised me that you wanted that car.

*Me **entristecía de** que ella me visitara sólo para investigar su libro.*
It made me sad that she visited me just to investigate her book.

The Past Subjunctive Formulas

The past subjunctive is used with the conditional tense to create contrary-to-fact speculation. "If I were the president, I would improve the country," is an example of such a sentence in English. The same sentence can be written in the opposite order: "I would improve the country if I were the president." The Spanish version uses the past subjunctive after the word "if" (*si*) and puts the other verb in the sentence in the conditional tense. The formulas below are meant to demonstrate that regardless of in which order the sentence is written, the verb that follows *si* is in the past subjunctive and the other verb is in the conditional:

si + past subjunctive + conditional

Si ellos fueran más inteligentes, no comprarían esta casa.

If they were smarter, they wouldn't buy this house.

conditional + si + past subjunctive

Ellos vendrían a mi fiesta si sus padres les permitieran.

They would come to my party if their parents would permit them.

Another use of the past subjunctive is after the conjunction *como si* ("as if" in English). Although the verb in the first clause may be in almost any tense, the verb that follows *como si* is always in the past subjunctive because it means that what follows is contrary to reality.

Ella hablaba como si fuera princesa.

She was talking as if she were a princess.

El gobierno gasta dinero como si no tuviera ningún límite.

The government spends money as if it had no limit.

Chapter Checkout

For the following sentences, write the verb in parentheses in the past subjunctive and underline the word or phrase that indicates that you must use the past subjunctive.

1. *Me sorprendió que tú _____ ir conmigo al baile. (querer)*
2. *No me alegraba de que Pepe _____ otra chica a la fiesta. (traer)*
3. *Tú nos tratas como si nosotros _____ tus empleados. (ser)*
4. *Marianela prefería que sus hijos _____ la mesa. (poner)*
5. *Ojalá que mi amor ___ conmigo. (estar)*

Answers: 1. *sorprendió; quisieras* **2.** *me alegraba; trajera* **3.** *como si; fuéramos* **4.** *prefería; pusieran* **5.** *Ojalá; estuviera*

CQR REVIEW

Use this CQR Review to reinforce and practice what you've learned in this book. After you work through the review questions, you'll be well on your way to understanding the Spanish language.

Chapter 1

1. If a word ends in a vowel, the natural stress is on the
   a. last syllable.
   b. next-to-last syllable.
   c. first syllable.

2. True or False: The letter *h* sounds the same in English and Spanish.

3. True or False: The letters *b* and *v* sound the same in Spanish.

4. What word has the same *c* sound as the word *cama*?
   a. *cantar*
   b. *centro*
   c. *ciencia*

Chapter 2

5. Translate to a "yes or no" question in Spanish: Does Jaime work here?

6. Write the appropriate question word:

   ¿_____ es la fecha de hoy?

7. Write the appropriate question word:

   ¿_____ libro leíste anoche?

8. Write the question word necessary to elicit the response in parentheses:

   ¿_____ almorzaste ayer? (en la cafetería)

Chapter 3

9. Write the appropriate present tense form of the verb for the following sentence:

Tú y yo _____ la comida muy bien. (cocinar)

10. Create a conjugation chart with the present tense forms of the verb *seguir.*

11. Create a conjugation chart with the present tense forms of the verb *perder.*

12. Translate to Spanish: Bela and Melina want to bring the sodas.

Chapter 4

13. Write the appropriate preterit tense form of the verb for the following sentence:

Thalia _____ un vestido de luces durante los premios. (llevar)

14. Create a conjugation chart with the preterit tense forms of the verb *almorzar.*

15. Create a conjugation chart with the imperfect tense forms of the verb *ser.*

Chapter 5

16. Translate to Spanish: Lolita will contradict the truth.

17. Translate to Spanish: I would leave.

18. True or False: All of the conditional tense endings have an accent on the letter *i.*

Chapter 6

19. Write the *él* form of the helping verb *haber* in the following tenses: present, preterit, and imperfect.

20. Create the past participle form for the following verbs: *tener, leer,* and *ver.*

21. Translate to Spanish: We have written many letters.

22. True or False: The past participle changes *o* to *a* when used after *haber* in a compound tense.

Chapter 7

23. Write the present subjunctive conjugation of the *yo* form for the following verbs: *seguir* and *tener.*

24. Write the present subjunctive conjugation of the *ellos* form for the following verbs: *conducir* and *dormir.*

Chapter 8

25. Decide whether the subjunctive or indicative is appropriate and write the correct form of the verb in parentheses:

No queremos que el mundo _____ contaminado. (ser)

26. Decide whether the subjunctive or indicative is appropriate and write the correct form of the verb in parentheses:

No dudo que Edmundo _____ vivir. (merecer)

27. True or False: The subjunctive is always used after expressions of certainty.

Chapter 9

28. Create the affirmative *tú* command for the following verbs: *dormir, tener, salir,* and *hablar.*

29. True or False: Pronouns are always attached to commands.

30. Creat the negative *tú* command for the following verbs: *pensar, repetir,* and *sentarse.*

31. Translate to Spanish: Call me. (using an *usted* command)

Chapter 10

32. Write the following sentence using a comparison formula: The girl is taller than her brother.

33. True or False: Adjectives of nationality are just like other adjectives in every way.

34. Where in a sentence are adjectives expressing quantity placed?

35. Select the correct form of the adjective for the following sentence: *Laura es la más _____ de sus amigos.*

    a. *bonito*
    b. *bonita*
    c. *bonitos*
    d. *bonitas*

Chapter 11

36. Write the correct preposition to fill in the blank:

Nosotros no consentimos _____ conducir a la fiesta.

37. Translate to Spanish: He always studies at night.

38. True or False: Any verb that is followed by a preposition in English is followed by a preposition in Spanish.

39. Determine whether *por* or *para* is appropriate and provide a reason:

Se venden los discos _____ veinte dólares.

Chapter 12

40. What pronoun would replace the underlined word in the following sentence?

Elena le da <u>consejos</u> a su hija.

41. Where do you place RID pronouns when using an affirmative command?

42. Conjugate the verb in the present tense with the appropriate reflexive pronoun:

Paulina _____ en la silla. (sentarse)

43. Rewrite the sentence using a pronoun instead of the words in parentheses:

El regalo es para _____. (mi hermana)

Chapter 13

44. Change the following sentence to the passive voice:

Pablo Picasso pintó la obra.

45. Write the correct exclamation word:

¡_____ *gran hombre es el jefe!*

46. True or False: Double negatives must be avoided in both Spanish and English.

47. Translate to Spanish: We have class unless it snows.

Chapter 14

48. Write the appropriate form of the verb in the blank:

Ojalá que ellos _____ anoche. (ganar)

49. Create the past subjunctive *tú* form of the following verbs: *entender, traer, conducir,* and *salir.*

50. Translate to Spanish: He spoke as if he were the president.

Answers

1. b **2.** False **3.** True **4.** a **5.** *¿Trabaja Jaime aquí?* **6.** *Cuál* **7.** *Qué* **8.** *Dónde* **9.** *cocinamos* **10.** *sigo, sigues, sigue, seguimos, seguís, siguen* **11.** *pierdo, pierdes, pierde, perdemos, perdéis, pierden* **12.** *Bela y Marina quieren traer los refrescos.* **13.** *llevó* **14.** *almorcé, almorzaste, almorzó, almorzamos, almorzasteis, almorzaron* **15.** *era, eras, era, éramos, erais, eran* **16.** *Lolita contradirá la verdad.* **17.** *Yo saldría.* **18.** True **19.** *ha, hubo, había* **20.** *tenido, leído, visto* **21.** *Hemos escrito muchas cartas.* **22.** False **23.** *siga, tenga* **24.** *conduzcan, duerman* **25.** *esté* **26.** *merezca* **27.** False **28.** *duerme, ten, sal, habla* **29.** False **30.** *no pienses, no repitas, no te sientes* **31.** *Llámeme.* **32.** *La muchacha es más alta que su hermano.* **33.** False **34.** In front of the nouns they modify. **35.** b **36.** *en* **37.** *Él siempre estudia por la noche.* **38.** False **39.** *por* (exchange) **40.** *los* **41.** Attached to end of command form. **42.** *se sienta* **43.** *ella* **44.** *La obra fue pintada por Pablo Picasso.* **45.** *Qué* **46.** False **47.** *Tenemos la clase a menos que nieve.* **48.** *ganaran* **49.** *entendieras, trajeras, condujeras, salieras* **50.** *Habló como si fuera el presidente.*

CQR RESOURCE CENTER

CQR Resource Center offers the best resources available in print and online to help you study and review the core concepts of Spanish. You can also find additional resources, plus study tips and tools to help test your knowledge, at www.cliffsnotes.com and www.cliffsnotes.com/extras.

Books

This CliffsQuickReview book is one of many great books about Spanish language concepts. If you want some additional resources, check out these other publications:

1001 Spanish Pitfalls, by Marion Peter Holt and Julianne Deuber, is designed to predict and eliminate the mistakes you will make as a typical English speaker learning Spanish. Barron's Educational Services, $11.95.

Book of Spanish Idioms provides a comprehensive listing and explanations of common idiomatic expressions in Spanish. This is extremely useful because idioms can not be understood simply by looking up each individual word in the dictionary. Passport Books, $8.50.

Spanish For Dummies, by Susan Wald and Juergen Lorenz, is designed to get you speaking Spanish quickly. This easy to understand book delivers another perspective on the grammar concepts you are learning. Wiley Publishing, Inc., $24.99.

501 Spanish Verbs, by Christopher Kendris, is as important as a dictionary if you want to produce written or spoken sentences in Spanish. This book charts all the forms of all the tenses of the 501 most common verbs in an easy-to-understand format. There is also a clear explanation of all the forms and tenses at the beginning of the book. Barron's Educational Services, $13.95.

The Concise American Heritage Larousse Spanish Dictionary provides the clearest and most detailed entries and includes many idiomatic expressions. Houghton Mifflin, $21.00

Wiley also has three Web sites that you can visit to read about all the books we publish:

- www.cliffsnotes.com
- www.dummies.com
- www.wiley.com

Internet

Visit the following Web sites for more information about Spanish language concepts (since Web sites constantly change, try a search on any Web browser by typing "Spanish Language").

About — www.spanish.about.com — contains lessons on subjects ranging from pronunciation to verb conjugation. It also features information on the history of Spanish, grammar, literature, teaching resources, and a word of the day. Students can post questions about Spanish in a chatroom.

AllExperts — www.allexperts.com/getExpert.asp?Category =1551 — is the site to use when you have a question about the Spanish language. There are all different sorts of experts willing to help you translate, prepare an individualized study plan, or help you with your Spanish homework.

Lingolex — www.lingolex.com/spanish.htm — is a very interesting site for learning basic Spanish. There is a chatroom where you can practice your Spanish, and fun activities to help you master some of the challenging grammatical concepts and improve your vocabulary.

Spanish Unlimited — www.spanishunlimited.com — is "the right place to learn Spanish and meet new friends." There are popular games, weekly lessons, Spanish jokes, and even a verb conjugator to help you use the correct form of any verb.

Webspañol — www.geocities.com/Athens/Thebes/6177/ — is an extremely popular site where you can download free Spanish language learning software, work on your pronunciation with an audio pronunciation guide, and find unique methods for reinforcing and practicing what you have learned.

CASLT/ACPLS — www.caslt.org/research/musicsp.htm — is a site for music lovers, hosted by the Canadian Association of Second Language Teachers. This fun site integrates music into your learning of Spanish. From the Beatles to *villancicos* (Christmas carols), to national hymns — you name it, it is here.

GLOSSARY

Accent mark If a word ends in any vowel or *n* or *s*, the natural stress is on the next-to-last syllable. The natural stress is on the last syllable for any word that ends in any consonant (except for *n* and *s*). When the stress of the word is somewhere other than on the natural stress, an accent mark is written on the appropriate vowel. Accent marks are also used to differentiate between two similar one-syllable words, such as *si* (if) and *sí* (yes).

Acronym A word that represents the first letter of each word in a list being used to help you remember a group of words or phrases.

Adjective A word that describes (modifies) a noun or pronoun. A Spanish adjective often follows the noun or pronoun it modifies and always matches the noun's gender and number. An adjective that indicates amount, number, or order usually precedes the word it modifies.

Adverb A word that modifies a verb, an adjective, or another adverb. Adverbs generally tell how, when, or where something happened.

Agreement There are many situations in which the number and gender of a word must "match" another word. If a noun is singular and feminine, any word that modifies that noun must be in a singular feminine form. Also, a conjugated verb must match (agree with) the subject that is responsible for the action of the verb.

Apocopated adjective If placed in front of a singular masculine noun, some adjectives must be in a shortened form. These are called "apocopated" adjectives.

Clarification When it is unclear what noun an indirect object is replacing, a clarification is written using the preposition *a* followed by a noun or pronoun.

Cognate A word that is similar in both Spanish and English. A cognate will either look similar or sound similar (but not both).

Compound subject When more than one noun or phrase serve as the subject, joined by a conjunction.

Compound word A noun that is composed of a verb in its *él* form followed by a plural noun. Compound nouns are always masculine and can be singular even though they end in *-s* (for example, *el rascacielos* or *el abrelatas*). The plural form looks like the singular (*los rascacielos* or *los abrelatas*).

Conditional tense The conditional tense is translated as "would [something]." In Spanish, the conditional is created by adding endings to the infinitive. It is used to indicate a condition that must be met in order for another verb in the sentence to occur.

Conjugation   The categorizing of verbs according to the forms used for each subject and in each tense.

Conjunctions   A word or phrase that serves to join two nouns or phrases together.

Definite article   The Spanish definite article must match the gender and number of the noun it modifies and is equivalent to the English word "the." Definite articles are used in front of a noun to indicate a specific person or thing: *el, la, los, las.*

Demonstrative   An adjective or pronoun that points out the relative distance of an object or person. "This" and "that" are singular demonstratives in English and "these" and "those" are plurals.

Dipthong   A combination of two vowels to form one syllable. This is caused by a strong vowel (*a, e, o*) combined with a weak vowel (*i, u*) or the combination of two weak vowels.

Direct object   The noun or pronoun that receives the action of the verb.

Expression   A group of words that have a specific meaning different from the translation of each individual word in the expression.

First person   Indicates that the subject of the verb is "I" or "we."

Formal   The forms of pronouns and verbs used when addressing someone in a respectful manner.

Future tense   In English, this tense is created by placing the helping verb "will" or "shall" in front of a verb to indicate that the action of the verb will occur in the future. In Spanish, the future tense is created by adding endings to the infinitive form of the verb.

Gender   All nouns in Spanish are either masculine or feminine, and all words that modify a noun will be in a form that agrees with the gender of the noun.

Helping verb   The helping verb *haber* is used to create the perfect tenses. In English, the helping verb forms are "have," "has," or "had."

Idiomatic expression   See "Expression."

Imperfect subjunctive   See "Past subjunctive."

Imperfect tense   This tense indicates a description or ongoing action in the past.

Indefinite article   There are four specific adjectives that are used in front of a noun to indicate that it refers to an indefinite person or thing. The singular forms *un* and *una* are equivalent to the English word "a." The plural forms *unos* and *unas* are equivalent to the English word "some." Spanish indefinite articles must match the nouns they modify.

Indirect object   Indicates for whom (or what) or to whom (or what) something is done.

Infinitive   The form of the verb that has not been conjugated will end in *-ar, -er,* or *-ir.* This is called the infinitive form of the verb and is what you find when you look up a verb in the dictionary.

Informal   When addressing someone in a friendly manner, informal forms of pronouns and verbs are used.

Interrogative pronoun   This is a question word.

Irregular verbs   A verb that does not follow the normal patterns of conjugated forms.

Mnemonic devices   Techniques that help you remember something.

Modify   The grammatical term for when one word describes another (for example, adjectives modify nouns).

Neutral pronoun   When a pronoun replaces an abstract concept or unknown thing, use the neutral pronoun *lo*.

Noun   A word that names a person, place, thing, animal, or idea.

Number   A reference to whether something is singular or plural. You must consider number with Spanish nouns, pronouns, adjectives, and verbs.

Object of a preposition   The noun or pronoun that follows and receives the action of a preposition.

Past participle   The past participle form of the verb generally ends in *-ado* or *-ido* unless it is irregular. It can be changed into an adjective or used with a helping verb.

Past subjunctive tense   The tense used when the subjunctive is necessary in a past tense sentence. It is technically called the "imperfect subjunctive" but is based on the preterit form of *ellos*.

Person   The pronoun and form of verb that indicates the person involved.

Personal *a*   The preposition *a* is placed in front of any word that refers to a person or people that serve(s) as the direct object of the sentence.

Possessive   An adjective or pronoun that shows ownership.

Potencial   The Spanish grammatical term for the conditional tense.

Preposition   A word that indicates the relationship between nouns, pronouns, or clauses.

Present perfect tense   Created when the helping verb *haber* is conjugated in the present tense and is followed by a past participle. In English, this is translated as "have [verb]-ed" or "have [verb]-en."

Present progressive tense   The present tense of the verb *estar* is used with the present participle (*-iendo*, *-ando*) form of the verb to indicate an ongoing action in the present.

Pronombre tónico   The case of pronoun that is used after a preposition.

Pronoun   A word that takes the place of a noun. A pronoun functions as the same part of speech and has the same person, number, and gender as the noun it replaces.

Second person   Indicates that the subject of the verb is "you."

Sequence of tenses   The rule that governs which of the subjunctive tenses should be used. The past subjunctive follows the conditional, preterit, or imperfect. The present subjunctive follows any command form or the present or future tense.

Stem   The stem of a verb is what is left when you remove the *-ar*, *-er*, or *-ir*.

Stem-changing verbs   A verb whose stem changes from *e>ie*, *o>ue*, or *e>i* in all forms except *nosotros/nosotras* and *vosotros/vosotras*.

Stress Very specific rules govern the syllable that is pronounced most strongly. This is called the natural stress of a word. A written accent mark indicates that a vowel is stressed that would not be stressed according to the rules that govern the natural stress of a word.

Subject The person, place, or thing responsible for the action of the verb.

Subject case Pronouns are grouped in cases. The pronouns used to replace a noun that is the subject of the sentence must come from the subject case.

Subjunctive indicator Specific verbs and expressions that express the types of situations that are followed by the subjunctive mood.

Subjunctive tense The subjunctive is a mood that is used after verbs that express situations such as doubt, emotion, an indirect command, and so on. There is a present subjunctive tense and a past (imperfect) subjunctive tense.

Suffix The ending of a word that often determines the part of speech of the word.

Superlative The extreme form of an adjective in English often ends in *-est,* but can also be irregular: "the most," "the least," "the best," "the worst." In Spanish, there are also a few irregulars,

but most superlatives are created with the article *el, los, la,* or *las* preceding the comparative *más* or *menos.* The conjunction *que* of the comparative form is replaced by the preposition *de.* Also, there is an absolute superlative that is formed by adding the suffix *-ísimo* to the appropriate ending of the adjective.

Tense The time indicated by the verb of a sentence.

Third person In English, the third person indicates that the subject of the verb is "he," "she," or "it" in the singular or "they" in the plural. The third person form of the verb in Spanish is used with the singular pronouns *él, ella,* and *usted* and the plural pronouns *ellos, ellas,* and *ustedes.*

Transitive verbs A verb that requires a direct object.

Umlaut A symbol over the letter *u* (ü) that indicates that the *u* is pronounced in situations when it normally would not be pronounced.

Verb A word expressing an action or a state of being.

Verb conjugation chart A chart that indicates what form of the verb is used with each subject pronoun for each verb tense.

Appendix
ANTONYMS AND SYNONYMS

Antonyms

Many classroom and standardized exams utilize questions requiring a student to provide the antonym (or opposite) of a word. The following lists of antonyms are helpful vocabulary words to have in your word arsenal. Learn each word's meaning as well as its opposite word. Don't forget to learn the stem change in parentheses following any stem-changing verb.

Verbs and their opposites

Verb	Antonym
aburrirse (to be bored)	*divertirse* (*e>ie*) (to have fun)
admitir (to admit)	*negar* (*e>ie*) (to deny)
alejarse de (to go away from)	*acercarse a* (to get close to)
amar, querer (*e>ie*) (to love)	*odiar* (to hate)
aparecer (to appear)	*desaparecer* (to disappear)
apresurarse (to hurry)	*tardar en* (to delay)
bajar (to go down, to lower)	*subir* (to go up, to raise)
bendecir (to bless)	*maldecir* (to curse)
cansar (to tire)	*descansar* (to rest)
cerrar (*e>ie*) (to close)	*abrir* (to open)
comprar (to buy)	*vender* (to sell)
dar (to give)	*recibir* (to receive)
dejar caer (to drop)	*recoger* (to pick up)
descubrir (to discover)	*cubrir* (to cover)
despertarse (*e>ie*) (to wake up)	*dormirse* (*o>ue*) (to fall asleep)
destruir (to destroy)	*crear* (to create)

Verb	**Antonym**
desvanecerse (to disappear)	*aparecer* (to appear)
elogiar (to praise)	*censurar* (to criticize)
empezar (*e>ie*) (to begin)	*terminar* (to finish)
encender (*e>ie*) (to light, to turn on)	*apagar* (to extinguish, to turn off)
entrar (to enter)	*salir* (to exit)
gastar (to spend [money])	*ahorrar* (to save [money])
hablar (to speak)	*callar* (to be quiet)
ignorar (to not know [a fact])	*saber* (to know [a fact])
jalar (to pull)	*empujar* (to push)
jugar (*o>ue*) (to play)	*trabajar* (to work)
juntar (to join)	*separar* (to separate)
levantarse (to get up)	*sentarse* (*e>ie*) (to sit down)
meter (to put in)	*sacar* (to take out)
nacer (to be born)	*morir* (*o>ue*) (to die)
perder (*e>ie*) (to lose)	*ganar* (to win) or *encontrar* (*o>ue*) (to find)
permitir (to permit)	*prohibir* (to prohibit)
preguntar (to ask)	*responder, contestar* (to answer)
prestar (to lend)	*pedir* (*e>ie*) *prestado* (to borrow)
quedarse (to stay)	*irse, salir, marcharse* (to leave)
quitarse (to take off)	*ponerse* (to put on)
recordar (to remember)	*olvidar* (to forget)
reír (*e>i*) (to laugh)	*llorar* (to cry)
sumar (to add)	*restar* (to subtract)
tomar (to take)	*dar* (to give)
unir (to unite)	*dividir, desunir* (to divide)
vaciar (to empty)	*llenar* (to fill)

Nouns and their opposites

Nouns ending in *-o* may also end in *-a, -os,* or *-as.* In the following list, if a noun is listed without an article and refers to a person, it can be masculine or feminine. All other nouns have a predetermined gender that is indicated by the definite article:

Noun	Antonym
amigo (friend)	*enemigo* (enemy)
el amor (love)	*el odio* (hatred)
la capacidad (ability)	*la incapacidad* (inability)
la dama (lady)	*el caballero* (gentleman)
la derrota (defeat)	*la victoria* (victory)
el descuido (carelessness)	*el esmero, el cuidado* (caution)
el éxito (success)	*el fracaso* (failure)
el fin (end)	*el principio* (beginning)
gigante (giant)	*enano* (dwarf)
la hembra (female)	*el varón* (male)
la ida (departure)	*la vuelta* (return)
la juventud (youth)	*la vejez* (old age)
la lentitud (slowness)	*la rapidez* (quickness)
la libertad (freedom)	*la esclavitud* (slavery)
la luz (light)	*la sombra* (shadow)
la llegada (arrival)	*la partida* (departure)
la mentira (lie)	*la verdad* (truth)
la paz (peace)	*la guerra* (war)
el peligro (danger)	*la seguridad* (security, safety)
la pobreza (poverty)	*la riqueza* (wealth)
el porvenir (future)	*el pasado* (past)
la pregunta (question)	*la respuesta* (answer)
el ruido (noise, sound)	*el silencio* (silence)
la salida (exit)	*la entrada* (entrance)
el sur (south)	*el norte* (north)
la vida (life)	*la muerte* (death)

Adjectives and their opposites

Remember that adjectives change to match the nouns or pronouns they modify. Below, the adjectives are listed in their singular masculine form. Adjectives ending in *-o* may also end in *-a, -os,* or *-as.* Other adjectives have a singular and plural form only.

Adjective	Antonym
antipático (mean)	*simpático* (nice)
ausente (absent)	*presente* (present)
bajo (short)	*alto* (tall)
bueno (good)	*malo* (bad)
caro, costoso (expensive)	*barato* (cheap)
cobarde (cowardly)	*valiente* (brave)
cómico (funny)	*trágico* (tragic)
común (common)	*raro* (rare)
corto (short)	*largo* (long)
débil (weak)	*fuerte* (strong)
delgado (thin)	*gordo* (fat)
diferente (different)	*mismo* (same)
desgraciado (unfortunate)	*afortunado* (fortunate)
distinto (different)	*semejante* (similar)
dulce (sweet)	*amargo* (bitter)
duro (hard)	*suave* (soft, smooth)
estrecho (narrow)	*ancho* (wide)
estúpido (stupid)	*inteligente* (intelligent)
fácil (easy)	*difícil* (difficult)
fatigado (tired)	*descansado* (rested)
flojo (lazy)	*aplicado* (industrious)
flojo (loose)	*apretado* (tight)
frío (cold)	*caliente* (hot)
feo (ugly)	*hermoso* (beautiful)
flaco (thin)	*gordo* (fat)
grande (big)	*pequeño* (small)
hablador (talkative)	*taciturno* (not talkative)
humilde (humble)	*orgulloso* (proud)
inocente (innocent)	*culpable* (guilty)
interesante (interesting)	*aburrido* (boring)
lejano (distant)	*cercano* (near)
limpio (clean)	*sucio* (dirty)
listo (clever)	*tonto* (foolish)

Adjective	Antonym
lleno (full)	*vacío* (empty)
mejor (better)	*peor* (worse)
menor (younger)	*mayor* (older)
moderno (modern)	*antiguo* (old)
mojado (wet)	*seco* (dry)
mucho (a lot)	*poco* ([a] little)
natural (natural)	*artificial* (artificial)
necesario (necessary)	*innecesario* (unnecessary)
occidental (western)	*oriental* (eastern)
oscuro (dark)	*claro* (light, clear)
perezoso (lazy)	*diligente* (diligent)
pesado (heavy)	*ligero* (light)
primero (first)	*último* (last)
privado (private)	*público* (public)
recto (straight)	*tortuoso* (winding)
sabio (wise)	*tonto* (foolish)
tranquilo (calm)	*turbulento* (restless)
triste (sad)	*feliz* (happy)
usual (usual)	*extraño* (unusual)
útil (useful)	*inútil* (useless)
viejo (old)	*joven* (young) or *nuevo* (new)

More useful words and their opposites

aquí (here)	*allí* (there)
arriba (above)	*abajo* (below)
bien (well)	*mal* (badly)
cerca de (near)	*lejos de* (far [from])
con (with)	*sin* (without) or *contra* (against)
delante de (in front of)	*detrás de* (behind)
despacio (slowly)	*aprisa* (quickly)
más (more)	*menos* (less)
tarde (late)	*temprano* (early)

Synonyms

It is extremely important to learn more than one Spanish word for the same thing because most standardized tests include a reading comprehension section in which the author purposefully uses a synonym for the word in the passage as the correct answer choice. Remember that, although you may choose to use one of the synonyms consistently when you are producing the language, there is no guarantee that the same word will be used by the other person producing the language when you are listening or reading Spanish.

Synonymous verbs

English	Spanish equivalents
to allow	*dejar, permitir*
to answer	*contestar, responder*
to approach	*acercarse a, aproximarse a*
to attempt	*tratar de, intentar*
to beg	*rogar (o>ue), suplicar*
to begin	*comenzar (e>ie), empezar (e>ie), principiar*
to break	*quebrar (e>ie), romper*
to choose	*elegir (e>i), escoger*
to cook	*cocinar, cocer (o>ue), guisar*
to continue	*continuar, seguir (e>i)*
to conquer	*conquistar, vencer*
to cross	*cruzar, atravesar*
to dare	*atreverse a, osar*
to delay	*posponer, diferir, aplazar*
to die	*fallecer, morir (o>ue)*
to disappear	*desaparecer, desvanecerse*
to end	*acabar, concluir, terminar*
to fight	*combatir, luchar, pelear, pugnar*
to find	*encontrar (o>ue), hallar*
to finish	*acabar, completar, concluir, terminar*
to flatter	*adular, halagar, lisonjear*
to frighten	*asustar, espantar*

English	Spanish equivalents
to get	*conseguir (e>i), obtener*
to get mad	*enfadarse, enojarse*
to go away	*irse, marcharse*
to hate	*aborrecer, odiar*
to have fun	*divertirse (e>ie), pasar un buen rato*
to invite	*convidar, invitar*
to leave	*partir, salir*
to love	*amar, querer*
to make fun of	*burlarse de, mofarse de*
to occur	*acaecer, acontecer, ocurrir, pasar, suceder*
to own	*poseer, tener*
to praise	*alabar, elogiar*
to put	*colocar, poner*
to raise	*alzar, elevar, levantar*
to remember	*acordarse de (o>ue), recordar (o>ue)*
to return	*regresar, volver (o>ue)*
to scare	*asustar, espantar*
to send	*enviar, mandar*
to shout	*dar voces, gritar*
to show	*enseñar, mostrar (o>ue)*
to stop	*detenerse, pararse*
to suffer	*padecer, sufrir*
to surprise	*asombrar, sorprender*
to take	*tomar, llevar*
to take a walk	*pasearse, dar un paseo*
to throw	*arrojar, echar, lanzar, tirar*
to try to	*intentar, tratar de*
to understand	*comprender, entender (e>ie)*
to wait for	*aguardar, esperar*
to walk	*andar, caminar, ir a pie*
to want	*desear, querer (e>ie)*

Synonymous nouns

English	Spanish equivalents
battle	*la batalla, el combate, la lucha*
beautiful	*hermoso, bello, guapo*
bedroom	*la alcoba, el dormitorio, el cuarto*
beggar	*el mendigo, el pordiosero, el limosnero*
bird	*el ave, el pájaro*
boat	*el barco, el buque, el vapor, la nave*
car	*el automóvil, el coche, el carro*
country	*la nación, el país, la patria*
devil	*el demonio, el diablo*
employee	*el dependiente, el empleado*
face	*la cara, el rostro, el semblante*
farmer	*el campesino, el labrador, el granjero*
fear	*el miedo, el temor*
fever	*la calentura, la fiebre*
food	*el alimento, la comida*
fright	*el espanto, el susto*
happening	*el acontecimiento, el suceso*
help	*la ayuda, el auxilio, el socorro*
husband	*el esposo, el marido*
jewel	*la alhaja, la joya*
joke	*la broma, la chanza, el chiste*
language	*el idioma, la lengua*
love	*el amor, el cariño*
mistake	*el error, la equivocación*
mountain	*la montaña, el monte*
newspaper	*el diario, el periódico*
nobility	*la nobleza, la hidalguez, la hidalguía*
owner	*el dueño, el propietario*
pain	*el dolor, la pena*
pastime	*la diversión, el pasatiempo*
permission	*el permiso, la licencia*

English	Spanish equivalents
place	*el lugar, el sitio*
priest	*el cura, el sacerdote*
prize	*el premio, el galardón*
ring (jewelry)	*el anillo, la sortija*
room	*la sala, la habitación, el cuarto*
scorn	*el desdén, el desprecio*
skill	*la destreza, la habilidad*
speed	*la prisa, la rapidez, la velocidad*
story	*el cuento, la historia*
student	*el alumno, el estudiante*
task, work	*la obra, la tarea, el trabajo*
tooth	*el diente, la muela*
train	*el tren, el ferrocarril*
waiter	*el camarero, el mozo*
wave	*la ola, la onda*
wife	*la esposa, la mujer*

More important synonyms

English	Spanish equivalents
again	*de nuevo, otra vez*
finally	*al fin, finalmente*
maybe, perhaps	*acaso, quizá(s), tal vez*
never	*nunca, jamás*
nevertheless, however	*sin embargo, no obstante*
often	*a menudo, con frecuencia, frecuentemente, muchas veces*
only	*solamente, sólo*
slowly	*lentamente, despacio*
since, inasmuch as	*ya que, puesto que*
sometimes	*a veces, algunas veces, de vez en cuando*
so that	*de manera que, de modo que*
still, yet, even	*aún, todavía*
then	*entonces, luego*

Index

irregular verbs, 24
 conditional tense, 71–73
 definition, 233
 future tense, 63–68
 imperative, affirmative commands,
 126–127
 imperfect tense, 57–58
 infinitives, 39–40
 infinitives, changing letters, 63
 present subjunctive mood, 101–103
 preterit tense, morphing verbs, 51–54
 preterit tense, very irregular, 54–55
 tú affirmative commands, 126–127
 yo irregular, 24

J-K-L

j (letter), pronunciation, 6
j-stem verbs, preterit tense, 53–54

la, 179
las, 143–144, 179
le, 180–181
lejos de, 241
les, 181
letters, pronunciation, 5-8
ll as separate letter, 4
lo, 179
los, 143–144, 179

M-N-O

mal, 241
más, 152–153, , 203, 239
means *(por),* 166
menos, 152–153, 239
mnemonic devices, 233
modify, definition, 233
motivation *(por),* 165

nationality, adjectives of, 142–143
need, subjunctive indicators, 105
negatives, 209–210
neutral pronouns, 233
nosotros(nosotras), 13, 135–136
nouns
 antonym listing, 236–237
 definition, 233
 possessive adjectives and, 146
 roles, identifying, 178
 synonyms, 242–243
numbers, 233

o (conjunction), 204–205
-o ending adjectives, 142
o>ue stem changers, 36–37
object of a preposition, 191, 233
object pronouns, 177–182
ojalá, 107, 221–222
opinion *(para),* 163
-oy verb ending, 26

P

para (preposition), 156, 162–167
 idiomatic expressions, 169
 P.R.O.D.D.S. acronym, 162
 verbs followed by, 171
para que (conjunction), 207–208
passive voice, 200–203
past participle, 74–79, 201–202, 233
past perfect tense, 81
past subjunctive, 215–223, 233
past tense. *See* imperfect tense; preterit
 tense
perfect tense, 74–78, 81–84
pero (conjunction), 203
person, definition, 233
personal *a,* 233
pluperfect tense, 81
plurals, adjectives, 143–144
poner, future tense, 65–66
por (preposition), 162–171
porque (conjunction), 208
possessives
 adjectives, 146–148
 definition, 233
 possessive pronouns, 193–195
potencial, 233
prefixes, verbs, 24
prepositions
 compound prepositions, 167–174
 definition, 233
 infinitives and, 175–176
 object of, definition, 233
 object of, pronouns, 191
 pronouns after, 191–192
 in questions, 211–212
 simple, 155–167
 verbs with, 171–174
 verbs with in English but not Spanish,
 174–176
present perfect tense, 79–80, 233
present progressive tense, 233
present subjunctive mood, 85-87, 100-103
present tense, stem-changing verbs, 31–39